ART THERAPY FOR SOCIAL JUSTICE

Radical Intersections

Edited by Savneet K. Talwar

Routledge
Taylor & Francis Group

NEW YORK AND LONDON

First published 2019
by Routledge
711 Third Avenue, New York, NY 10017

and by Routledge
2 Park Square, Milton Park, Abingdon, Oxon, OX14 4RN

Routledge is an imprint of the Taylor & Francis Group, an informa business

© 2019 Taylor & Francis

The right of Savneet K. Talwar to be identified as the author of the editorial
material, and of the authors for their individual chapters, has been asserted in
accordance with sections 77 and 78 of the Copyright, Designs and Patents Act 1988.

Library of Congress Cataloging-in-Publication Data
Names: Talwar, Savneet K., editor.
Title: Art therapy for social justice : radical intersections / edited by Savneet
    K. Talwar.
Description: New York : Routledge, 2019.
Identifiers: LCCN 2018011654| ISBN 9781138909052 (hardcover : alk. paper) |
    ISBN 9781138909069 (pbk. : alk. paper) | ISBN 9781315694184 (e-book)
Subjects: LCSH: Art therapy. | Art therapists. | Multiculturalism.
Classification: LCC RC489.A7 A76943 2019 | DDC 616.89/1656—dc23
LC record available at https://lccn.loc.gov/2018011654

ISBN: 978-1-138-90905-2 (hbk)
ISBN: 978-1-138-90906-9 (pbk)
ISBN: 978-1-315-69418-4 (ebk)

Typeset in Bembo
by Swales & Willis Ltd, Exeter, Devon, UK

ART THERAPY FOR SOCIAL JUSTICE

Art Therapy for Social Justice seeks to open a conversation about the cultural turn in art therapy to explore the critical intersection of social change and social justice. By moving the practice of art therapy beyond standard individualized treatment models, the authors promote scholarship and dialogue that opens boundaries; they envision cross-disciplinary approaches with a focus on intersectionality through the lens of black feminism, womanism, antiracism, queer theory, disability studies, and cultural theory. In particular, specific programs are highlighted that re-conceptualize art therapy practice away from a focus on pathology towards "models of caring" based on concepts of self-care, radical caring, hospitality, and restorative practice methodologies. Each chapter takes a unique perspective on the concept of "care" that is invested in wellbeing. The authors push the boundaries of what constitutes art in art therapy, re-conceptualizing notions of care and wellbeing as an ongoing process, emphasizing the importance of self-reflexivity, and reconsidering the power of language and art in trauma narratives.

Savneet K. Talwar, PhD, ATR-BC, is a professor in the graduate art therapy program at the School of the Art Institute of Chicago. She has published articles in *Arts in Psychotherapy, Art Therapy: Journal of the American Art Therapy Association,* and *Gender Issues in Art Therapy.* Her current projects are *Wandering Uterus Project: A DIY Movement for Reproductive Justice* and *CEW (Creatively Empowered Women) Design Studio,* a craft, sewing, and fabrication enterprise for Bosnian and South Asian women at the Hamdard Center in Chicago. She is also the past associate editor of *Art Therapy: Journal of the American Art Therapy Association.*

CONTENTS

FIGURES AND TABLE

Figures

Table

CONTRIBUTORS

Rumi Clinton, MAAT, LPC is a graduate of the School of the Art Institute Chicago's Master of Arts in Art Therapy Program. Whether drawing comics or practicing art therapy, Rumi focuses on the overlapping axis of personal identities and social change through art making. Rumi's clinical practice has been focused on adult mental health and drawing from feminist, harm reduction, narrative, and relational-cultural frameworks. Rumi's most recent clinical work includes research on comics as art therapy with veterans completed at Jesse Brown VA Medical Center in Chicago. They currently work at the Alzheimer's Association's national office with caregivers and families of those living with dementia.

Leah Gipson, MAAT, ATR-BC is an assistant professor in the art therapy department at the School of the Art Institute of Chicago. Her current research interests include womanism, black feminism, black church, and the use of cultural spaces to explore the politics of individual and social change. She uses her professional experience as a healthcare and human service provider to develop counter-public projects that address gender, racial and economic systems of inequality in Chicago's West Side neighborhoods. Her current projects are: The Rectory, for which she received the Propeller Fund Award 2016 for the Austin neighborhood studio co-op, co-creator of DIVISIVE, a radio show, and Care Session at Homan Square. Her publications are, "Challenging Neoliberalism and Multicultural Love in Art Therapy" and "Is Cultural Competence Enough? Deepening Social Justice Pedagogy in Art Therapy" published in *Art Therapy: Journal of the American Art Therapy Association.*

Luisa Ospina, MAAT, LPC is a Colombian-born art therapist and artist living in Vancouver, Canada. She completed her Master of Arts in Art Therapy at the School of the Art Institute of Chicago. Her clinical practice and research are focused on the intersection of trauma, identity, culture, and social issues with individuals of various age groups. She works from a client-centered, harm-reduction framework and emphasizes the importance of the therapeutic alliance. Luisa's artistic practice examines the relationship between the personal and the public to highlight systems of oppression.

Sangeetha (Sangi) Ravichandran, MAAT, ATR is an activist scholar, an art therapist and a PhD student at the University of Illinois at Chicago in the sociology program. Her current research examines criminalization, medical industrial complex, immigration, race, and gender through an intersectional and interdisciplinary lens. She serves as the Associate Director at the first ever Arab American Cultural Center on a college campus at UIC, building a space that is centered in arts and culture of the Arab world. She also does research for the Institute for Research in Race & Public Policy at UIC. She currently organizes with Love & Protect, a Chicago-based collective to end criminalization of survivors of violence. She also serves the Chicago Desi Youth Rising collective in an advisory capacity. Her mixed media art practice entails commentary on social justice issues and she has exhibited her work in the US, India, and Canada. Through her research, art/therapy practice and activism, she hopes to collectively build a world that is geared towards gender and healing justice.

Teresa Sit, MAAT, LPC is a Chicago area art therapist working in the field of hospice and palliative care. In addition to her work as an art therapist, Teresa continues her work as a professional photographer, specializing in events and portrait sessions.

Savneet K. Talwar, PhD, ATR-BC is a professor in the graduate art therapy program at the School of the Art Institute of Chicago. Her current research examines feminist politics, critical theories of difference, social justice and questions of resistance. Using a cross interdisciplinary approach, she is interested in community-based art practices; cultural trauma; performance art and public cultures as they relate to art therapy theory, practice and pedagogy. She is the author of a number of articles and has published in *Arts in Psychotherapy, Art Therapy: Journal of the American Art Therapy Association*, and *Gender Issues in Art Therapy*. Her current projects are: *Wandering Uterus Project: A DIY Movement for Reproductive Justice* and *CEW (Creatively Empowered Women) Design Studio*, a craft, sewing, and fabrication enterprise for Bosnian and South Asian women at the Hamdard Center in Chicago. She is also the past Associate Editor of *Art Therapy: Journal of the American Art Therapy Association*.

Salamishah Tillet, PhD is the Robert S. Blank Presidential Associate Professor of English and Africana Studies at the University of Pennsylvania. She is the co-founder of A Long Walk Home, a Chicago based national nonprofit that uses art to empower young people to end violence against girls and women.

Her writing has appeared online and in print in *The Atlantic, The Chicago Tribune, The Guardian, The Nation, NPR, The Root,* and *Time,* and she regularly contributes to *The New York Times.* She is the author of *Sites of Slavery: Citizenship and Racial Democracy in the Post-Civil Rights Imagination* and is currently working on a cultural memoir on Alice Walker's *The Color Purple* and a book on the civil rights icon, Nina Simone.

Scheherazade Tillet, MAAT is an art therapist, social documentary photographer, and community organizer. She received her BA in Child Development from Tufts University and her Master of Arts in Art Therapy from the School of the Art Institute of Chicago. In 2003, she co-founded A Long Walk Home (ALWH), a Chicago-based national nonprofit, that uses art to empower young people to end violence against girls and women. Currently, she is the artistic director of the award-winning multimedia performance, "Story of a Rape Survivor (SOARS)," a 20-year project in which Scheherazade documented her sister, Salamishah's recovery from sexual violence. In addition, as Executive Director of A Long Walk Home, Scheherazade inaugurated the Girl/Friends Leadership Institute, a yearlong artist-activist program that empowers girls and young women in Chicago to be social justice leaders in their schools, communities, and Chicago at large. Currently, Scheherazade is working on the following multimedia art projects: *The Visibility Project, The Prom Sendoff: A Rite of Passage for African-American Girls in Chicago,* and the curator of the traveling exhibition, *Picturing Black Girl/Hood.*

Chun-Shan (Sandie) Yi, MAAT, MFA, ATR is an artist, art therapist and disability rights activist whose practice is based both in the USA and Taiwan. She is a PhD candidate in Disability Studies at the University of Illinois at Chicago, and an arts administrator for Bodies of Work: Network of Disability Art and Culture. Her research interests include Disability Arts and Culture, social justice based art therapy, arts based research, and accessibility in the arts and culture. Her academic publications include, "From Imperfect to I Am Perfect: Reclaiming the Disabled Body through Making Body Adornments in Art Therapy" (2013) and *Disability Culture, Social Justice and Power in Museum Service and Accessibility Practices* (2015). She is currently writing her dissertation on Crip Couture to explore the intersections of disability and fashion.

INTRODUCTION

Savneet K. Talwar

This book takes a cultural turn to explore the relationship between art therapy, ideas of cultural change, and social justice in private and public art therapy spaces. The term "cultural turn" refers to a movement that began in the 1970s and impacted several disciplines in the humanities and social sciences; its purpose was to challenge positivist epistemologies by considering the role that culture, politics, and social policies played in everyday life. Mainstream psychology, counseling, and art therapy have sought to explain human behavior at an individual level. They uncritically emphasize self-expression as a means to uncover the hidden psychological truth that can make a person "whole," an approach that ignores the social and cultural conditions that shape the daily lives of the less advantaged. The challenge to mainstream frameworks has come from feminists of color and queer art therapists (contributors to this book) who emphasize the effects of social policies on mental and physical wellbeing. This book takes a cross disciplinary approach to include and discuss intersectionality, black feminism, womanism, antiracism, queer theory, disability studies, and cultural theory as they might enrich the practice of art therapy.

Who can doubt that art therapy, like society at large, stands at a critical juncture? Powerful forces are at work to erode the gains made in individual freedom. We witness increased violence towards non-normative bodies, the deregulation of health care, curtailment of women's access to health care and reproductive justice—all raising questions about the therapist's social responsibility. Basic tenets of the profession, enshrined in its code of ethics, are under legislative attack from those who wish to curtail access to services sought by members of the LGBTQ community. The authors, all of whom share a vision of social justice, urge art therapists to begin by stepping back and examining central concepts that define therapy: theories about healing, the body, and the therapeutic in order to begin to evaluate how mental health practices have replicated power structures that need dismantling.

Essays in this book focus on art therapy programs in Chicago, but take up themes applicable across other communities. The authors' cross disciplinary approach is intended to stimulate critical thinking about programs that respond to the needs of the community rather than provide fixed recipes. Believing that the profession of art therapy must continually undergo examination, the authors here stress the therapist's need to exercise self-reflexivity, while recognizing that the practice of art therapy is socially constructed and operates within a systemic context. The first part of the book questions the epistemological frameworks of art therapy that stand in the way of a social justice vision. The second part is focused on praxis, to envision new paradigms of care that I call "radical intersections" for art therapy practice.

In Chapter 1, "Beyond Multiculturalism and Cultural Competence: A Social Justice Vision in Art Therapy," I explore the concepts of diversity and inclusion and what it means to "do multiculturalism." I further problematize concepts of multicultural competence to set the platform for a social justice approach to examine the history of mental health to locate art therapy in a broader social, cultural, and historical context. In Chapter 2, "Critiquing Art Therapy: History, Science, and Representation," I point out the historical influence of social policies and laws that have justified stratification and inequality. The chapter considers the history of eugenics, a pseudo-scientific endeavor that shaped discourses of the body. Locating the influences of art therapy within the twentieth-century re-humanizing project in psychology, I investigate the history of mental health and fascination with the artistic renderings of the mentally ill and the advent of photography and empirical categorization of normalcy and deviancy. I end the chapter questioning what the future of an art therapy, that is located in a cultural construct, should look like.

In Chapter 3, "Identity Matters: Questioning Trauma and Violence through Art, Performance, and Social Practice," I take an intersectional perspective to understanding the power of art in addressing trauma and violence. Offering examples from social practice, performance, and public art, I examine how an intersectional approach can deepen the discourse about the body, identity, and citizenship. Using examples of public responses to *9/11*, the *Black Lives Matters movement*, *Say Her Name project*, and *Gone But Not Forgotten*, among other projects, I illustrate the ways in which artists, cultural workers, and activists have used art to highlight the social policies that have justified inequality.

Chapter 4, "Intersectional Reflexivity: Considering Identities and Accountability for Art Therapists," is coauthored by Savneet K. Talwar, Rumi Clinton, Teresa Sit, and Luisa Ospina, and focuses on intersectional reflexivity. The four authors use a critical art-based inquiry to explore their narratives from personal, social, and political perspectives. They illustrate the complexity of identity formation, its performance, and negotiation in the social structures of everyday life. By examining the relationships between the personal and political, the private and public, they show how a critical, art-based inquiry can offer a window into the contradictions of lived experience.

In Chapter 5, "Envisioning Black Women's Consciousness in Art Therapy," Leah Gipson takes a personal and historical perspective to discuss Black women's corrective responses to invisibility in art therapy. She asks "what ideas and strategies from Black women can help to analyze professional norms [of art therapy] that maintain the violent outcomes of systemic oppression in the everyday lives of people of color?" Gipson couches her analysis in her own lived experiences, applying a womanist methodology as a means to analyze the work of three deceased Black art therapists—Georgette Seabrooke Powell (1916–2011), Sarah Pollard McGee (1930–2002), and Lucille D. Venture (1919–2006)—and the contributions of contemporary Black art therapists. She offers a long-awaited historical perspective on an issue that has largely been missing in art therapy.

The second part of the book turns to new paradigms of care that I call "radical intersections" for art therapy practice. The contributing authors offer a range of programs that illustrate the incorporation of social justice and advocacy models into art therapy practice. Each of the chapters has a foundation in a particular theoretical framework focusing on intersectionality through the lens of Black feminism, feminist pedagogy, disability studies, and post-colonial theory. The emerging theme in these chapters re-conceptualizes art therapy practice away from uncovering pathology and towards "models of caring." The authors frame art therapy in concepts of self-care, radical caring, hospitality, and restorative practice methodologies. Each chapter takes a unique perspective on the concept of "care" that is invested in wellbeing. In addition, the authors have carefully chosen language to describe the people they serve. Readers will notice that the word client is rarely used, rather words like Girl/Friends, members, community members, consumers, and participants are used to shift the power differential inherent in traditional therapeutic relationships. A significant contribution of these chapters is 1) they push the boundaries of what constitutes art in art therapy; 2) they re-conceptualize notions of care and wellbeing as an ongoing process; 3) they emphasize the importance of self-reflexivity; and 4) they ask art therapists to reconsider the power of language and art in trauma narratives.

In Chapter 6, "'You Want to Be Well?' Self-Care as a Black Feminist Intervention in Art Therapy," Salamishah Tillet and Scheherazade Tillet offer a radical perspective on self-care as a form of social action integral to the Girl/Friends Leadership Institute. Using the historical meaning of "Girl/Friends" to build lasting relationship among the participants, the authors propose a "self-care" approach under the rubric of black feminism for destigmatizing therapy and counseling with black girls. The Girl/Friends program uses a combination of art therapy, social justice, and community development models to apply an intersectional approach to self-care practice. As part of the program, the Girl/Friends attend workshops on intersectional feminisms, social justice, activism, and advocacy, meditation and yoga to integrate self-care as part of their everyday lives. A self-care methodology at Girl/Friends, therefore, is about making an ethical and political commitment to the wellbeing of its participants and their community. The program centers on engagement with the stories of trauma, invisibility, and health on an individual and community level, and thus addresses the impact of violence, racism, sexism, abuse and other forms of oppression towards developing the Girl/Friends artist-activist identity. The concept of self-care, therefore, blurs the boundaries between the personal and political, becoming an act of political resistance, finding one's voice, and healing. Incorporating public protests and activism along with individual therapy, forms a significant aspect of raising critical consciousness among the Girl/Friends to finding their voice and gain a sense of empowerment.

In Chapter 7, "Radical Caring and Art Therapy: Decolonizing Immigration and Gender Violence Services," Sangeetha (Sangi) Ravichandran argues for decolonizing immigration and gender violence services. She offers a historical critique of the essentializing models that have informed the gender violence movement with terms like "the battered women's syndrome." By offering an intersectional analysis she conveys the complexity of how race, gender, and class simultaneously act on the structural and political levels to represent violence against women of color. Working as an art therapist at Apna Ghar (our home), a domestic violence shelter for immigrant women in Chicago, she takes an active role in decolonizing services using art-based approaches to further the role of activism, advocacy, and therapy for immigrant communities through the concept of "radical caring."

Chapter 8, "Res(crip)ting Art Therapy: Disability Culture as a Social Justice Intervention" by Chun-Shan (Sandie) Yi brings a critical perspective to art therapy from a disability culture standpoint. She questions the foundational principles of art therapy and its limits when working with people with disabilities using a medical/ deficit model. Yi argues for an intersectional framework informed by disability studies to explore a community art-based practice with a sustainable social justice focus. The medical model rests on the notions of the normative to categorize and define the disabled body. She calls attention to the limits of both the medical and social models, pointing towards a political/relational model—a radical social model centered on a feminist framework of disability. Such a model rescripts the ableists' cultural practices by moving the disability narratives from pathology to identity.

Finally, in Chapter 9, "'The Sweetness of Money': The Creatively Empowered Women (CEW) Design Studio, Feminist Pedagogy and Art Therapy," I write about the CEW Design Studio. In its fifth year of operation, the CEW Design Studio leans on a feminist pedagogy to conceptualize labor and crafting (knitting and crocheting) through a trauma-informed approach. This chapter outlines the

FIGURE I.1 Robert Martin Narciso, *Art Therapy*® (2017)

community studio approach to a hospitality model to develop restorative spaces for wellbeing that primarily serves Muslim, refugee, and immigrant women. In particular, it speaks to the joy of crafting and its impact on community and social transformation.

To conclude, Robert Martin Narciso's image *Art Therapy*® (Fig I.1) is particularly appropriate for the critical take of this book. Narciso made the sculpture from cardboard, tissue paper and LED lights to recall the neon signs of a Walgreens drug store. He exhibited the piece as part of the final graduate art therapy show at the School of the Art Institute of Chicago. In likening art therapy to Walgreens, a neoliberal and capitalist venture, Narciso highlights the corporatization of both the profession and education of art therapy. He draws on the work of contemporary artists like Bruce Nawman and Glenn Ligon—who use neon signs to grapple with issues of identity through the confrontational nature of neon signs to ask that art therapy confront its identity as a profession.

As a viewer, my first encounter with *Art Therapy*® was one of amusement at seeing the word art therapy written in a Walgreens font. The sheer size of the neon sign, 2.5 × 14 × .5 ft, leads one to consider the cultural role of art therapy and the use of text as art. The familiarity conveyed by the font creates a resonance, yet also a dissonance at reading the word "Art Therapy" rather than "Walgreens." This conceptual piece engages in an open-ended dialogue about using text as a symbolic act as well as a form of art narration. For art therapists, the work asks that we continually consider questioning the purpose and power of language, art, and art therapy, issues taken up by the authors in this book.

PART I

Theoretical Framework

1

BEYOND MULTICULTURALISM AND CULTURAL COMPETENCE

A Social Justice Vision in Art Therapy

Savneet K. Talwar

For 30 years, I have led a hyphenated life in the United States: Indian-American, Sikh, middle class, brown skinned, and able-bodied. I am all too familiar with the challenges of negotiating my identity and privilege as a U.S. citizen and a university professor. On an everyday basis, I am hyperaware of my representation as a woman of color working in a predominantly white institution. My education and experiences have taught me to examine my interactions in a systemic context and to question the subtle power arrangements that surround me. Most often, the expressions of disparities in perceived cultural capital are not overt; rather, they are subtle combinations of what is said and what is not said, who is included and who is not.

My position as an educator has offered me the opportunity not only to teach diversity and difference, but also to be an advocate in my institution. That said, my experiences have not always been comfortable ones, especially since I mostly work with a white faculty, teaching mostly white students, in an overwhelmingly white institution. Although the struggle to increase diversity can have gratifying rewards, it is emotionally exhausting. Like many art therapy programs, mine requires a course in multiculturalism, yet understanding the complexity of identity and difference cannot be achieved in one 15-week class. In order to truly embrace a framework that addresses diversity and inclusion, issues of identity and difference must be addressed across the curriculum. This means addressing trauma and violence from an intersectional perspective that takes into account poverty, racism, sexism, classism, homophobia, and other forms of social oppression. Art therapists must understand how deep-seated inequalities—social, economic, and political—have shaped the psychological make-up of the people they serve, and examine the role of the arts and social action in the delivery of mental health services. Art therapists tend not to take into account factors such as economic development, engaged citizenship, and colonialism that have shaped health care and the delivery of mental health services. The justice work needed to address stigma and prejudice must include advocacy and action to counteract racism, sexism, ableism, classism, and heterosexism, and thus to make multiculturalism and human rights central to mental health services (Chung & Bemak, 2012; Goodman & Gorski, 2015; Talwar, 2015a).

Understanding diversity and inclusion has become even more urgent in the face of the 2016 election. In all my years of living in the U.S., I have never felt more unsafe and acutely aware of my existence and representation as a brown-skinned person. The tolerance and even celebration displayed by a cross-section of Americans, from political elites to blue-collar workers, in the face of the xenophobia and racism perpetuated by the 45th president is deeply disturbing. That Donald Trump has called Muslims "radical Islamist terrorists," Mexicans "criminals" and "rapists," and can make denigrating remarks about women and their bodies demonstrates clearly that racist and sexist language is acceptable, even appealing, to a large segment of the electorate. Trump's popularity requires us to question what diversity and multiculturalism mean in the twenty-first century. His vehement attacks on racial, ethnic, gendered, and sexual minorities evoked anger and anxiety in my colleagues, students, and friends. The success of his candidacy calls to mind questions of the power, limits, and creditability of hate speech and, particularly, Ahmed's (2012) inquiry into how some bodies become those of strangers. Why do hatred and fear stick to some bodies? And which bodies have the right to citizenship?

Trump's insistence that he does not believe in being "politically correct" points to how the politics of difference and diversity have been obfuscated and exploited (Grzanka, 2014). His hate speech and arrogance reveal the extent to which white privilege and power continue to operate in shaping, through affect and emotions, a collective narrative around non-white bodies. Trump uses othering to drive his narrative of us vs. them. The brown, Muslim, Sikh, immigrant, undocumented, and more are "not us," and in this way he redefines who we are and what is ours. Narratives of "us versus them," Ahmed (2004) argues,

> threaten to take away from what "you" have, as the legitimate subject of the nation, as the one who is the true recipient of national benefits. The narrative invites the reader to adopt the "you" through working on emotions: becoming this "you" means developing a certain rage against the illegitimate others (immigrants, refugees), who are represented as "swarms" in the nation.
>
> (p. 1)

The effectiveness of hate and fear, in Trump's case, alerts us to the ways in which the work of diversity has served to identify difference, but has not uprooted the social, economic, and political conditions that continue to contribute to inequality and oppression in the U.S.

For art therapists, the understanding of diversity and its application in practice need to move beyond mere recognition of difference. When multiculturalism and diversity rely on political correctness it only reinforces race, class, gender, and sexuality as biological attributes associated with pathology or deviancy; a context is created that runs the risk of replicating the power arrangements that need dismantling (Gorski & Goodman, 2015; Talwar, 2015a). Thus, to have a more effective understanding of diversity and multiculturalism there needs to be an examination of how history, institutions, and public policies have reinforced the systems of white power and privilege that continue to colonize our everyday lives, research, and our art therapy practice. Gorski and Goodman (2015) argue that the danger lies in the well-meaning counselors and therapists who, without understanding the context of culture, history, and oppression, may do harm to the people they serve. In this chapter, I explore diversity and inclusion and what it means to "do multiculturalism." I argue that to decolonize the practice of art therapy one has to include a social justice framework informed by critical inquiry and praxis for developing "critical consciousness."

What Do We Mean by Diversity and Inclusion?

Why are multiculturalism and diversity important? What do they do? Why should art therapists understand their effect on practice? What do "equality," "social justice," and "equal opportunity" (Ahmed, 2012; Anderson & Collins, 2007) mean for art therapy practice? The U.S. is founded on the principle of equality, but historically it has been denied to many. Now, however, there is a legal framework that "guarantees protection from discrimination and equality of treatment for all citizens before the law" (Anderson & Collins, 2007, p. 1). Several social movements—civil rights, feminism, the Lesbian, Gay, Bisexual, Transgender, and Queer (LGBTQ) rights movement, and the Americans with Disabilities Act (ADA)—have reshaped how the normative is conceived in mental health services. In the fight for equality, several of these movements have overlapped to reveal the ways in which social, economic, and public policy contributed to unequal conditions in the U.S. (Anderson & Collins, 2007; Talwar, 2015a). In Chapter 2, I examine the historical discourses that have shaped the representation of racial, ethnic, gendered, disabled, and sexual bodies, and in particular how nineteenth- and twentieth-century scientific movements have molded public perception.

Multiculturalism and diversity require that we examine the systems of power and stratification that have produced language to define categories of difference: race, class, gender, and other socially constructed differences. Categories of difference are reinforced when they are seen as natural and unchangeable biological or physiological aspects of life. Such conceptions are inherently essentialist, since they refer to supposedly innate human conditions (Ore, 2009). Against immutability, the social constructionist argues that we learn difference as a result of our social interactions. Creating meaning and value around difference is a cultural process, and depends on one's social positioning. As Burger and Luckman (1966) point out, the creation of a "social order" is not a natural process, but one that is produced and constructed by individuals. A social constructionist's approach, therefore, asks that the "reality" of things be questioned: what power relationships exist, who is included and who is left out, and how have power arrangements been normalized. As such, it is important that art therapists examine the essentializing language that has promoted reductive conceptions of human nature.

Identity and difference have generally been ignored in favor of universalizing psychological theories that lean on medical models (Gorski & Goodman, 2015). When assessing treatment and prognosis, the models have located psychic distress in the individual, in the belief that individuals have control over their lives and their environment. A social constructionist's perspective encourages deeper inquiry, recognizing that in order to ameliorate the psychological effects of oppressive cultural practices on a client's life, art therapists need to understand how childhood abuse, trauma, and psychological disorders are systemic issues (Talwar, 2010). Questioning the predominant concepts and frameworks for practice also means questioning how certain epistemological frameworks have shaped the profession of art therapy.

Over the course of the last two decades, a number of art therapy scholars have made efforts to centralize multiculturalism (Awais & Yali, 2013; Dufrene, 1994; Doby-Copeland, 2006; Hiscox & Calisch, 1998; George, Greene, & Blackwell, 2005; Gipson, 2015; Robb, 2014; Talwar, Iyer, & Doby-Copeland, 2004; Talwar, 2015a; ter Maat, 2011). Despite their work, approaches to the practice of art therapy still fail to take into account the importance of difference. Trauma and neuroscience have emerged as the new frontiers of research (Hass-Cohen & Carr, 2008; King, 2016; Talwar, 2007) but they, too, impose the kinds of essentializing principles that theories of identity and difference caution against. Current publications in art therapy and neuroscience, for example, offer techniques and protocols for treating trauma, but rarely is there a case study that takes into account the client's social context or intersectional identities. Acknowledging that not everyone starts on an equal playing field is the beginning of properly contextualizing views of trauma, or considering attachment and affect regulation from the intersection of culture, identity, and emotions that have been shaped by inequality: the economic resources denied to urban schools, the scarcity of jobs and reliable shelter, unsafe neighborhoods and food deserts, little access to affordable childcare, and shortage of health care and mental health support.

Well-meaning art therapists have worked in poor neighborhoods or in developing and war-torn countries, offering art materials for self-expression and therapy. There is a misleading idea that passing out art materials is an act of social justice. Although these motives are laudable, concepts of "art as healing" can only go so far when poverty is rampant and people do not have enough food to eat, clothes to wear, or predictable shelter. To expand the investigation of normalization and intersectionality, art therapists have to consider how identity is complicated when politics, emotions, language, and embodiment intersect with race, class, gender, sexuality, religion, disability, and other markers of difference. It is important that one questions the assumptions that underscore art therapy practice. What critical discourses does art therapy ignore at its peril?

There is a neoliberal idea of art therapy as a means of problem solving through "self-expression" and "art as healing." When the psychological construct of "healing" remains a personal responsibility, insight, and reforming behavior, therapists run the risk of ignoring how emotions like sorrow, loss, and anger are agents in the formation of identity, especially in communities that have long histories of oppression. A social model of art therapy, one that is rooted in social justice praxis, examines trauma not as a psychological condition alone, but as one that is linked to a person's position in society and culture (Lupton, 1997). Art therapists, therefore, need to reexamine how art therapy has privileged concepts of "art for healing," "wholeness," "sublimation," and "the self," in the service of individualized and privatized models of practice. A social model of art therapy locates concepts of diversity at the center of its practice. "Doing multiculturalism" means helping our clients understand and challenge oppression on a social-cultural level. In order to do so, art therapists need to question the assumptions upon which art therapy continues to be practiced. When art therapists move from modernist art therapy concepts invested in a single "truth" to be uncovered as part of becoming "whole," to incorporating postmodernist concepts—ones that draw from feminism, antiracism, intersectionality, and queer theory, all of which advocate for multiple truths and realties—they have begun to embrace a practice invested in principles of social justice. In this context, healing and wholeness become what Alarcón (1996) calls "subjectivity-in-process" (p. 138). This means that "identity," "wholeness," and "the self" are abstractions of process, personal processes that are constantly changing because becoming never ceases (Alarcón, 1996).

When art therapy is considered from a social and wellness model, art therapists have to reflect on the ethics of empathy, language, and storytelling (Shuman, 2005). The ethics of empathy and telling other people's stories demand that art therapists ask whose stories have been told and how. Often, medical and clinical language has described the lives of clients in skeptical rather than affirmative ways. Art therapists need to consider the impact of language when representing their clients. Descriptions such as: lack of insight, uncooperative, non-compliant, treatment resistant, and the analysis of art as primitive, defensive, or controlling, uphold assumptions reflecting negative expectations of the client that impede attunement and understanding. One of the key components of engaging with others people's lives has been mutual sharing through conversation, careful listening, and empathy. According to Shuman (2005), empathy is the key component that holds the promise of understanding others.

Yet, for her, empathy is not just "wearing another person's shoes;" rather, it is engaging, through a critical reflexive methodology, with stories as expressions located within a historical context in order to deconstruct how individuals are composed not just psychically but also historically.

If art therapists are to make a commitment to "doing multiculturalism," they must question the universalist concepts of art therapy practice and the ethical dimension to art and healing as a universal concept. They must move identity and difference from the margins to the center of art therapy practice, examine the texts used in training art therapists, understand and name white power and privilege, acknowledge the history of discrimination in the U.S. and the field of art therapy, and finally, embrace a self-reflexive stance. In "doing multiculturalism" Madison (2012) invites us to consider questions like the following:

1. How do we reflect upon and evaluate our own purpose, intentions and frames of analysis?
2. How do we predict consequences or evaluate our own potential to do harm?
3. How do we create and maintain a dialogue of collaboration between ourselves and others in our research and projects?
4. How is the specificity of the local story relevant to the broader meanings and operations of the human condition?
5. How—in what location or through what intervention—will our work make the greatest contribution to equity, freedom, and justice?

(p. 5)

Problematizing Multicultural Competence

The American Art Therapy Association (AATA), like many other human service organizations—the American Counseling Association (ACA), American Psychological Association (APA), National Association for Social Workers (NASW)—has introduced required education in multicultural competencies, but there remains a lack of understanding of how these competencies are connected to larger systems of oppression (Talwar, 2015a). The current tripartite model of multicultural competencies (knowledge, awareness, and skills) has become foundational for mental health practices (Gorski & Goodman, 2015). This model has mainly been devised as a means to increase the cross-cultural sensitivity of mental health professionals engaged in the treatment of individuals. It emphasizes a client-centered approach of listening with intentionality to elicit the cultural perspective of the client, seeking meaning by understanding the client's lived experiences and knowledge (Anderson & Goolishian, 1992). Although the model contributes to understanding cross-cultural and ethical dimensions of practice, "cultural competence" needs to move beyond just raising awareness of art therapists. Gipson (2015) states,

If the field truly embraces social justice, our training should equip students (and art therapists) to reach new understandings of their identities in relationship to systems of domination and dehumanization, and to formulate useful alternatives in solidarity with targeted communities. Approaching social justice in art therapy requires a more complex engagement with social issues than an introduction to new terminology and recognition of privilege.

(p. 142)

Art therapists need to contextualize identity and difference, in the design and delivery of services to avoid "replicating the existing systems of power and privilege" (Gorski & Goodman, 2015, p. 2). Additionally, they need to pay attention to the "discourses of the body" and how the body has historically been the grounds for "defining and policing the normal, the deviant and the pathological" (Ballantyne & Burton, 2005, p. 406).

Issues of political and institutional oppression have become a particular concern to counselors, psychologists, and art therapists. The work of therapists becomes increasingly difficult in the face of bills passed like the one in the state of Tennessee (HB 1840), which allows counselors and therapists to refuse services to clients whose behaviors, therapy goals, or chosen therapeutic outcomes conflict with the counselor's or therapist's "sincerely held principles" or religious beliefs. The bill, on the one hand, can be seen as well meaning, adhering to the "do no harm" ethics of practice. Yet, on the other hand, laws like HB 1840 call into question the ethics and foundations of practice for therapists. While laws are created to enforce and regulate citizenship, "ethics embody morals and values that supersede legal issues when laws come into conflict with basic human rights" (Talwar, 2017, p. 102). The AATA (2013) ethical principles and the ATCB (2016) ethics code define the values needed to safeguard the people we serve. Their purpose is to ensure responsible practice and check discriminatory attitudes, in order to promote social justice, advocacy, and human rights (Corey, Corey, & Callanan, 2015). Refusing "professional service to anyone on the basis of age, gender identity, race, ethnicity, culture, national origin, religion, sexual orientation, disability, socioeconomic status, or any basis proscribed by law" (AATA, 2013) is a breach of ethics. Following laws like Tennessee HB 1840 is an act of discrimination. Such laws raise questions around the ethics of practice, cultural competence, sociopolitical trauma, and the role of diversity and inclusion in art therapy practice. When the ethical obligations of art therapists collide with their personal values, they must return to the professional code of ethics and ask: What is my responsibility to my clients? How do my personal values and beliefs have the potential to harm others and reinforce discrimination? And ultimately, what is my position in the face of restrictive and discriminatory laws?

The center of therapeutic practice lies in the art therapist's ability to listen and help clients adjust psychologically within their social world, its politics of marginalization and the traumatic experiences that are situated in the context of state sanctioned laws (Karcher, 2017). Sajnani (2016) argues that it is "in moments like these that the false borders between art, therapy and politics have felt the most dangerous" (p. 1). Pointing to sociopolitical trauma and oppression Karcher (2017) and Kuri (2017) ask that art therapists look to an intersectional framework to expand the conceptualization of trauma on non-normative bodies that have been targets in the current political climate.

In addition to legal considerations it is necessary to examine the well-established diagnostic criteria that therapists are required to use in documenting their work. Classification and representation lie at the heart of psychological diagnoses catalogued in the *Diagnostic Statistical Manual (DSM)*. First published in 1952 by the American Psychological Association (APA), the *DSM* was compiled on the basis of clinical research, yet it was also shaped by drug and insurance companies, the legal system, and policy makers. To take the most obvious example, theories from biology, medicine, and psychoanalysis were used to support the diagnosis of homosexuality as a psychiatric disorder in the first *DSM*, confirming a longstanding social and religious stigma. It was not until 1973, following momentous social shifts and protests, that homosexuality was declassified as a psychiatric disorder. Even though the *DSM* has been praised for standardizing psychiatric diagnoses, many critics, including the National Institute of Mental Health, argue that the *DSM* is a biased and unscientific reference manual (Insel, 2013). Yet, despite the ongoing concerns over its validity, reliability, and cross-cultural applicability, the *DSM* is the most popular tool for treating psychiatric patients worldwide. Maintaining a healthy skepticism of the *DSM* is vital to well-informed treatment. The *DSM* is a capitalistic project: the APA earns five million dollars a year from its publication, and it brings untold wealth to the drug companies whose products it endorses. In the early twentieth century psychologists undertook a re-humanizing project in support of the wellbeing of those suffering distress. This re-humanizing project has now become a multimillion dollar industry that in one way or another has impacted every individual in the U.S., from pharmaceutical companies, psychiatrists, and therapists, to the self-help book industry, and publishers of art therapy coloring books. "Mindfulness" has become a common term that has penetrated the vocabulary of every American, giving rise to phone apps for relaxation and meditation, and drawing to relieve anxiety. Gipson (2017) and Kuri (2017) consider it an ethical mandate for art therapists to confront the field's engagement with neoliberal and capitalist agendas.

In the current social and political climate, understanding identity and difference means recognizing laws that are discriminatory, and upholding the ethical responsibility of art therapists. Hamrick and Byma (2017) ask art therapists to address the knowledge gap and recognize the "contemporary realities of racism, cis-heteropatriarchal sexism, and ethno-religious prejudice in the field, to critically analyze whiteness, and to take steps to dismantle white supremacy in the study and practice of art therapy" (p. 106). For art therapists, having a critical understanding of diversity, multiculturalism, cross-cultural, and social justice practices becomes essential to promoting just practices of care.

What Is Social Justice?

Chung and Bemak (2012) suggest that social justice is the "fifth force" in counseling. (The psychoanalytic paradigm is considered the first force, followed by cognitive behavioral therapy as the second. Existential and humanistic theories are the third force, followed by multiculturalism as the fourth.) Including a social justice focus means expanding concepts of multiculturalism and cultural competence. A social justice paradigm focuses on community building, empowerment, sustainability, equity, and justice in a domestic and international context. It expands the vision of art therapy.

Social justice is based on the concept of human rights and equality for all. Chung and Bemak (2012) note that a social justice paradigm is not just based in identity politics, but is located within the legal systems and the laws that govern everyday life. It transcends race, class, gender, sexuality, religion, and disability. An underlying assumption equates social justice to access, and to fair and just treatment for all. Social justice in the mental health field (art therapy, counseling, or psychology), therefore, translates into understanding how clients are positioned in society and if they have equal and fair access to resources and benefits. A social justice paradigm broadens the scope of practice to incorporate a critical perspective on the ways subjectivity is socially and politically constructed, and the ways history and language produce representations of non- normative identities. As Bell (2008) notes, "The question is not 'Who am I?' but 'How am 'I' a subject—in history, in language, and in material ways?'" (p. 174). In such a framework, the starting point of the therapeutic is based in an examination of the institutions, policies, and history that make citizens subjects the topic of this implicit discourse. A social justice oriented art therapy practice thus means complicating the modernist perspectives that continue to dominate art therapy: the focus on the individual and the unconscious, art and healing as a road to the inner self, and emphasis on increasing self-awareness (Burt, 2012). This also requires a critical examination of the language used to define human beings, their lives, and the therapeutic (Spaniol & Cattaneo, 1994).

Some counselors and art therapists have called for decolonizing art therapy in order to connect cultural competence to social justice frameworks and open paths for envisioning new paradigms of care that are rooted in ethical decision-making (Gorski & Goodman, 2015; Sajnani, 2016; Talwar, Moon, Timm-Bottos, & Kapitan, 2015). The term "decolonizing" means breaking down the hegemonic structures that rule daily life; in the words of Lorde (1984), using the masters' tools to dismantle the master's house. Decolonizing art therapy requires rethinking the purpose of "art." Taking a social justice perspective is not enough if art therapy practices are not focused on challenging the power hierarchies that are embedded in systems and structures of therapeutic practice. A decolonizing view asks that art therapy projects be committed to critical interventions that link critical inquiry and praxis, projects highlighted in this book. By doing so, multiculturalism, and cross-cultural, and cultural competence, informed by ethical decision-making, will function as the cornerstone of art therapy practice to make "the links between practice, culture, diversity, and identity as they relate to social justice" (Talwar, 2015a, p. 100).

Moving Towards Critical Consciousness

In the last decade, psychologists, counselors, and art therapists have drawn attention to the need for critical thinking around issues of identity construction and difference (Goodman & Gorski, 2015; Gipson, 2015; Prilleltensky & Nelson, 2002; Talwar, 2010, among others). The term "critical" entails challenging the theories and frameworks that inform art therapy practice, but may also reinforce inequality. By recognizing the prevailing power structures, art therapists can become advocates for reducing the systems of domination and dependence that entrap the people they serve (Lévesque, 2007).

Art therapists are adept at developing treatment plans using critical thinking to analyze and evaluate the lives of their clients, their psychic distress, and their level of functioning. But in order to have a more nuanced practice, they have to incorporate critical consciousness to understand the social oppressions facing their clients. Paulo Freire (1970) who coined the term "critical consciousness," suggests that individuals live in a relational world, not in a vacuum. He argues that social justice occurs when political action is taken *with* people who are oppressed, not *for* them. Developing critical consciousness means acknowledging the "link between trauma, oppression, power, privilege and the historical inequities embedded in social relationships" (Talwar, 2015b, p. 843). Critical consciousness, according to Ward (2007), involves, "Knowing and learning how to interpret one's own experience, trust one's own voice, and give legitimacy to one's own perspective" (p. 247). She outlines three ways to instill critical consciousness: 1) *reading* and *naming* socially marginalizing patterns by recognizing how media images and stereotypes have informed lived experiences of racial, classed, gendered, sexual, disabled, and religious minorities; 2) exploring ways to respond to the socially negative images by *"opposing them"* : disrupting racists, sexist, or homophobic micro aggressions by speaking up; and finally 3) *"replacing"* the negative images with positive images of pride. As Golub (2005) argues, social action art therapy is ideally a participatory, collaborative process that emphasizes art making as a vehicle through which communities name and understand their realities, identify their needs and strengths, and transform their lives in ways that contribute to individual and collective wellbeing and social justice

Understanding difference and inequality, thus means examining the disparities and oppression that exist in American society. The disparities experienced are not random; rather, they exist as part of a powerful historical and social system that has structured individual and collective existence on the basis of race and class. The pseudo-scientific knowledge produced by the eugenics movement in the early twentieth century constructed notions of biological inferiority that shaped social policy and laws to justify stratification and inequality in society. As Weber (2001) stated, the U.S. is,

> Founded on the ideals "all men are created equal," power and privilege, in fact, are distributed not only along individual but also along group lines so that some groups are privileged—whites, heterosexual, upper classes, men—while others are oppressed - people of color, gays, bisexuals, lesbians, the working classes, the poor, and women. This tension—between the ideals of individual equality and the reality of systemic group inequality—is a long-standing source of controversy and contest in U.S. society.
>
> *(p. 4)*

Race, class, gender, sexuality, and physical ability are social constructs. Social science has traditionally examined them as independent variables even when there happens to be an overlap under specific conditions. For example, studying racial differences and similarities between whites, blacks, Latinos, and Asians cannot happen without understanding the historical implications of how each group was incorporated into the U.S. (Dill & Zambrana, 2009).

In the twenty-first century, art therapy cannot continue to just address the behavior and the minds of individuals to understand their conscious and unconscious experiences. Art therapists have to engage in understanding the complexity of human life and behavior within a historical and cultural context (Gorski & Goodman, 2015) to avoid promoting essentializing notions of human behavior and development (Talwar, 2010). In conclusion, examining the history and theories that give rise to discourses of race, gender, sexuality, and disability as part of the nation building project in the U.S., along with Britain, and Germany, means looking at the eugenics movement of the late nineteenth and twentieth century, which I will explore in Chapter 2.

References

Ahmed, S. (2004). *The cultural politics of emotion*. New York, NY: Routledge.
Ahmed, S. (2012). *On being included: Racism and diversity in institutional life*. Durham, NC: Duke University Press.
Alarcón, N. (1996). Conjugating subjects in the age of multiculturalism. In A. F. Gordon & C. Newfield (Eds.), *Mapping multiculturalism* (pp. 127–148). Minneapolis, MN: University of Minnesota Press.
American Art Therapy Association (AATA). (2013). Ethical principles for art therapists. Retrieved from http://arttherapy.org/aata-ethics/

Anderson, H. & Goolishian, H. (1992). The client is the expert: A not knowing approach to therapy. In S. McNamee & K. J. Gergan (Eds.), *Therapy as social construction* (pp. 25–32). Thousand Oaks, CA: Sage.

Anderson, M. L. & Collins, P. H. (2007). *Race, class, and gender: An anthology* (6th Ed.). Belmont, CA: Thomson Wadsworth.

Art Therapy Credentials Board, Inc. (ATCB). (2016). *Code of Ethics, Conduct, and Disciplinary Procedures*. Retrieved from www.atcb.org/Ethics/ATCBCode

Awais, Y. J. & Yali, A. M. (2013). A call for diversity: The need to recruit and retain ethnic minority art therapy students in art therapy. *Art Therapy: Journal of the American Art Therapy Association, 30*(3), 130–134. doi.10.1080/07421656.2013.819284

Ballantyne, T. & Burton, A. (Eds.) (2005). *Bodies in contact: Rethinking colonial encounters in world history*. Durham, NC: Duke University Press.

Bell, E. (2008). *Theories of performance*. Los Angeles, CA: Sage Publications.

Burger, P. L. & Luckman, T. (1966). *The social construction of reality*. Garden City, NY: Anchor books.

Burt, H. (2012). Multiple perspectives: Art therapy, postmodernism and feminism. In H. Burt (Ed.), *Art therapy and postmodernism: Creative healing through a prism* (pp. 17–31). London, England: Jessica Kingsley Publishers.

Corey, G., Corey, M., & Callanan, P. (2015). *Issues and ethics in the helping professions* (9th Ed.). Pacific Grove, CA: Brooks/Cole.

Chung, R. & Bemak, F. (2012). *Social justice counseling: The next step beyond multiculturalism*. Los Angeles, LA: Sage Publications.

Dill, B. T. & Zambrana, R. E. (Eds.) (2009). *Emerging intersections: Race, class, and gender in theory, policy and practice*. Piscataway, NJ: Rutgers University Press.

Doby-Copeland, C. (2006). Cultural diversity curriculum design: An art therapist's perspective. *Art Therapy: Journal of the American Art Therapy Association, 23*(1), 81–85. doi.10.1080/07421656.2006.10129330

Dufrene, P. M. (1994). Art therapy with Native American clients: Ethical and professional issues. *Art Therapy: Journal of the American Art Therapy Association, 11*(3), 191–193. doi.10.1080/07421656.1994.10759083

Freire, P. (1970). *Pedagogy of the oppressed*. New York, NY: Continuum.

George, J., Greene, B., & Blackwell, M. (2005). Three voices on multiculturalism from the art therapy classroom. *Art Therapy: Journal of the American Art Therapy Association, 22*(3), 132–138.

Gipson, L. (2015). Is cultural competence enough? Deepening social justice pedagogy in art therapy. *Art Therapy: Journal of the American Art Therapy Association, 32*(3), 142–145. doi.10.1080/07421656.2015.1060835

Gipson, L. (2017). Challenging neoliberalism and multicultural love in art therapy. *Art Therapy: Journal of the American Art Therapy Association, 34*(3), 112–117. doi.10.1080/0 7421656.2017.1353326

Golub, D. (2005). Social action art therapy. *Art Therapy: Journal of the American Art Therapy Association, 22*(1), 17–23. doi.10.1080/07421656.2005.10129467

Goodman, R. D. & Gorski, P. C. (Eds.) (2015). *Decolonizing "multicultural" counseling through social justice*. New York, NY: Springer.

Gorski, P. C. & Goodman, R. D. (2015). Introduction: Towards a decolonized multicultural counseling and psychology. In R. D. Goodman & P. C. Gorski (Eds.), *Decolonizing "multicultural" counseling through social justice* (pp. 1–10). New York, NY: Springer.

Grzanka, P. R. (Ed.) (2014). *Intersectionality: A foundations and frontier reader*. Boulder, CO: Westview Press.

Hamrick, C. & Byma, C. (2017). Know history, know self: Art therapists' responsibility to dismantle white supremacy. *Art Therapy: Journal of the American Art Therapy Association, 34*(3), 106–111. doi.10.1080/07421656.2017.1353332

Hass-Cohen, N. & Carr, R. (2008). *Art therapy and clinical neuroscience.* Philadelphia, PA: Jessica Kingsley.

Hiscox, A. R. & Calisch, A. C. (Eds.) (1998). *Tapestry of cultural issues in art therapy.* Philadelphia, PA: Jessica Kingsley.

Insel, T. (April 29, 2013). Director's blog: Transforming diagnosis. National Institutes of Mental Health. Retrieved www.nimh.nih.gov/about/director/2013/transforming-diagnosis.shtml

King, J. (2016). *Art therapy, trauma and neuroscience: Theoretical and practical perspectives.* New York, NY: Routledge.

Kuri, E. (2017). Toward an ethical application of intersectionality in art therapy. *Art Therapy: Journal of the American Art Therapy Association, 34*(3), 118–122. doi.10.1080/07421656.2017.1358023

Lévesque, F. (2007). *Critical art therapy: A third perspective.* Retrieved from www.lulu.com/product/ebook/critical-art-therapy-a-third-perspective/11771260

Lorde, A. (1984). *Sister outsider.* Freedom, CA: Crossing Press.

Lupton, D. (1997). Foreword. In S. Hogan (Ed.) *Feminism and art therapy* (p. xii–xix). London, UK: Jessica Kingsley.

Karcher, O. P. (2017). Sociopolitical oppression, trauma, and healing: Moving towards a social justice art therapy framework. *Art Therapy: Journal of the American Art Therapy Association, 34*(3), 123–128. doi.10.1080/07421656.2017.1358024

Madison, S. D. (2012). *Critical ethnography: Method, ethics and performance* (2nd Ed.). Washington, DC: Sage Publications.

Ore, T. (2009). *The social construction of difference and inequality: Race, class, gender and sexuality* (4th Ed.). New York, NY: McGraw-Hill.

Prilleltensky, I. & Nelson, G. (2002). *Doing psychology critically: Making a difference in diverse settings.* New York: Palgrave Macmillan.

Robb, M. (2014). National survey assessing perceived competence in art therapy graduate students. *Art Therapy: Journal of the American Art Therapy Association, 31*(1), 21–27. doi.10.1080/07421656.2014.873691

Sajnani, N. (2016). Borderlands: Diversity and social justice in drama therapy. *Drama Therapy Review, 2*(1), 1–3.

Shuman, A. (2005). *Other people's stories.* Chicago, IL: University of Illinois Press.

Spaniol, S. & Cattaneo, M. (1994). The power of language in the art therapeutic relationship. *Art Therapy: Journal of the American Art Therapy Association, 11*(4), 266–270. doi.10.1080/07421656.1994.10759100

Talwar, S. (2007). Accessing traumatic memory through art making: An art therapy trauma protocol (ATTP). *Arts in Psychotherapy, 34*(1), 22–35. doi.10.1016/j.aip.2006.09.001

Talwar, S. (2010). An intersectional framework for race, class, gender, and sexuality in art therapy. *Art Therapy: Journal of the American Art Therapy Association, 27*(1), 11–17. doi.10.1080/07421656.2010.10129567

Talwar, S. (2015a). Culture, diversity and identity: From margins to center. *Art Therapy: Journal of the American Art Therapy Association, 32*(3), 100–103. doi.10.1080/07421656.2015.1060563

Talwar, S. (2015b). Creating alternative public spaces: Community-based art practice, critical consciousness, and social justice. In D. Gussak, & M. Rosal (Eds.),

The Wiley-Blackwell handbook of art therapy (pp. 840–847). Oxford, England: Wiley Blackwell.

Talwar, S. (2017). Law, ethics and cultural competence in art therapy. *Art Therapy: Journal of the American Art Therapy Association, 34*(3), 102–105. doi.10.1080/07421656.2017.1358026

Talwar, S., Iyer, J., & Doby-Copeland, C. (2004). The invisible veil: Changing paradigms in the art therapy profession. *Art Therapy: Journal of the American Art Therapy Association, 21*(1), 44–48. doi.10.1080/07421656.2004.10129325

Talwar, S., Moon, C., Timm-Bottos, J., & Kaptian, L. (2015, July). *Decolonizing art therapy: Social justice and new paradigms of care.* 46th Annual Conference of the American Art Therapy Association, Minneapolis, MN.

ter Maat, M. (2011). Developing and assessing multicultural competence with a focus on culture and ethnicity. *Art Therapy: Journal of the American Art Therapy Association, 28*(1), 4–10. doi.10.1080/07421656.2011.557033

Ward, J. V. (2007). Uncovering truth, uncovering lives: Lessons of resistance in the socialization of Black girls. In B. Leadbeater & N. Way (Eds.) *Urban girls revisited* (pp. 243–260). New York, NY: New York University Press.

Weber, L. (2001). *Understanding race, class, gender and sexuality: A conceptual framework.* New York, NY: McGraw-Hill.

2

CRITIQUING ART THERAPY

History, Science, and Representation

Savneet K. Talwar

In 2008, Abigail Fisher sued the state of Texas after she was denied admission to the University of Texas at Austin (UT Austin). She claimed that the university denied her, a white woman, admission due to her race while offering admission to less qualified students of color, a violation of the Equal Protection clause of the Fourteenth Amendment. In 2009, the district courts upheld the legality of UT Austin's admissions policy. The case was then taken to the U.S. Supreme Court. In 2013, the Supreme Court, in *Fisher v. University of Texas*, ruled that strict scrutiny be applied to UT Austin's admission policy to determine the constitutionality of a race-sensitive admissions policy, thus sending the case back to the appeals court. In 2015, Fisher and her lawyer Edward Blum, a conservative activist, tweaked the case, arguing

> that UT's "qualitative" diversity interest is in fact illegitimate. It depends on the assumption that, as a group, minorities admitted through the Top Ten Percent Law are inherently limited in their ability to contribute to the university's vision of a diverse student body, merely because many come from majority-minority communities.
>
> *(as cited in Marcotte, 2015)*

Blum's argument, in essence, stated that it is racist to give students of color with middling grades admission, and asked the court to strike down affirmative action policies for college admissions. During the oral argument Justice Antonin Scalia stated,

> There are those who contend that it does not benefit African-Americans to get them into the University of Texas where they do not do well, as opposed to having them go to a less-advanced school, a less—a slower-track

school where they do well. One of the briefs pointed out that most of the black scientists in this country don't come from schools like the University of Texas. They come from lesser schools where they do not feel that they're being pushed ahead in classes that are too fast for them.

(Fisher v. Texas, p. 67)

In a similar vein, Justice Roberts questioned, "What unique perspective does a minority student bring to a physics class?" raising the issue of what diversity accomplishes.

Although Justice Scalia's remarks drew gasps in the courtroom, his opinion rests on a longstanding view that the potential for education and achievement is rooted in racial and ethnic identity. His argument, which is essentially that intelligence is rooted in biology, continues the legacy of white supremacy in characterizing race as a biological phenomenon "rather than a power phenomena or purposeful societal arrangement" (Gorski & Goodman, 2015, p. 3). Conversely, the narrow focus on race as a claim for discrimination by Fisher ignores her class and gender privilege, or the ways in which she has benefited from being a white woman raised in a wealthy suburb of Houston. At the same time, Justice Roberts' remark about non-white bodies in the physics classroom offers the ignorant view that the role of brown and black bodies is to expand the experience of white students, rather than to learn physics.

Cases like *Fisher v. University of Texas* are often framed to focus on a single marker of difference, in this case race, while overlooking gender and class privilege. Intersectionality scholar Grzanka (2014) argues that "the reality of social structures, including the law, media, education, government, and economy, is much more complicated than a zero sum game" (p. xiii). When we privilege

> one dimension of inequality (e.g., race *or* gender *or* class) and which derive ideas, knowledge, and policy from that single dimension [suggest] such that all members of a racial, gender, or class group are thought to have essentially the same experience of race, gender, or class. Single-axis paradigms generally position racism and sexism as *parallel* or *analogous*, as opposed to *intersecting* or *co-constitutive*, phenomena.
>
> *(p. xv)*

When cases like *Fisher v. University of Texas* are viewed from an intersectional lens, race, class, gender, and sexuality are viewed as constituents in the production and construction of inequality. The Justice's remarks about diversity, in 2015, and "what diversity is" hearken back to the history of racial science and its continued impact on the representation of bodies of color.

Although the concept of diversity is commonplace in the U.S. and is central to health, education, employment, and the human service professions, there remains an urgent need to deconstruct the hegemony of whiteness and its social construction. When the highest ranking justice of the United States, sworn to enforce laws that uphold equality, ascribes to theories of biological inferiority there remains an urgent need to question the legacy of scientific racism that continues to influence laws, policy, and ideas that perpetuate white supremacy. Finally, it is also important to question the language used by the justices. The term "minority" has become associated with race and ethnicity. From a sociological perspective, the term minority refers to social groups that have less social capital and power, rather than to their numerical statistic (Barzilai, 2010).

The aim of this chapter is to examine the power of law and images in supporting discourses of the body—the normative, deviant, or pathological—as they were used in the eugenics movement of the nineteenth and twentieth centuries and subsequently inherited by the field of art therapy. Eugenics was a scientific endeavor intended to improve humankind. The movement relied heavily on visual media and documentation to garner support by citizens as a call to civic responsibility. But the findings of the eugenics movement fostered racist governmental policies that have had a lasting impact on the representation of racial minorities, people with disabilities, the mentally ill, the LGBTQ community, as well as on the educational and criminal justice systems. I locate the origins of art therapy within the movement identifying deviant and pathological bodies, as part of psychology's "re-humanization" mission in the early twentieth century. Whereas psychology purported to understand human behavior and the mind, art therapy elevated the artistic renderings of the mentally ill to material objects that made pathology of the mind visible. Since images are fundamental to the practice of art therapy and are considered to be a "visual representations of an internal state" (Junge & Asawa, 1994, p. 7), a critical examination of the uses of images in art therapy requires problematizing the ways in which art therapy has participated in promoting reductive visual representations of human beings by drawing on psychological frameworks. I argue that theories emerged in the twentieth-century eugenics movement as a way to make meaning of bodies that were principally viewed within a social and cultural context. Examining art therapy within a broader historical discourse helps clarify its methodologies and how its viewing practices have been shaped. Doing so helps to evaluate the purpose, intentions, and frames of analysis that produced its fundamental concepts.

In this chapter, I outline a brief history of mental health and how it was shaped within discourses of popular culture that reinforced the normative versus deviant body. I examine the material conditions that shape subject formation—immigration status, criminality, and disability in addition to race, class, gender, and sexuality—and the role played by photography. What are the methodological and epistemological frameworks that have contributed to shaping knowledge about bodies? What are the social, political, and moral forces that have molded our ways of seeing? Lastly, what impact did this knowledge have in shaping art therapy and its analysis of images? I contend that mainstream art therapy emerged from early discourses of the body that mirrored positivism (language, techniques, and visual representations) in the pursuit of psychology's re-humanization project.

Beginnings of Mental Health

In 1812, Benjamin Rush offered his thoughts on madness in his book entitled *Medical Inquiries and Observations upon the Disease of the Mind*. One of the first psychiatric texts to be published in the United States, Rush's book recounts his observations and views on various forms of mental disorder. Although he offers detailed observations and classifications of mental disorders—advising medical treatments such as bleeding, blisters, and psychological terror—his book also argues for the humane treatment of the mentally ill. His counsel that the mentally ill should be treated with great kindness reflected reformists' practices, known as the moralists' treatments (Whitaker, 2002), is of particular interest to art therapy. The idea of moral treatment involving a rethinking of the insane was inspired by the work of the French physician Philippe Pinel, who was highly skeptical of medical remedies. For Pinel, medical treatments were often injurious, and frequently arose out of "prejudice, hypotheses, pedantry, ignorance and authority of celebrated names" (Pinel, as cited in Whitaker, 2002, p. 21). Pinel advocated for actively listening to patients, getting to know them, and providing meaningful activities, rather than idleness, to heal the

FIGURE 2.1 Pinel à la Salpêtrière, Salon de 1876

Printed by permission of the British Museum

wounded mind. As part of the treatment, art making was introduced as a way to tap into the patients' emotions (Hogan, 2001). Pinel's relationship with the mentally ill was captured in a painting by Tony Robert-Fleury, in 1876, entitled *Pinel Unchaining the Insane at the Hospital of Salpêtrière*, Paris (Figure 2.1). The painting illustrates the humanitarian work of Pinel, also known as the father of psychiatry and a much celebrated hero of the past (MacGregor, 1989).

Around the same time, the Quakers were developing a form of their own moral treatment rooted in their religious beliefs, which became the most significant influence on the care of the mentally ill in nineteenth-century America. The first moral-asylum was opened by the Philadelphia Quakers in 1817, with several other states following suit. Between 1833 and 1841, 16 public asylums were opened in the U.S., all promising to provide moral treatment to the mentally ill. A significant effort, related to emergence of occupational therapy, was made to keep the patients busy using a variety of activities like reading and writing, poetry, sewing, gardening, and other domestic activities. The Quakers were thought to employ the healing hand of kindness, where love, empathy, and creating a gentle environment were the key focus (Hogan, 2001; Whitaker, 2002).

From 1841 to 1883 the Quaker physician Thomas Kirkbride oversaw the Pennsylvania Hospital for the Insane, including the institute's construction on expansive grounds. It housed occupational therapy suites, libraries, and swimming pools that allowed the patients a variety of recreational and educational opportunities. He added a greenhouse, a museum, and meticulously kept gardens, stating

> that every object of interest that is placed in and about the hospital for the insane, that even every tree that buds, or every flower that blooms, may contribute in its small measure to excite a new train of thought, and perhaps the first step towards bringing back to reason, the morbid wanders of the disordered mind.
>
> *(Scull as cited in Whitaker, 2002, p. 31)*

Kirkbride defined the doctor–patient relationship as the critical element of the curative process, along with empathy and compassion. Between the 1840s and 1850s, Dorothea Dix also worked tirelessly to bring humane care to all mentally ill Americans, who had generally been shut up in poor houses or in local prisons. This enlightened movement briefly stalled, if not ended, in the face of, first, economic pressure that translated into political and, second, a misguided quest for scientifically valid categorizations of the mentally ill.

Eugenics: Constructing the Normal and the Abnormal

Davis (1997), a disability studies scholar, explores the lasting influence of the eugenics movement on contemporary society in representing what is normal. He wrote that,

We live in a world of norms. Each of us endeavors to be normal or deliberately tries to avoid that state . . . We rank our intelligence, our cholesterol,
our weight, height, sex drive, bodily dimensions along some conceptual
line from subnormal to above-average . . . Our children are ranked in
school and tested to determine where they fit within the normal curve of
learning and intelligence.

(p. 3)

The concept of the normal is so entrenched in everyday life that to understand
the disabled, criminal, or mentally ill body it is necessary to return to the construction of normality to understand the problem. Davis (1997) attributes the
hegemony of the normal to the eugenics movement. He argues that eugenics
was "part of a notion of progress, of industrialization, and the ideological con-
solidation of power of the bourgeoisie. The implications of the hegemony of
the normal are profound and extend to the very heart of cultural production"
(p. 12). In this sense, racialized, classed, and gendered bodies are always marked

FIGURE 2.2 Eugenics logo

Printed by permission of the Cold Spring Harbor Laboratory Archives

with ideological meaning. The historical movements and social reasoning that both formed and perpetuated discursive practices of colonialism and the visual technologies through which subjects were formed and produced (Gonzàlez, 2008) lie at the heart of identity and difference.

Using the symbol of a tree as the growth of science (Figure 2.2), the eugenicist's slogan was "like a tree eugenics draws its materials from many sources and organizes them in a harmonious unity." Eugenics drew from and shaped knowledge in the fields of anthropology, psychology, psychiatry, genetics, biology, genealogy, anatomy, sociology, law, and more. Although eugenicists propounded theories of biological inferiority, which emerged in the nineteenth and twentieth centuries as a means to scientifically investigate human character and link behaviors of certain groups to social and economic differences (Hogan 2001), the main goal of eugenics was to improve the human race (Stokopf, 2009). Originating in Britain, eugenics spread to Germany and the U.S., eventually having a global impact. It was only after World War II that eugenics lost its influence. Promoted as a progressive science and supported by the educated elite, eugenics became the "basis for racist governmental practices, including the sterilization of Britons and Americans, and the mass murder of millions of Jews, together with Slavs, Gypsies, and homosexuals, in Germany and Poland during World War II" (Maxwell, 2008, p. 1).

The eugenicists expertly used visual technologies, especially photography, in promoting their agenda. The search for empirically valid categories of difference to form a baseline norm is interwoven with the eugenics movement in the U.S. and England. As a movement it would reshape the treatment of the mental illness and the field of psychology. The American Eugenics Movement maintains an archive of over 27,000 images (www.eugenicsarchive.org/eugenics/). A topic search of the archive yields a range of categories, from Better Babies contests, to birth and population control, criminality, family trait forms, immigration, race and ethnicity, race mixing, sterilization, poverty and degeneracy, physical and intellectual development, and mental illness. The eugenicists were particularly interested in mental illness because, to them, the mentally ill were a growing burden on society. And since most mentally ill people were wards of the state, the researchers had easy access to personal and family records, as well as access to the patients for interviews. Some of the first data to emerge as evidence that "social inadequacy" might be in the genes came from research data in mental institutions (Stokopf, 2009; Lowe, 1998; Whitaker, 2002). Classifying the information into categories such as feeblemindedness, criminality, insanity, and dependency, a spectrum of normality and pathology (Figure 2.3) began to come into existence. The mental asylums and hospitals became the laboratories for the eugenicist researchers. Their work began to shape the ways in which people were categorized, especially how race, ethnicity, gender, and sexuality defined the norms of "good citizenship" and "moral codes of conduct" to protect society, the body politic, using evidence of criminality and insanity (Davis, 1997).

Two of the first groups to be identified as a risk to American society were immigrants and individuals with disabilities. The influx of large numbers of

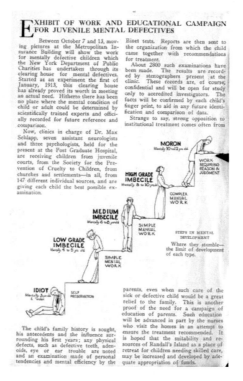

FIGURE 2.3 Educational campaign for juvenile mental defectives (1904)

Printed by permission of the American Philosophical Society

immigrants happens to have coincided with the eugenics movement. Harry Laughlin, Eugenics Office Superintendent, lobbied the House of Representatives Committee on Immigration to limit immigration from "undesirable" countries, those mainly in Eastern Europe and the Mediterranean (the Eugenicists were of Western European and Scandinavian descent). He used flawed data to argue that a large number of incoming immigrants showed traits of social inadequacy (www.eugenicsarchive.org/eugenics/list2.pl).

Following the work of Charles Darwin, his cousin Sir Frances Galton began the Eugenics Movement in England. Using evolutionary theory, Galton laid the groundwork for eugenics through norms of "fitness," placing the disabled body to the periphery as the "defective." The eugenicists become obsessed with the elimination of "defectives," those who were categorized as the feebleminded, criminal, and insane (Whitaker, 2002). The movement led to forced sterilization laws that impacted people with intellectual and physical disabilities, criminals, and the mentally ill. Between 1897 to 1909 states like Michigan, Indiana, Pennsylvania, Washington, and California passed sterilization laws, and the Supreme Court made sterilization constitutional in 1927, in the case of *Buck v. Bell* (Figure 2.4).

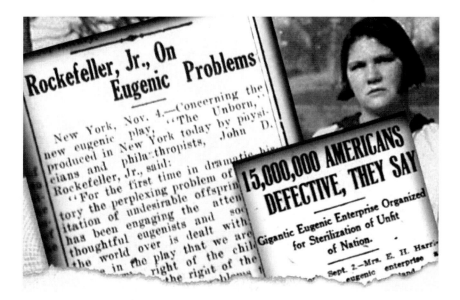

FIGURE 2.4 *The Salem Daily Capital Journal* printed Thursday, November 4, 1915

Justice Oliver Wendell Holmes justified the decision and stated, "It is better for all the world, if instead of waiting to execute degenerate offspring for crime, or to let them starve for their imbecility, society can prevent those who are manifestly unfit from continuing their kind" (Garcia, 2013, para 8).

The Role of Photography

The invention of photography played a powerful role in the eugenics movement. Photography became the tool to document human beings and provide the objective evidence to justify scientific findings, and it gave legitimacy to the civilizing mission of colonial imperialism. Photographs captured the contrast between the civilized and the primitive (Figure 2.5), thus instituting cultural hegemony (Gramsci, 1971) and discourses of knowledge and power (Foucault, 1980).

Foucault (1980) claimed that images don't exist in a vacuum; rather they are instruments of power. His concept of "discourse" relates to systems of power that work within a given society, and to the cultural practices and rules that historically create meaning. The eugenics archives housed at Cold Springs Harbor Laboratory in New York, powerfully created and shaped knowledge of bodies in relationship to race/ethnicity, class, gender, and sexuality. The detailed categorization of photographs made the racial, gendered, and sexual body transparent as a legible and categorizable document, and one that reinforced and served the ideology of middle-class norms by visually exemplifying concepts such as deviance and the perverse (Sekula, 1986).

FIGURE 2.5 Two Aiomne women of Papua New Guinea, measured by Lord Moyne and colleague (1935)

Printed by permission of the Pitt River Museum

The eugenicists methodically documented non-normative bodies, using photography as a means to support the growing medicalization of bodies. Detailed photographic images were taken to capture salient aspects of the body. One powerful example is the work of Alphonse Bertillon who, in 1876, took systematic frontal and profile photographs of criminal suspects for a biometric database. He supplemented the photographs with detailed measurements to document unique features of suspects. His database, supported by the popularization of phrenology and eugenics, was rooted in the belief that facial features could be used to distinguish between superior and inferior races, thus providing empirical evidence for theories of biological inferiority. Bertillon gained tremendous popularity in the U.S. when his classification system was introduced, in 1887 (http://apa.nyu.edu/hauntedfiles/biometric-policing-more-local-police-using-facial-recognition-software/). Bertillon's system created a unique way to identify and track suspects and repeat offenders. As scientific evidence it was also read from political, economic, cultural, and historical perspectives. The architects of eugenics, empowered with authority on the basis of its objectivity and rationality, mapped the body to produce and construct identities in the twentieth century (Terry, 1995).

Fascination with the body became a source of scientific inquiry into the construction of perversion. Through clinical surveillance, psychiatry, and diagnosis, the body is territorialized, becoming an object that could be measured, zoned, mapped and read as text as in Bertillon posters of physical features in the *Musée des Collections Historiques de la Préfecture de Police*. In critiquing scientific discourse, new media, and technology, Terry (1995) argues that photography in particular became a means of popularizing representations of difference based on race, ethnicity, gender, and sexuality. Visual images illustrated deviancy from the normative and played a critical "role in the hegemonic production of a standardized normative subjectivity" (p. 139). Terry adds that homosexuals were one of the "internal others," "alongside criminals, prostitutes, and the feeble minded – whose bodies were believed to carry the germs of ruin" (p. 139). Science and medicine were installed as keepers of the public trust. Social inequality was a matter of biology.

Eugenics had a profound effect on the lives of immigrants, people of color, the disabled, and anyone who existed outside the "mythical norm." As Smith (1999) argues, eugenicists defined "race" as a biological characteristic and used the definition to bring clearly into focus the concept of whiteness and the normal body. Photography and eugenics combined to support the moral and biological superiority of whiteness. Struken and Cartwright (2001) stressed that photography

> became an integral part of both the scientific profession and the regulation of social behavior by bureaucratic institutions of the state. It is used in the law to designate evidence and criminality, in medicine to document pathologies and define a visual difference between the "normal" and "abnormal," and in the social sciences, such as anthropology and sociology, to enable the creation of the subject positions of the researcher (anthropologist) and the object of the study (in many cases, defined as the "native").
>
> *(p. 95)*

The system of categorization created by eugenics was fixed and unchangeable, promoting essentialism: that human behavior is predetermined on the basis of genetics and biology (Ore, 2009).

While the eugenics movement had social ramifications for racial/ethnic and sexual minorities, poor and working class individuals, it also impacted social and education policy. In pursuing its aim of improving the human race, the science of eugenics produced a visual archive of normativity through categories of deviancy and social pathologies. The camera again becomes the tool for creating images of otherness. Accepted as a scientific practice by the medical and biological sciences, including social sciences such as anthropology, eugenics created a colonial discourse (Struken & Cartwright, 2001) that continues to impact underrepresented racial, ethnic, and gender non-conforming people even today. Eugenics pedagogy failed to consider the real depth of individual problems, such as poverty, lack of healthcare or childcare, unhygienic living conditions, or unemployment. As Tucker (1994) argues in *The Science and Politics of Racial Research*, the political purpose of the scientific study of human difference and the abilities of different races was to rationalize social and political inequality. He offers a chronological history of the use of science to support ideas of genetic and intellectual inferiority that continue to impact the racialization of people of color and their everyday experiences.

After World War II, the idea of race and biological inferiority as an organizing principle slowed to a halt, but race has remained a persistent concept as a "regressive, colonial taxonomy that masquerades as a progressive multiculturalism" (González, 2008, p. 4). While many scholars agree that race is a social, not a biological, construct, the long history of pseudo-science, eugenics, and image production continues to impact the politics of representation and present people as "racialized" subjects. González (2008) states that "Race discourse can thus be understood as the process or experience of *subjection* through which people are transformed into signs of culturally preconstituted subject positions" (p. 3), as such "race discourse *produces* the subject it supposedly describes" (p. 4).

Gilroy (2000) noted that visual culture played a vital role in promoting racial beliefs. European and U.S. imperialism made sure that photographs didn't just remain in the service of racial science; they became popular among the home population of colonial powers who consumed them out of taste for novelty as much as pride in the imperial project, a development alongside concerns about the nation's health, helped lay the foundation for the public's later interest in the racial-type photography of eugenicists (Maxwell, 2008).

Racialists' belief penetrated every aspect of visual culture: newspapers, cartoons, paintings, comic books, illustrations, postcards, posters, and more. It was not until 1945 that critical voices began to challenge the definition and norms of race as a biological condition. The rise of the anti-colonial movement in the 1940s and the civil rights movement in 1950s began the process of challenging racialist attitudes and practices. In 1951 the UNESCO Foundation condemned the biological basis of race that, for the most part, led to the Holocaust. As Maxwell (2008) states,

> What was condemned in this moment, and is arguably still regarded with horror and distaste by many people today, were the attempts of powerful individuals and governments to apply biological definition of race and its corollary of eugenics, to the task of nation and empire building, at the expense of the humanitarian values and the basic human rights that we have come to associate with "civilized" society.
>
> *(p. vii)*

Despite the fact that the eugenics movement has been written out of the history of textbooks, it nonetheless has left an insidious impact on educational policies, representation of immigrants and people of color, mental illness, the LGBTQ community, and more. To this end, it is important to examine how the field of psychology participated in eugenics research, which in turn engendered a fascination with the art of the mentally ill. What are the cultural and political intersections that produce the circumstances in which the art of the mentally ill provides a visual narrative to reinforce colonial practices of the normal versus abnormal, or the primitive versus civilized? And, what are the circumstances that produce art therapy?

Locating Art Therapy

Psychiatry was a key contributor to the concepts of degeneration and madness. It formulated the language and indictors of the pathology of the degenerate or primitive mind (criminal or insane) used in the eugenics movement. MacGregor's (1989) *The Discovery of the Art of the Insane* offers a window into the early discourses that culturally shaped viewing and interpreting practices of the artistic renderings of the mentally ill. He argues that art had been produced by the mentally ill throughout history and initially it was considered to be mindless antics. It is not until the nineteenth century that a systemic interest in the art of the mentally ill emerged. Both Hogan (2001) and MacGregor (1989) contend that while art produced by the mentally ill was viewed with fascination, it also becomes a subject for scientific research.

Cesare Lombroso (1835–1909) developed theories of genius and insanity by examining the art of the mentally ill in the nineteenth century. As a criminologist, anthropologist, and psychiatrist, his early work focused on "characterology." He was particularly interested in the relationship between mental and physical characteristics. Lombroso systematically researched the physical characteristics (jaws, brain size, and more) associated with criminal psychopathology to produce indicators for sociopathic and criminal behavior. As someone focused on diagnosis and pathology, he assembled a large collection of drawings and paintings from mentally ill patients as "providing a visual evidence for mental pathology" (MacGregor, 1989, p. 93).

Hogan (2001) observes that the writings and publications produced a generalized view of criminality and mental illness as inherited rather than produced by the social conditions and struggles of everyday life. For Lambroso, symbolism as a form of primitive self-expression or "atavism" (Hogan, 2001), gave rise to reductionist language characterizing criminals and the mentally ill as savages, degenerates, insane, mad, deviant, deficient, and more. He also took an analytic approach to classifying the art of the mentally ill through his research. He tried to demonstrate the link between "primitive civilizations and the atavistic characters of much insane art" (MacGregor, 1989, p. 100).

Lambroso's research laid the foundation for the eugenicists who were using their research and documentation to map the "deviant" and "deficient" body. At the same time psychoanalysts like Freud, Kris, Jung, and others were producing studies on the behavior and the inner worlds of their patients. Paralleling this discourse was the publication by a European psychiatrist who was influenced by the work of Lambroso (MacGregor, 1989), Hans Prinzhorn (1922), whose book *Bildnerei der Geisteskranken* (*The Artistry of the Mentally Ill*), reproduced images drawn by asylum patients across Europe. The intersection of art, psychological theories, psychopathology, and the information gathered by the eugenicists about the material body created the moment in which art therapy began to emerge as a new technique to make the human mind transparent, a readable text.

The precursors of art therapy directly relate to the intellectual and sociological developments of the late nineteenth and early twentieth century. The views put forward by eugenicists influenced the child study movement, anthropological study of non-Western cultures, education theories, and the personality theories of psychoanalysts that defined norms of care in psychiatric settings (Junge & Asawa, 1994). Using the ideals of normative behavior and deviancy, psychiatrists like Lambroso, and others, such as Traddieu, and Simon, examined the art of their patients (MacGregor, 1989). At the same time, psychologists influenced by intelligence testing developed diagnostic drawing tests, like "House-Tree-Person" (Buck, 1948) and Machover's (1949) "Draw-a-Person" test, to tap into personality characteristics, therefore promoting reductionist categories when evaluating drawings and what they mean. This research was based on the assumption that drawings were a "visual representations of an internal state" (Junge & Asawa, 1994, p. 7), despite the absence of reliable evidence. The search for universals meant ignoring the individual's social and cultural context in favor of norms of human behavior based on models of artistic development.

Emulating the research methods of psychology, art therapists embraced linear concepts of human development, to create assessment instruments that claimed to identify psychopathologies (Kramer & Schehr, 1983; Kwiatkowka, 1978; Rubin, 1978; Ulman & Dachinger, 1975, among others). Vick (2003) points out that, "Even today, the notion that artworks in some way reflect the psychic experience of the artist is a fundamental concept in art therapy" (p. 8). Even though different approaches for viewing the mind and psychological development have been proposed (Rubin, 2001), the principles and framework within which art therapy is enacted have remained the same: transference, countertransference and the concept of the unconscious revealed through images. The theoretical terrain has varied as some art therapists looked for the ways that defense mechanisms were symbolically revealed in images relating to adaptive and maladaptive behaviors (Levick, 1983), while others documented the correlations between developmental stages and the imagery in clients' drawings (Rubin, 1978). The main goal of the relevant studies was to document, "how unresolved conflicts led to fixations in these stages and manifested in the drawings of children and adults" (Junge & Asawa, 1994, p. 183). As a result, many art therapists have uncritically followed the artistic, cognitive, and developmental theories that Lowenfeld (1949) and Piaget (1950) based on their encounters with children in clinical settings and without concern for the social and cultural influences on their development.

Drawing on the standardized methods of research and projective drawing assessments that evolved during the twentieth century (Hammer 1958; Machover, 1949), art therapy mirrored psychology's pseudo-scientific method of collecting visual data in the hope of finding a set of universals: images that can be used to assess the client's functionality or pathology or development. Projective drawing tests become widely used for evaluation and diagnosis and continue to be employed with children and adults today (Vick, 2003). There is no proven validity to the projective drawing tests or the art therapy assessments devised by various art therapists in the last several decades.

The emergence of art therapy as a field has been attributed to four women—Edith Kramer, Hanna Yaxa Kwiatkowska, Margret Naumburg, and Elinor Ulman (Junge & Asawa, 1994; Vick, 2003). Although Naumburg is considered to be the "mother of art therapy," it is Ulman who had a significant impact in defining the field. Despite other voices and conceptions of art therapy, Ulman's (1975) article "Art Therapy: Problems of Definition," was a major force in locating art therapy within a psychoanalytic framework (Talwar, 2016).

Wix (2000) critiques the history of art therapy to reflect on the missing history, tracing the artistic roots of art therapy. In the face of the strong push to embrace psychoanalytic theories, Wix points to the work of Mary Huntoon. Huntoon practiced art therapy in Kansas from the 1930s through the late 1950s. Huntoon began working at the Menninger's Clinic and then continued at the Winter Veterans Administration Hospital, in Kansas, both under the administration of Dr. Karl Menninger. Wix (2000) questions why Huntoon is a little known figure in art therapy, asking "Was she left out of history because she practiced art therapy from an artistic rather than a psychoanalytic perspective?" (p. 169). As Ault states, "Art Therapy was 'something else.' It meant art analysis done by a handful of women on the East Coast and was spelled with a capital A.T." (as cited in Wix, 2000).

Wix's (2000; 2010) analysis points to the separation of the art from therapy that came to define art therapy. The push by the east coast art therapists to embrace psychoanalytic terminology was perhaps self-defensive, since many of the early practitioners, like Ulman and Kramer, worked in psychiatric units treating adults, children, and adolescents. To legitimize the field in the eyes of psychiatry, art therapists employed projective drawing tests, standardized drawing tests, art and psychopathology, and studies of artistic development (Rubin, 2001). Several of the early ideas around assessment and studies of artistic development have little to no validity cross-culturally. The idea that drawings reveal some pathology or deep-seated emotional conflict remains a socially constructed and essentializing concept.

An important overlooked aspect of the history of art therapy is the work of east coast art therapists of color, who from the beginning raised issues related to identity and difference (Dye, 1981; Joseph, 1974; Lomoe-Smith, 1979; McGee, S., 1979; McGee, S. E., 1981; Venture, 1977) interjecting race and ethnicity as important elements in the treatment process. Sarah McGee writes about working with migrant families to address parent child relationships. Her husband, Scuddie McGee, a psychologist, writes about the importance of understanding the specific therapeutic issues with black families. Other articles and presentations in the early conferences focus on the cultural influences on Native American (Dye, 1981), and Hispanic (Lomoe-Smith, 1979) clients. It is not surprising that issues of culture and identity were central in the treatment focus of the early art therapists of color. Parallel to this process is the tight control of the American Art Therapy Association and its mission by white art therapists, including the control of the journal by Elinor Ulman for 23 years (Talwar, 2016). Under the circumstances, the early art therapists of color were pushed to the margins, as were issues of culture, identity, and difference by privileging a universalist vision of artistic rendering that would become a window into the pathology and the mind of the patient. It is not until the 1990s and later that art therapists of color begin to advocate for the importance of culture and the social implications of practice that resulted in the cultural competencies (Boston, 2015; Potash, Doby-Copeland, Stepney, Washington, Vance, Short, Boston, & Ballbé ter Maat, 2015; Talwar, Iyer, and Doby-Copeland, 2004; Talwar, 2015, among others) impacting art therapy educational curriculum.

Conclusion

This chapter focused on the epistemological frameworks and the methods used to produce "knowledge" about non-normative bodies. Examining the history of the eugenics movement, the role of psychiatry and psychology in particular, I outlined the ways in which photography and "scientific" research become methodological tools for collecting, coding, measuring, and disseminating information about race, poverty, gender, and sexuality. The underlying ideology of eugenics was characterized by the belief in the power of heredity and genetics in determining physiological and mental traits essential to characteristics of fitness. The result confirmed the belief in the inferiority of some races and superiority of others.

Undoing the damage caused by the eugenics ideology required several social movements. One was the civil rights movement of the 1950s, when black Americans fought to end racial segregation and discrimination, demanding their legal and political rights to protection from discrimination and recognition of their equality. A second was feminism, which took strength from the civil rights movement to advocate for economic and political equality on the basis of gender. First wave feminists were the suffragists who won the right to vote in 1920. Second wave feminists fought for fair wages. Feminists of color broadened the scope of issues affecting women by advocating for reproductive rights, as well as family and work place parity (Mohanty, 2003). A third was the fight to declassify homosexuality as a psychiatric disorder, which succeeded in 1973, and was followed in the 1980s by the demand for an effective AIDS policy. The gay rights movement challenged the dominant discourse of heteronormativity, and led to the legalization of same-sex marriage, in 2015. Fourth and finally, the decades of harm done to people with disabilities by the "compulsory sterilization" decision passed by the Supreme Court, in 1927, were finally recognized when the United States Congress, in 1990, passed the Americans with Disabilities Act.

The Immigration Act of 1924 limited who could enter the U.S. based on a quota system, completely excluding people from Asian countries. It is not until the Immigration Act of 1965 that the quota system was abolished, opening the borders to Asian, African, and Latin American countries. The laws that governed American citizenship have a long history of racial discrimination and bias. African Americans were denied their rights as citizens, since slavery was legal. Despite bans on slavery, runaway slaves had to be returned to their owners. It is not until 1965 that individuals from Asian, African, and Latin American countries could become American citizens. Central to these laws are miscegenation laws that enforced racial segregation, criminalizing interracial marriage. It is not until 1967 and *Loving v. Virginia* that the Supreme Court overturned miscegenation laws.

I conclude by returning to Justice Scalia's remarks during oral argument in the 2013 case *Fisher v. University of Texas* and the bias they reveal. The belief that educational potential is dependent on what is called "race" continues to remain a prominent one among many U.S. politicians and lawmakers. Tucker (1994) writes about the little known history of the *Brown v. Board of Education* decision of 1955, when a group of scientists testified as expert witnesses to overturn the case based on racial differences by presenting the research on biological inferiority from the eugenics movement. Lowe (1998) points to the impact of eugenics on contemporary education and policy. He argues that the controversies over education and intelligence testing are a direct result of the lasting influence of eugenics. Two decades ago, Richard Herrnstein and Charles Murray, authors of *The Bell Curve* (1994), claimed that race and class differences were caused largely by essentially immutable genetic factors, concluding that low IQ scores were due to inborn cognitive limits (Gould, 1994). The book has been widely criticized for its racism and misleading data, reminiscent of the influence of eugenics on education policy in the 1920s.

To conclude, as part of providing services in mental health care, art therapists need to examine the historical conditions that have produced reductive narratives of non-normative identities in order to imagine change. This entails disrupting the taken for granted universalizing principles of art therapy, psychology, and counseling that maintain the status quo. As Denzin (2006) and Thomas (1993) contend, to move beyond "what is" to "what could be" it is imperative to think of individuals not just as psychological beings, rather as part of history, institutions, political systems, social spaces, and practices that define his/her/their positionality. Art therapists must begin "resisting domestication" (Madison, 2012, p. 6) to use their skills, resources, and privilege to penetrate and open borders that suppress or undermine the stories of clients. A critical approach means that art therapists are committed to emancipatory practices and social justice from an intersectional perspective. Chapter 3 takes up the theoretical frameworks in art therapy that need to shift to include difference. How can attention to discourse, knowledge-making, lived experience and daily practices be included theoretically in art therapy to account for difference? Finally, what should the future of art therapy look like?

References

American eugenics movement image archive. www.eugenicsarchive.org/eugenics/

Barzilai, G. (2010). *Communities and law: Politics and cultures of legal identities*. Ann Arbor, MI: University of Michigan Press.

Boston, C. (2015). Art therapy and multiculturalism. In D. Gussak, & M. Rosal (Eds.), *The Wiley-Blackwell handbook of art therapy* (pp. 822–828). Oxford, England: Wiley Blackwell.

Buck, J. N. (1948). The H-T-P test. *Journal of Clinical Psychology, 4*(2), 151–159.

Davis, L. J. (1997). *The disability studies reader* (4th Ed.). New York, NY: Routledge.

Denzin, N. K. (2006). Pedagogy, performance and autoethnography. *Text and Performance Quarterly, 26*(4), 333–338. doi.org/10.1080/10462930600828774

Dye, S. K. (1981). The Native American: Developing cultural foundations as a tool for problem solving and expression. In A. D. Maria (Ed.), *Art therapy: A bridge between worlds, Proceedings of the 12th Annual Conference of the American Art Therapy Conference* (pp. 32–33). New York, NY.

Fisher v. Texas, Supreme Court brief, December 9, 2015. Retrieved from www.supreme-court.gov/oral_arguments/argument_transcripts/14-981_p8k0.pdf

Foucault, M. (1980). *Power and knowledge: Selected interviews and other writings, 1972–1977*. New York, NY: Pantheon.

Garcia, S. (2013, July 10). 8 shocking facts about sterilization in U.S. history. *Policy. Mic*. Retrieved from https://mic.com/articles/53723/8-shocking-facts-about-sterilization-in-u-s-history#.IV8ZMCAB1

Gilroy, P. (2000). *Against race: Imagining political culture beyond the color line*. Cambridge, MA: Harvard University Press.

González, J. A. (2008). *Subject to display: Reframing race in contemporary installation art.* Cambridge, MA: MIT Press.

Gorski, P. C. & Goodman, R. D. (2015). Introduction: Towards a decolonized multicultural counseling and psychology. In R. D. Goodman & P. C. Gorski (Eds.), *Decolonizing "multicultural" counseling through social justice.* New York, NY: Springer.

Gould, S. (1994) Curveball. In S. Fraser (Ed.), *The bell curve wars: Race, intelligence, and the future of America* (pp. 11–22). New York, NY: Basic Books.

Gramsci, Antonio (1971) *Selections from the prison notebooks of Antonio Gramsci.* New York, NY: International Publishers.

Grzanka, P. R. (Ed.) (2014). *Intersectionality: A foundations and frontier reader.* Boulder, CO: Westview Press.

Hammer, E. F. (Ed.) (1958). *The clinical application of projective drawings.* Springfield, IL: Charles C Thomas.

Herrnstein, R. & Murray, C. (1994). *The bell curve: Intelligence and class structure in American life.* New York, NY: Free Press Paperbacks

Hogan, S. (2001). *Healing Arts: The history of art therapy.* London, England: Jessica Kinsley Publishers.

Joseph, C. (1974). *Art therapy and the third world.* Paper presented at the fifth Annual convention of the American Art Therapy Association, New York.

Junge, M. B. & Asawa, P. P. (1994). *A history of art therapy in the United States.* Mundelein, IL: American Association of Art Therapy.

Kramer, E. & Schehr, J. (1983). An art therapy evaluation session for children. *American Journal of Art Therapy, 23*(3), 3–12.

Kwiatkowka, H. Y. (1978). *Family therapy and evaluation through art.* Springfield, IL: Charles C Thomas.

Levick, M. F. (1983). *They could not talk so they drew: Children's styles of coping and thinking.* Springfield, IL: Charles C Thomas.

Lomoe-Smith, J. (1979). Cultural influences in art therapy with Hispanic patients. In L. Gantt's (Ed.), *Focus on the future: The next ten years, Proceedings of the 10th Annual Conference of the American Art Therapy Conference* (pp. 17–22). Washington, DC.

Lowenfeld, V. (1949). *Creative and mental growth.* Indianapolis, IN: Mcmillam Publishing Co.

Lowe, R. (1998). The educational impact of eugenics. *International Journal of Educational Research, 27*(8), 647–660. doi. org/10.1016/S0883-0355(98)00003-2

Machover, K. (1949). *Personality projections in the drawings of the human figure.* Springfield, IL: Charles C Thomas.

Madison, S. D. (2nd Ed.) (2012). *Critical ethnography: Method, ethics and performance.* Washington, DC: Sage Publications.

Marcotte, A. (Dec 12, 2015). Abigail Fisher deserves an "F" for her race-baiting Supreme Court Case aimed at boostingsubpar white students. Retrieved from www.alternet.org/news-amp-politics/abigail-fisher-deserves-f-her-race-baiting-supreme-court-case-aimed-boosting

Maxwell, A. (2008). *Picture perfect: Photography and eugenics, 1870–1940.* Brighton, England: Sussex Academic Press.

McGee, S. (1979). Art therapy as a means of fostering parental closeness in a migrant preschool. In L. Gantt (Ed.), *Focus on the future: The next ten years, Proceedings of the 10th Annual Conference of the American Art Therapy Conference* (pp. 32–35). Washington, D.C.

McGee, S. E. (1981). The Black family: Culture specific therapeutic needs. In A. D. Maria (Ed.), *Art therapy: A bridge between worlds, Proceedings of the 12th Annual Conference of the American Art Therapy Conference* (pp. 34–36.) New York, NY.

MacGregor, J. M. (1989). *The discovery of the art of the insane.* Princeton, NJ: Princeton University Press.

Mohanty, C. (2003). *Feminism without borders: Decolonizing theory, practicing solidarity.* Durham, NC: Duke University Press.

Ore, T. (2000). *The social construction of difference and inequality: Race, class, gender and sexuality* (4th Ed.). New York, NY: McGraw-Hill.

Piaget, J. (1950). *Psychology of the child.* New York, NY; Basic Books.

Potash, J., Doby-Copeland, C., Stepney, S., Washington, B., Vance, L., Short, G., Boston, C., & Ballbé ter Maat, M. (2015). Advancing multicultural and diversity competence in art therapy: American art therapy association multicultural committee 1990–2015. *Art Therapy: Journal of the American Art Therapy Association, 32*(3), 146–150.

Prinzhorn, H. (1922). *Bildnerei der Geisteskranken: ein Beitrag zur Psychologie und Psychopathologie der Gestaltung.* Retrieved from http://digi.ub.uni-heidelberg.de/diglit/prinzhorn1922

Rubin, J. A. (1978). *Child art therapy: Understanding and helping children through art.* New York, NY: Van Nostrand Reinhold.

Rubin, J. A. (2001). *Approaches to art therapy: Theory and technique.* Philadelphia, PA: Brunner-Routledge.

Sekula, A. (1986). The body and the archive, *October, 39*(Winter), 3–64.

Smith, S. (1999). *American archives: Gender, race, and class in visual culture.* Princeton, NJ: Princeton University Press.

Stokopf, A. (2009). The forgotten history of eugenics. In W. Au (Ed.), *Rethinking multicultural education: Teaching for racial and cultural justice* (pp. 45–52). Milwaukee, WI; Rethinking Schools Ltd.

Struken, M. & Cartwright, L. (2001). *Practices of looking: An introduction to visual culture.* Oxford, England: Oxford University.

Talwar, S. (2015). Culture, diversity and identity: From margins to center. *Art Therapy: Journal of the American Art Therapy Association, 32*(3), 100–103. doi.10.1080/07421656.2015.1060563

Talwar, S. (2016). Is there a need to redefine art therapy? *Art Therapy: Journal of the American Art Therapy Association, 32*(3), 116–118. doi.org/10.1080/07421656.2016.1202001

Talwar, S., Iyer, J., & Doby-Copeland, C. (2004). The invisible veil: Changing paradigms in the art therapy profession. *Art Therapy: Journal of the American Art Therapy Association, 21*(1), 44–48. doi.org/10.1080/07421656.2004.10129325

Terry, J. (1995). The seductive power of science in the making of deviant subjectivity. In J. Halberstam & I. Livingston (Eds.), *Posthuman bodies* (pp. 135–161). Bloomington, IN: Indiana University Press.

Thomas, J. (1993). *Doing critical ethnography.* London, England: Sage.

Tucker, W. (1994). *The science and politics of racial research.* Chicago, IL: University of Illinois Press.

Ulman, E. (1975). Art therapy: Problems of definition. In E. Ulman & P. Dachinger (Eds.), *Art therapy in theory and practice* (pp. 3–13). New York, NY: Schocken.

Ulman, E. & Dachinger, P. (1975). *Art therapy in theory and practice.* New York, NY. Schocken Books.

Venture, L. (1977). *The Black beat in art therapy experiences.* Unpublished dissertation, Union Institute (formerly Union Graduate School), Cincinnati, OH.

Vick, R. (2003). A brief history of art therapy. In C. A. Malchiodi (Ed.), *Handbook of art therapy* (pp. 5–15). New York, NY: Guilford Press.

Whitaker, R. (2002). *Mad in America: Bad science, bad medicine, and the enduring mistreatment of the mentally ill.* New York, NY: Basic Books.

Wix, L. (2000). Looking for what's lost: The artistic roots of art therapy: Mary Huntoon. *Art Therapy: Journal of the American Art Therapy Association, 17*(3), 168–176. doi. org/10.1080/07421656.2000.10129699

Wix, L. (2010). Studios as locations of possibility: Remembering a history. *Art Therapy: Journal of the American Art Therapy Association, 27*(4), 178–183. doi.org/10.1080/07421 656.2010.10129388

3

IDENTITY MATTERS

Questioning Trauma and Violence through Art, Performance, and Social Practice

Savneet K. Talwar

This chapter takes an intersectional perspective in exploring the power of art in addressing violence and trauma. Artists, activists, and cultural workers have used arts-based methodologies to demonstrate the link between critical inquiry and praxis when critiquing the social and personal consequences of violence, trauma, shame, and stigma. I contend that when affect, memory, and feelings become the subject and method of analysis, feelings can be something useful in creating spaces for expression, creativity, and hope. When art practice links trauma, the body, feelings, memory, affect, and subjective formation to the social construction of race, class, gender, sexuality, or disability, it encourages an analysis of power relationships to question the status quo with the aim of transforming relationships.

For a mental health context, intersectionality offers a critical framework for social workers, counselors, art therapists, and others (Murphy et al., 2009). There is a position that responsibility of wellbeing and treatment outcomes is the client's personal responsibility, irrespective of any effects of poverty, homelessness, or violence. Hill Collins and Bilge (2016) contend that intersectionality is not a heuristic methodology, but rather a synergetic way of *thinking* and *doing* social justice work. For me, as an art therapist, when intersectionality is linked to the body through critical art-based methodologies, it offers a powerful means to foreground the embodiment of fear, hate, and shame, to uncover how "emotions work to shape the 'surface' of individual and collective bodies" (Ahmed, 2004, p. 1). Ahmed (2004) asks us to consider emotions as a force that holds and binds the social body. As such, emotions "operate between to 'make' and 'shape' bodies as form of action, which also involve orientation towards other" (p. 2). An intersectional analysis of race, class, gender, sexuality, and disability inevitably leads to memory, emotions, and the body to convey the embodiment of culture.

In this sense an analysis of power, privilege, and oppression can be useful when creating spaces for creativity and hope.

I begin with a brief description of intersectionality, what it is, and how an art based methodology can add to an intersectional discourse around identity and difference as they are located in the materiality of the body. Through select works of art, performances, and examples of activism, I show how artists, activists and cultural workers have raised questions about society, violence, trauma, and the body. The art projects I explore focus on the intersection of the personal with the social to create counter narratives that offer a structural analysis, raising questions about the cultural production of identity and difference, and illuminating the systems of oppression that need dismantling.

Intersectionality

Intersectionality emerged out of the scholarly work of black feminists, lesbians of color, queer, and disability scholars (Anzaldúa, 1987; Crenshaw, 1989; Collins, 1990; Garland-Thomson, 2011; Grzanka, 2014; Zinn & Dill, 1996; Weber, 2001). Although their work takes place across disciplines (women studies, sociology, American studies, cultural studies, gender and sexuality studies, disability studies, and law), the conversation that links them is based on the understanding that "knowledge is always political." From this standpoint they offer "critiques of dominant epistemologies and avenues for producing new, counterhegemonic knowledges" (Grzanka, 2014, p. 32). Intersectionality can be thought of as a methodical tool when analyzing the *dimensions of difference*, such as racism, heterosexism, ableism, patriarchy, class-based oppression, and other forms of systemic and institutionalized discrimination (Shin, 2015; Talwar, 2015). Intersectionality as a mode of analysis has been informed by and transformed by critical race theory, black feminism, disability studies, queer theory, and others in critiquing the social construction of identities (theories applied in Part II of this book). In this sense, the relevance of intersectionality is not "what it is," but rather "what it does" (Cho et al., 2013, p. 795).

The term "intersectionality" has been credited to Crenshaw (1989), who argued that discrimination in the lives of women of color, especially black women, did not neatly fit within single-axis categories of "racism" or "sexism." Rather, it is a product of both race and gender, which, I argue, are experienced "in" and "on" the body. Thus, a feminist epistemology of knowing and reflecting on black women's experience has meant, for Crenshaw, examining issues of violence, health care, reproduction, and other forms of oppression from an intersectional perspective. The goal is not to isolate parts of a woman's representation, but instead to see her life and experiences as in their totality. For example, reproductive justice means advancing a discussion of women and their bodies that takes into account their community and includes environmental factors of oppression, violence, and trauma. An intersectional analysis, therefore, focuses on acknowledging that individuals occupy multiple social locations and recognizes the complexity—rather than a reductive singularity—of human experience (Thorton-Dill & Zambrana, 2009; Talwar, 2010). An art therapy practice informed by intersectionality explores the embodiment of lived experience from personal, social, and political perspectives.

Intersectionality has now been adopted by activists and organizations that advocate for people of color, the LGBTQ community, the disabled, and those incarcerated.

Hill Collins and Bilge (2016) state that

> Intersectionality is a way of understanding and analyzing the complexity in the world, in people, and in human experience. The events and conditions of the social and political life and the self can seldom be understood as shaped by one factor. They are generally shaped by many factors in diverse and mutually influencing ways. When it comes to social inequality, people's lives and the organization of power in a given society are better understood as being shaped not by a single axis of social division, be it race, or gender or class, but by many axes that work together and influence each other. Intersectionality is an analytic tool that gives people better access to the complexity of the world and of themselves.
>
> *(p. 2)*

Intersectionality is currently being incorporated into various health and law practices—social work, criminal justice, disability justice, counseling, psychology, art therapy—as a way to articulate the relationship between knowledge production (how we come to know what we think we know) and how we practice. A practice based in intersectionality rejects received opinion and seeks a richer context for social inequality. It encourages the examination of the layers of power relationships to understand the embodiment of lived experiences with the aim of transformation. It is a tool for empowerment (Hill Collins and Bilge, 2016).

Figure 3.1 is a diagram developed by the Canadian Research Institute for the Advancement of Women (CRIAW) to show the intersecting dimensions of individual identity and experience. The innermost circle refers to the unique circumstances of the individual as they relate to power, privilege, and identity. It captures the individual's lived experiences, the social structures that have shaped the material body and cultural memory. The second circle relates to socialization through the markers of difference that impact individuals and their social positioning. For example, a study conducted by Metzl (2009) following Hurricane Katrina examined the wellbeing of individuals following exposure to a natural disaster. She found a direct relationship between age, race, and socioeconomic status. Stress scores were lower among affluent white survivors than for those who lacked economic resources, who were mostly African Americans. She concludes

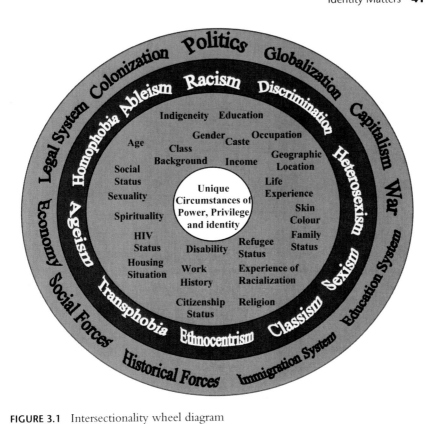

FIGURE 3.1 Intersectionality wheel diagram

Printed with permission from the Canadian Research Institute for the Advancement of Women

that creative thinking and resilience are likely affected by class status and social privilege. Resources and social capital are directly related to access to education, good health care, safe neighborhoods, and the satisfaction of everyday needs. The interaction of the first and second circles is the basis of discrimination. The fourth or invisible circle represents the outside forces, some structural—legal, economic, educational, and political—that shape identity, the body, and citizenship practices. Examining identity, therefore, means deconstructing the structures of power and oppression that are instrumental in the production of identity.

Bell (2008), a performance studies scholar, contended that citizenship and identity are carefully policed and we are punished when we perform history incorrectly. History always weighs on the body and its materiality. Foucault (1977) posited that *bodies are docile* in his book *Discipline and Punish*. He argues that discipline creates docile bodies, which are ideal for achieving the goal of citizenship, reached through cooperation and the desire to fit within society. Good citizenship relies on internalizing disciplinary powers in order to self regulate the body. Power over bodies, therefore, is mostly invisible, producing participation and behaviors sanctioned by society. Intersectionality as a methodology asks that we investigate the visible and invisible systems of power to allow for a deeper analysis of social categories of difference and the disciplinary powers that have sanctioned shame, violence, and trauma, thus stigmatizing the performance of non-normative bodies. Garland-Thomson (2011), a feminist disability studies scholar, argues for a collaborative, interdisciplinary inquiry, with a self reflexive critique that investigates how subjectivities are a complex system of representation that "mutually construct, inflect, and contradict one another" (p. 15). For her "these systems intersect to produce and sustain ascribed, achieved, and acquired identities – both those that claim us and those that we claim for ourselves" (p. 15). The interaction between the personal and social is a political one.

Identity Matters

Intersectionality begins with a focus on identity. Using intersectionality as an analytical tool to understand the social constructedness of identity has been a process of individual and collective empowerment for many disenfranchised groups. Although identity categories such as race, class, and gender, remain central for an intersectional analysis, intersectionality has come under attack in the academy as promoting identity politics, itself questioned on two grounds. The first is that identify politics only reinforces the categories of difference it proposes to complicate. As such, it promotes an essentialist framework due to a lack of attention to intra-group difference. The second is that identity politics is rooted in individual and group experiences rather than in a critique of structures of domination (Singh, 2015). Grzanka (2014) answers the criticism by noting that although intersectionality holds identity central to its analysis, intersectionality is much more than just identifying and naming aspects of individual identity. "Intersectionality is a structural analysis and critique insomuch as it is primarily concerned with how social inequities are formed and maintained; accordingly, identities and the politics thereof are the *products* of historically entrenched, institutional systems of dominance and violence" (Grzanka, 2014, p. xv). The emphasis is not simply on identity or the "self," but rather, and more importantly, on the systems of power and privilege by which identities are produced and policed. As illustrated in the previous chapter, to have a more complex understanding of human experience we need to consider approaching identity categories as a network of power relationships that are embedded in history. Cohen (2005) argues that while identity politics destabilizes the assumed categories and binaries, it reinforces the dichotomies. She calls for destabilization, but not the "destruction or abandonment of identity categories" (p. 45). She emphasizes the importance of the multiplicity and interconnectedness of identities, noting that they provide promising avenues for *destabilization and radical politicization.* At the same time, she rejects any analysis that ignores the usefulness of categories, roles, and shared experiences of oppression in building resources, shaping consciousness, and acting collectively.

Artists, activists, and community artists have brought an intersectional analysis to critical social issues impacting disenfranchised communities, for example, violence, and trauma in communities of color. By examining violence in poor communities as a structural issue, rather than on an individual basis, an intersectional analysis brings to light how gender, race, and class overlap to create inequality. Facilitating narratives of the body politic from an intersectional perspective that is imbued with cultural meaning, those responsible for works of art and community projects can raise questions about trauma and violence within a social discourse. In this chapter, I examine what happens when trauma is treated as a cultural and social discourse rather than an individual psychic condition in medical/psychiatric terms. What would an intersectional analysis look like if emotions, memory, culture, and history become central categories along with identity markers of race, class, gender, and sexuality? What role can art and creativity play in subject formation and repairing the fractured spaces in culture?

Trauma, Memory, and the Body Politic: Art and the Public Sphere

To define trauma, body, and memory as cultural, we have to question the relationship between these three concepts. Trauma, its effects on the body and memory, has traditionally been defined through medical or clinical models. The *Diagnostic Statistical Manual of Mental Disorders* (*DSM*-IV) saw trauma as having a direct impact on the body and memory, possibly affecting the capacity to work, relate to others, even the impairment of everyday functions. Trauma is generally diagnosed as a *Post-Traumatic Stress Disorder* (PTSD) resulting from "exposure to actual or threatened death, or serious injury or other threats to one's physical integrity" (p. 463). The *DSM*-V added "sexual violation" to physical integrity. The definition of trauma within the *DSM* tends to limit trauma to personal experiences, whether direct or witnessed. How does the discourse of trauma shift when it is moved outside the confines of the hospital or clinic? What does a social and cultural discourse of trauma look like? The goal is not to dismiss individual models of trauma, but rather to open a conversation about public spheres and the role art has played in trauma discourses.

Artists, activists, and cultural workers have questioned the social and cultural discourses surrounding violence and trauma. A social discourse of trauma can lead to an interdisciplinary exploration that, in turn, can generate spaces of resistance, empower citizens, and critique the aesthetics that surround the embodied expression of culture, its racial, and gender codes (Garoian, 1999). Expanded beyond an individual diagnosis, trauma studies becomes a useful field to understand how public cultures are formed around traumatic events (Cvetkovich, 2003). In this sense, trauma as a shared emotional reality helps us examine the intersection of memory and history, what Struken (1997) calls "cultural memory." Cultural memory is one that is shared outside the avenues of historical discourse.

It relates to subcultures where trauma is central in the formation of identities and shared meaning. By engaging in questions that are located in cultural, social, and political issues, artists and activists have raised questions about cultural memory as it relates to communities impacted by trauma and violence.

Cultural memory is a useful concept in understanding the multiple narratives that emerged in the aftermath of 9/11, a horrific and tragic event etched into the personal and historical memory of every person in the U.S. Within a couple of hours the world stopped on that day. Taylor (2000), who witnessed the event in New York, writes that "We stood transfixed, watching, witnesses without a narrative, part of a tragic chorus that stumbled onto the wrong set" (p. 237). As a national trauma, 9/11 produced entangled narratives surrounding citizenship as it related to race, ethnicity, and religion. While many people responded with patriotic gestures like raising the U.S. flag, expressing unity and national fervor, the backlash soon developed against communities of color, especially the Muslim or turbaned Sikh communities. The racial and ethnic tensions created enmity between friends and within the general public. The nationalism fueled by the media and President Bush gave way to the rhetoric of the "war on terror," that pointedly represented Muslims and brown skinned people as outsiders, the "other." In that moment, well meaning brown skinned people became the object of suspicion, fear, and hatred.

Amid the hate and fear, artists, activists, and community workers played a significant role in creating spaces to pay homage to those who lost their lives or loved

FIGURE 3.2   9/11 Shrines

Printed with permission from Magnum Photos

ones in the twin towers. Small shires emerged throughout New York City and else-where around the country (Figure 3.2). Candles, flowers, photographs, American flags, handwritten prayers, and other objects sprang up everywhere, supplementing the hundreds of photographs of loved ones, asking, "Have you seen this person?" Such images and objects became a representation of the public memory and trauma of 9/11. Memory theorist Huyssen (1995) states that "representation is central to memory and comes after the event." And he continues:

> The past is not simply there in memory, but it must be articulated to become memory. The fissure that opens up between experiencing an event and remembering it in representation is unavoidable. Rather than lament-ing or ignoring it, this split should be understood as a powerful stimulant for cultural and artistic creativity.
>
> *(p. 3)*

In the days following 9/11, memory came to be represented in small shrines, vigils, public art, and memorials as a way to show solidarity and collective remembering. Struken (1997) calls this kind of public remembering *technologies of memory*, that is, a form of social practice that people enact to show solidarity in social, political, or institutional practices. These social spaces that create avenues for collectively *seeing* and *feeling* to engage with the traumatic event can move anxiety, fear, or depres-sion to empathy, compassion, and shared meaning. Cultural memory, therefore, resists romanticizing the notion of nationalism or collective mourning as a form of healing and solidarity. Rather, the focus is on the analysis of power dynamics and the nationalistic rhetoric that sanctioned violence towards Muslims, Sikhs, or brown skinned people, promoting xenophobia and Islamophobia in the name of American unity. The work of cultural memory is to "resist progressive discourses of history and focus on definitions of 'Americaness' as simultaneously established, questioned and refigured" (Struken, 1997, p. 13). Investigating cultural memory means questioning who is sanctioned to speak, or who is considered "other," and who has the right to participate in narratives of American citizenship.

Roadside shrines are also common public sites to commemorate cultural memory when someone has been a victim of a sudden or unexpected accident. A common type of memorial is a shrine graced with photos, teddy bears, articles of clothing, etc. at the location where the person was last alive. Often, such shrines are found in poorer neighborhoods, especially when young people lose their life to police or community violence. Such shrines are a way to turn individual or family loss into community loss.

Art and Cultural Memory: Naming and Violence

On October 7, 2015, a group of 25 people gathered at the Hamdard Center in Chicago to attend a sewing circle for *Gone But Not Forgotten: A Memorial Quilt for Victims of Police Violence.* Sitting in a circle, participants introduced themselves and shared their interest in attending the quilting circle. The group's participants varied in age, race, and ethnic background. There was an older white gentleman, a Quaker minister, along with a young white woman from his meeting house, a young mother with her 12-year-old daughter, two young women friends from the neighborhood, among other attendees from diverse backgrounds. Participants introduced themselves and shared their reasons for attending the circle. Some admitted to curiosity about the project, while others spoke of their desire to be in a community of like-minded people and wanting to make a difference. Some of the attendees knew very little about the police shootings in Chicago other than what they had heard on the news and were interested in learning more. The consensus was that people were interested in making a difference.

The evening began by Rachel Wallis, the organizer, offering a brief history of the project. Prior to *Gone But Not Forgotten* she collaborated with Thelma Uranga for *Untitled (Homicide Quilt) 2014* as part of the Chicago stitching collective El Stitch y Bitch. In making the quilted map of the City of Chicago, participants embroidered 415 names of people who were victims of gun violence in 2013. Fifteen collaborators embroidered the names and shared their views on police brutality, the role of Chicago police in their neighborhoods, and the high rate of violence in some neighborhoods versus others. The disproportional nature of violence is starkly visible as one witnesses the quilt (Figure. 3.3). Wallis states, "during the quilting process there was just not enough space to fit the names of the victims so they could be read. We had to embroider names one over the others" (personal communication, September 12, 2016). The quilt is a visual reminder of how the interactions of race and class have defined the segregated geography of Chicago. It offers a critical look at police brutality as it is linked to certain neighborhoods: racially segregated spaces of violence and poverty. During this project Wallis became aware that, although the city of Chicago maintained a fairly accurate record of homicide victims, there was no public record for people killed by the officers of Chicago Police Department. *Gone But Not Forgotten* is an attempt to restore to memory the names of the victims killed by the police, for whom no records exit.

After the introductions for the *Gone But Not Forgotten* workshop, four small circles were formed. I was part of the four circle keepers and sewing instructors. The participants were asked to join one of the circles. Each person in my group was given a handout with the name, age, and date of the death of a victim of police violence. Some of the handouts had an image of the deceased along with a brief biography (Figure 3.4). The participants were asked to embroider the name of the deceased printed on the 10-inch quilt square held in the embroidery hoop. Some participants knew how to embroider, but many did not. After helping people with different levels of sewing skills, the embroidery process began. The first hour was spent on teaching, and facilitating the embroidery process. The last half hour was spent reading the biographies of the victims. Each participant began by

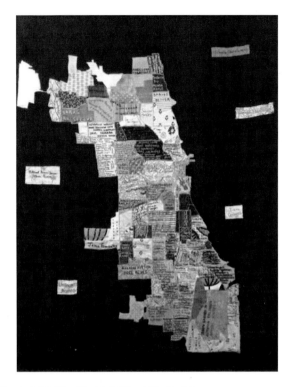

FIGURE 3.3 Rachel Wallis, *Untitled (Homicide Quilt)*

Printed with permission from Rachel Wallis

reading the name, age, and date of death of the victim followed by sharing the individual's biography. The biographical statements initiated conversations about racism, police accountability, community violence, and need for transformative justice in Chicago's south and west side communities

Wallis, a Chicago resident, is a self-taught crafter, print maker, fiber artist, activist, and social practice artist. Her aim as a quilter is to bring the attentive power of crafting to communities to contemplate issues of racism, poverty, gender, violence, and trauma. For her, the process of quilting, focusing on embroidering the name of each individual victim, became a way to mourn the deaths and memorialize the lives of each victim. The practice of repeating a name, followed by reading his or her biography is akin to traditions of mourning and remembering those who have passed on. Wallis says that for her, the focus is on the importance of recognizing each individual, regardless of his or her crime or what they did. She further states that, "the process of embroidering names is a means of remembering as well as creating a public record of those who died at the hands of the police" (personal communication, September 12, 2016). Her main goal is to create spaces for dialogue to talk about police violence and ways to stop it in Chicago.

FIGURE 3.4 Rachel Wallis, *Gone But Not Forgotten* collaboration with El Stitch y Bitch

Printed with permission from Rachel Wallis

Wallis says that when she set out to compile a list of the names of the victims, she could not find any record. "Despite the widespread outrage about police killings and misconduct, and an ongoing Justice Department investigation into the Chicago Police Department, there was no public record of individuals who have been killed by the police" (personal communication, September 12, 2016). She began to compile her own archive by researching police records, newspaper articles, and obtaining information directly from families of victims in Chicago. She collaborated with We Charge Genocide, a non-profit organization that looks into murder cases involving police. She collected the names of 144 individuals killed by Chicago Police or who died while in custody over the period from 2006 to 2015. The collaborative project generated six 40 × 40 feet quilts that have been exhibited in several venues.

During the two-year project (2014–2016), Wallis held 15 quilting circles to keep alive the memory of the victims of police violence. The community dialogues involved over 200 people in the north, west, and south side of Chicago. The quilting circles were a way to process the loss and trauma of police violence and its impact on mostly poor, black and Latinx communities. For Wallis, these conversations encourage community members to "engage in radical empathy, and to remember that victims of police killings are more than statistics or another headline on the nightly news" (personal communication, September 12, 2016). Both projects, *Gone But Not Forgotten* and *Untitled (Homicide Quilt) 2014*, center on highlighting systemic racism and social inequality in Chicago through the power of "naming."

Wallis's project coincides with the rise of Black Lives Matter (BLM). BLM is a movement that came about after the shooting of Trayvon Martin by George Zimmerman in Florida. It became headline news for its protests in the aftermath of the shooting of Michael Brown, in Ferguson, MO, in August 2014. The movement addresses the dehumanization and violence against black people, and to poverty, racial profiling, police brutality, and racial inequality. BLM is invested in making the invisibility of violence against black bodies visible. Using social media as a platform, the movement has become a transgressive symbol for affirming the lives of "Black queer and trans folks, disabled folks, **Black-undocumented folks**, folks with **records, women** and **all Black lives** along the gender spectrum" (http://blacklivesmatter.com/). An important national project, Say Her Name, emerged paralleling the BLM movement in an effort to challenge anti-black racism and police brutality against black women.

Say Her Name is a movement led by feminists of color for racial justice that focuses on the lives of black girls and women impacted by systemic racism and police violence. Organized by Kimberlé Crenshaw and others, the movement is an effort to highlight the invisibility of black women who are killed by law enforcement. A recent report from the African American Policy Forum (2015) states that while the current racial justice movement has clearly framed the police killings of black men and boys, their racial profiling and criminalization, little attention has been paid to violence against black women. A gender inclusive movement, Say Her Name aims to "shed light on black women's experiences of police violence in an effort to support a gender inclusive approach to racial justice that centers on all black lives equally" (p. 3). The report takes a black feminist perspective to demand the recognition that black girls, women, transgender, and non-transgender, lesbian, and heterosexual black women are equally venerable to state policing and are "profiled, beaten, sexually assaulted, and killed by law enforcement" (p. 3). Say Her Name is a vigil in the memory of and to "mobilize around the stories of black women who have lost their lives to police violence" (p. 4). As such, the project brings an intersectional analysis (gender, race, gender identity, and sexual orientation) to understand the victimization of black women. Each Say Her Name event is about remembering and breaking the silence to acknowledge the relationship between black women's experiences and law enforcement.

On July 23, 2015, Project NIA and the Chicago Light Brigade collaborated to demand justice for the death of Sandra Bland as part of the Say Her Name movement (Figure 3.5). Bland, a Chicago resident and activist, lost her life in police custody on July 13, 2015, in Waller County, Texas. She was on her way from Chicago to Texas Prairie View University to begin a new job, when she was pulled over by a police officer for failing to signal a lane change. She was charged with assault and held in custody. Bland was found dead in her cell three days later. The Say Her Name vigil, led by Mariame Kaba, a long time Chicago-based black activist, advocate, and organizer has been instrumental in advocating for

FIGURE 3.5 Say Her Name

Photo courtesy of Sarah Jane Rhee

community-based alternatives to end policing and youth incarceration in communities of color. The Chicago Light Brigade is a group of community organizers who use creative ways to perform and bring attention to social issues; among them battery-powered LEDs mounted on boards are used to make political statements. The Say Her Name vigil got underway as the evening light began to fade and people started to gather and line up along the Chicago river bridge on Michigan Avenue. The protesters raised signs with the name of Sandra Bland (Figure 3.5), alternating it with Say Her Name (Figure 3.6). The crowd carried large and small lights, singing "this little light of mine." Protesters loudly chanted the names of Sandra Bland, along with those of Sarah Lee Circle Bear, a 24-year-old Indigenous woman who had died in custody in south Dakota, and Rekia Boyd, an unarmed black woman gunned down by a Chicago police officer in 2012 (Hayes, 2015). Other projects in Chicago, such as Project NIA, Black Youth Project 100 and A Long Walk Home, organized by art therapist Scheherazade Tillet, have used art, performance, and protest gatherings to creatively bring attention to the impact of police brutality on black citizens in Chicago.

Another powerful example of naming that predates the above projects is the NAMES project AIDS Memorial Quilt, established in 1987. The NAMES project used naming as a key strategy for raising public awareness of AIDS and the marginalization of the gay community. The NAMES project consists of more than 48,000, 3 × 6 foot quilts, each memorializing someone who died of AIDS. Lovers,

FIGURE 3.6 Say Her Name

Photo courtesy of Sarah Jane Rhee

family, and friends have made the quilts using clothing, stuffed toys, dolls, photographs, and other personal memorabilia. Many of the quilts incorporate letters
and biographies that speak of the loss of a loved one and those who have been left
behind. The quilts have come from communities around the world. The NAMES
project was instrumental in bringing the politics of identity to the forefront, especially in the U.S. in the 1990s. While many LGBTQ activists have focused on
the political impact of the quilt—demanding inclusion, public policy to support
healthcare, and contesting issues of "morality and responsibility" (Struken, 1997,
p. 185)—for many others its therapeutic value lies in the making, memorializing,
and building a community to grieve with. The quilts have been displayed in many
venues. The entire collection has been shown at the Mall in Washington, DC,
five times (1987, 1988, 1989, 1992, and 1996). The NAMES project has been
the largest community arts project and continues to work towards AIDS awareness and HIV prevention education. The vast display on the Mall of 45,000 quilts
demonstrates the enormity of the impact of the AIDS pandemic.

> The quilt has created a particular kind of community in which loss and
> memory are actively shared, even among the highly fractured and divided
> groups—the gay population, black and Latino inner city populations—that
> deal with the AIDS epidemic.
>
> *(Struken, 1997, p. 185)*

In similar ways Wallis's *Untitled (Homicide)* quilt highlighted the impact of violence in the predominantly black and Latino south and west sides of Chicago.

In the mid 2000s, the NAMES project redefined its purpose to meet contemporary needs, specifically the impact of the AIDS pandemic on the African American community. The Call My Name project draws attention to the enormous impact of HIV/AIDS in the black community to raise awareness to break the persistent silence in recognizing the loss of those who have lost their lives to AIDS. Since the pandemic began, 42 percent of blacks have been diagnosed with HIV/AIDS. In 2007 in the 47,000 quilt archive, fewer than 400 of the panels honored black people who lost their lives as a result of HIV/AIDS. Call My Name encourages friends, families, and community members to create quilts to honor the memory of a loved one to raise awareness in the African American community (http://edition.cnn.com/2008/LIVING/05/02/bia.aids.quilt/index. html?eref=rss_latest).

Throughout life, an individual's name is "embodied" in relationships with family, friends, partners, lovers, and co-workers. When a person dies, especially in western cultures, his or her name is engraved on the head stone. There are the war memorials in large and small towns with the names of men who lost their lives in the First and Second World Wars. The Vietnam memorial bears only the names of the fallen soldiers carved on black marble. Naming is a way to honor, remember, and memorialize people. When an individual's death comes with the social stigma of HIV/AIDS, or from police violence kept officially unacknowledged, the result is effectively to erase his or her public memory. But behind that loss are the unjust laws, government policies, discrimination, and prejudice that result in death, yet fail to raise public outrage. According to Wallis, naming is thus an invitation for common citizens to participate in a radical ethics of care and empathy. It asks viewers not to dismiss the systems of discrimination that marginalize racial, gendered, sexual minorities, but to take part in the process of restoring the cultural memory. Furthermore, these projects offer an invitation to contemplate the history of racism, homophobia, and xenophobia to establish a collective sense of solidarity and mourning. They use the process of naming each victim in an attempt to construct a counter archive or counter narrative to highlight systemic and institutionalized discrimination.

Performing Disidentification

Social interactions are layered with language. The role of language, spoken and written, has been central in the production of knowledge about bodies. Laws and policies govern how bodies perform in everyday life, as theorized in the previous chapter. To understand the power of language, performance studies have sought to explain the enactment of culture in everyday life and how it can produce meaningful change (Conquergood, 2002; Denzin, 2004). Jones (2002) contends that performance ethnography is about "how culture is done in the body" (p. 7).

Performance studies thus "critique cultural discourses and practices that inhibit, restrict or silence [their] identity formation, agency, and creative production" (Garoian, 1999, p. 3); its goal is deconstructing social and historically determined speech as a means of enabling agency. This section examines how writers, artists, lay people participating in protests, and staged performances, use the power of language to decode the discriminatory history of race, class, and gender, to critique the process of "othering." The strategies used are referred to as "talking back" by hooks (1998) and "disidentification" by Muñoz (1999).

Naming has been integral to remembering and memorialization, but language has also played a role in disidentification, specifically in the counter-narratives and polemics of feminism, civil, and LGBTQ rights. Performing disidentification (Muñoz, 1999) is a means to the "remaking and rewriting of a dominant script" (p. 23). Disidentification, thus, becomes a means to problematize identity and to rethink the encoded messages attached to minoritarian bodies. It is about exposing universalized accounts that sanction discriminatory practices as a way to empower minoritarian identities and identification (Muñoz, 1999). Performing disidentification offers an alternative understanding of the methods of cultural resistance in disrupting established meaning.

Ta-Nehisi Coates used the power of language to name the everyday prejudices that have produced discourses surrounding black bodies. Coates's (2015) book *Between the World and Me*, a letter written to his son, explores the cultural production of black bodies, their exploitation and control through institutional and systemic violence. He refers, time and again, to the embodiment of fear and the intergenerational trauma (my words) of racism that impacts black bodies on a daily basis. Coates writes:

> The destroyers are mostly men enforcing the whims of our country, correctly interpreting its heritage and legacy. It is hard to face this. But all our phrasing—race relations, racial chasm, racial justice, racial profiling, white privilege, even white supremacy—serves to obscure that racism is a visceral experience, that it dislodges brains, blocks airways, rips muscle, extracts organs, cracks bones, breaks teeth. You must never look away from this. You must always remember that the sociology, the history, the economics, the graphs, the charts, the regressions all land, with great violence, upon the body.
>
> *(p. 10)*

Coates's book brings to the foreground the politics of identity and the history of racial injustice in performing disidentification, a revolutionary gesture that organizations like Black Lives Matter (BLM) advocate. As a gesture of disidentification, BLM has been instrumental is gaining media and public attention to highlight the trauma of bodies caught in an unending cycle of police brutality. Considered the twenty-first-century civil rights movement, BLM makes visible the racial injustice

that has disproportionally impacted the lives of black men, women, gender non-conforming, and trans lives. BLM, like the civil rights movement of the 1950s and 1960s, has used the power of imagery and text in fighting for racial, economic, and political justice (Figure 3.7). In particular, using text and bodies in the act of naming and "talking back" can be seen in the historical protests, speeches, and marches on labor issues in the black community. For hooks (1998), coming to voice, moving from silence to speech, is an act of resistance. In similar ways performance studies contextualizes such acts of protest as transgressive in nature. Performing disidentification can thus be an act of "intervention, a method of resistance, a form of criticism, a way of revealing agency" (hooks, 1998, p. 9).

One of the best known historical figures, Sojourners Truth (1851), gave the provocative speech "Ain't I a Woman" to highlight the politics of identity at the intersection of race, class, and gender, using language and talking back as a tool of resistance. Born as a slave in New York, Truth was emancipated in 1827 under the New York Anti-Slavery Law. She dedicated her life to abolitionism and the fight for equal rights for black men and women. The speech, given at the Women's Rights Convention in Akron, Ohio, on May 29, 1851, is a remarkable example of the politics of identity to offer an alternative narrative of race and gender. As an anti-slavery advocate she notes,

> That man over there says that women need to be helped into carriages, and lifted over ditches, and to have the best place everywhere. Nobody ever helps me into carriages, or over mud-puddles, or gives me any best place! And ain't I a woman? Look at me! Look at my arm! I have ploughed and planted, and gathered into barns, and no man could head me! And ain't I a woman? I could work as much and eat as much as a man—when I could get it—and bear the lash as well! And ain't I a woman? I have borne thirteen children, and seen most all sold off to slavery, and when I cried out with my mother's grief, none but Jesus heard me! And ain't I a woman?
> *(www.sojournertruth.com/p/aint-i-woman.html)*

Naming injustice as a form of resistance has been seen in a number of labor justice issues. In 1968 the Memphis sanitation workers led a strike. The phrase "I AM A MAN!" had been drawn from "Am I Not a Man and a Brother?" used in the abolition movements of England and the U.S. In 1787, Josiah Wedgwood created the phrase for a medallion that became the anti-slavery campaign logo. In the sanitation strike, each worker carried a protest sign that read "I AM A MAN!" to expose the inhumane working conditions and the need for economic and social justice. The strike was a result of the deaths of two sanitation workers, who were crushed by a malfunctioning garbage truck (Figure 3.7). The long history of neglect and abuse of black employees led to a strike by 1,300 black men from the Memphis Department of Public Works, demanding recognition for better on-the-job safety and a decent wage. The slogan "I AM A MAN!" has been used as a civil rights declaration and a statement for independence against oppression and claims to humanity. The protest challenged centuries of dehumanization and the impact of slavery and Jim Crow. By using text as a visual strategy to perform disidentification—moving the collective politics of identity into the public sphere, inserting bodies that have been denied visibility—the sanitation workers, after months of negotiation, achieved an agreement for increased wages and better working conditions.

In 1988, 20 years later, artist Glenn Ligon appropriated the sign *Untitled (I Am a Man)* carried by the 1,300 sanitation workers in Memphis to evoke the history of language and race in inscribing black identity and masculinity. The black text I AM A MAN is painted on a white background using a mixture of oil paint and enamel. The artist's mixing enamel and oil resulted in a cracked white surface that starkly reflects the words "I AM A MAN" in black (Figure 3.8). The cracking signifies the passage of time, and the words evoke the cultural memory of inhumane working conditions in the 1960s, which continue to hold similar power over black bodies to the present day.

Over the years Ligon has appropriated sentences from literary texts written by several historical black authors to raise questions about the history of slavery and to foreground the role of the civil rights movement in exposing the unjust systems that "inscribe" the black body in contemporary society. Ligon's use of text shows how language is directly related to social signification and illustrates how prejudice and discrimination continue to be part of the fabric of contemporary life. Ligon,

FIGURE 3.7 I AM A MAN march

With permission photo © Richard L. Copley

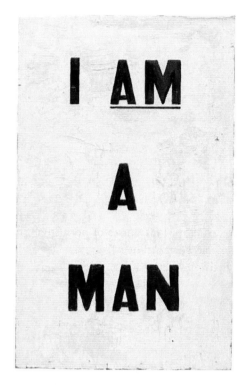

FIGURE 3.8 Glenn Ligon, *Untitled (I Am a Man)*, 1988, oil and enamel on canvas, 40 × 25 inches (101.6 × 63.5 cm)

© Glenn Ligon; Courtesy of the artist, Luhring Augustine, New York, Regen Projects, Los Angeles, and Thomas Dane Gallery, London

like Coates, centralizes the embodiment of the history of fear and hate that is produced and reproduced through the power of language in contemporary America. In another painting, *Untitled (I Feel Most Colored When I Am Thrown Against a Sharp White Background)*, Ligon uses black oil sticks to stencil text on a wooden door painted white. The sentence "I Feel Most Colored When I Am Thrown Against a Sharp White Background" is taken from Zora Neal Hurston's essay, "How it feels to be colored me." Ligon repeats it again and again until the words are incomprehensible, bleeding into one another during the process of stenciling. Ligon states that he tried for six months to perfect the letters so they could be read, but oil paint smears easily. The smudging, smearing, and disappearance of the letters eventually became interesting and the focus turned to the disappearance of language. The term "I" signifies an individual or the body that has been erased by words and language. It is the racialized black body that stands as the marker of difference that makes the body visually recognizable. The racialization of identity conjures up the silhouette of violations and violence evoking the history of slavery, theories of biological inferiority, the prison industrial complex, and the numerous cases of police brutality and murder of black men and women at the hands of police. As Saltzman (2006) contends, "In each of Ligon's paintings the experience of the black subject in a white world remains, for all its material occlusion and eventual erasure, stubbornly, vividly present" (p. 48).

Using similar strategies of disidentification and talking back, disability activists have turned to performance, art, film, and writing as a way to highlight issues surrounding the representation of disability and the body. Goffman's (1963) work has been influential in drawing attention away from the individual body as "defective" and to the social structures that shape public conceptions of stigma and shame. He was particularly interested in the ways a stigma was apparent to others, in contrast to how those who disclose their disabilities experience their circumstances. The disability justice movement, using the arts, has actively taken to public spaces to disrupt discourses of normativity by highlighting the insidiousness of the medical establishment in producing stigmatizing language and terminology of the disabled body.

My first experience of the disability justice movement came in the fall of 2010 with a performance at the Theater Arts Project at the Insight Center for Arts in Rogers Park, Chicago. Entitled "Stories of Lives Challenged with Mental Illness and Liberation," the public performance offered a glimpse into the lives of three adults who self-identified as mentally ill. They spoke of exploring their personal experiences as they came to accept their mental health disability and its negative social consequences. The stories were particularly focused on mental health as a "disability" versus an "illness." Disability studies scholars, critiquing the language used to define mental health, are concerned with three main contexts: the medical, social, and political. Medical models focus on mental health issues from a place of illness and sickness, thus promoting ableism. Disability studies scholars (Kuppers, 2003; Mackelprang & Salsgiver, 2009) contest the term *mental illness*, preferring *mental health disability* as a minority identity. For them, people with mental health disability may seek medical help, but also "exist independently of mental health service systems" (Mackelprang & Salsgiver, 2009, p. 289). Although the stories at the Theater Arts Project highlighted the lives of each individual and the social trauma that intersects identity, the power of the performance was in conveying the social frameworks that silence and shame people struggling with a mental health disability, along with the importance of resilience, relationships, and love.

Having worked as an art therapist over the past 25 years with people affected by various forms of mental health disabilities, I was struck by the power of performance, especially in the way it brought personal narratives into the public sphere. In particular, I was intrigued by how effectively the performers' stories touched me as an audience member, raising questions about the role of a public voice and visibility in moving the personal experiences and stories from the periphery to the center, that is, beyond the closed doors of a therapy space and into the public sphere. My experience of the performance led me to question the relationship between art, language and creativity, and especially what it means to "talk back" (hooks, 1998) or become the "speaking subject" rather than an object of psychological and medical discourses. What is the role of creativity in giving voice and agency to those who have lived at the margins of society? How have psychotherapeutic practices molded political anxieties, and reinforced methods that have continually reinscribed the disabling conditions of clients? How can autobiography and life history narratives offer a "politics of possibilities" (Madison, 1998) in shaping subjects, audience, and performers? The current ideas surrounding the disability justice and arts movement directly relate to issues of the body politic, social justice, and citizenship rights in bringing attention to cultural trauma through strategies of disidentification.

In the spring of 2014, I encountered Sins Invalid, "a performance project on disability and sexuality that incubates and celebrates artists with disabilities, centralizing artists of color and queer and gender-variant artists as communities who have been historically marginalized from social discourse" (www.sinsinva lid.org/mission.html). *Sins* is based in the Bay area in Berkeley, California, and is organized by Patti Berne and Leroy Moore Jr. *Sins* focuses on complicating epistemologies of normativity by making intersectionality central to their vision. The video *Sins Invalid: An Unshamed Claim to Beauty in the Face of Invisibility in the Darkness* (Lamm & Berne, 2014), examined in detail here, is a multimedia performance exploring the intersection of sexuality, beauty, and the disabled body. Central to their performances is the claim that disability is not a single-axis issue; rather the experience of disability is intersectional. One of the goals for *Sins* is to show the multiplicity of identities among the performers—people of color, queer, trans, gender variant individuals, from different ethnic backgrounds and with physical, emotional, sensory, and cognitive challenges, including those with chronic and severe illness. They present a wide range of experiences of the disabled body and disability culture. *Sins* strives to make visible the social inequity experienced by individuals with disability, especially the medical and therapeutic community that have imposed narratives of "cure and treatment" over "sex, love, and desire." As performer, Leslie Frye argues in the video, "disability sexuality is missing from mainstream culture. Even looking around you, you do not see disabled sexuality; you do not see disabled people being sexual. . . . Disabled people are asexualized a lot." The performances in the video vary, challenging us to think of sex and love beyond the socially ascribed able-bodied narratives and to set aside the misperceptions of the disabled body as sexless and undesirable. *Sins* asks its viewers to critically examine how the disabled body is juxtaposed within "abled-bodied epistemologies" (Mitchell & Snyder, 2001). By starting with the power of knowledge, Pattie Berne asks us to question the social constructedness of disability, the invisibility of disabled bodies and "the lack of venues to celebrate their bodies as beautiful, disabled, and HOT!" *Sins* offers a space for a disability justice performance project to explore how discourses of science, history, and public policy have defined disability and sexuality.

Performing disidentification is a way to disrupt the power of binary thinking, of either/or, normal/abnormal, or valid/invalid. *Sins*, in this sense, uses performance and theater in public venues to challenge the viewer's complicity with able-bodiedness. If and when disabled bodies have appeared on stage or Hollywood films, their purpose has been to suggest a lack of, to exploit an illness or a defective body to uphold able-bodied narratives. But when the entire performance, as in the case of *Sins*, is about disabled bodies, it destabilizes the power of the normative. By inverting power relationships, *Sins* asks it viewers to think of the complexity of identity beyond able-bodied narratives. As performer Cara Page states, "There is no right or wrong body, of a conscious revolutionary mind."

Taking the risk to raise the taboo subjects of sex and disability, Maria Palacios highlights the misperceptions of disabled people in her performance. As a feminist of color, writer, poet, author, spoken word performer, polio survivor and disability activist, she says,

> I learned to survive on my own, and on my own learnt about sex and love. And confused the two at times. For myself, trying to define womanhood and the white heterosexual able-bodied impossibility of things, because I was raised to believe I would never have sex, never get married, never have children, never grow up, never grow-up.
>
> *(Sins Invalid, 2016)*

Confessing that her body is imperfect only if seen through the lens of society's expectations of beauty, she speaks to the delicateness and innocence of her body, despite the harsh medical treatments, the orthopedic shoes and braces she has had to wear all her life. Recalling the discomfort of casts, memories of white coats and indifferent hands, she says, "treating my legs is another example of what another cripple looks like," repeating, "another example of what another cripple looks like, another example of what another cripple looks like" (Sins Invalid, 2016). Palacios talks back to able-bodied terminology, thus extending the conversation/contestation of what McRuer (2006) characterizes as "crip theory." The disability justice movement has reclaimed the term "crip" as an insider term to represent disability culture. Crip theory, on the one hand recognizes and challenges the knowledge and power of language by stigmatizing the disabled body, and on the other it celebrates identities that do not easily fit within the discourse of normativity.

The next performance on the video contests discourses of normativity. It shows a dark screen with a ray of light falling on the theater curtain to allude to the past. A voice in the background begins recounting the historical legacy of medical science and doctors visiting schools to study physical disabilities. Invoking the famous case of eugenics researcher Harry Laughlin of Virginia, who, in 1914, defined the "5 Ds" of those who should not reproduce—degenerate, dependent, deficient, delinquent, defective—the voice states: "eugenics was both a social movement and state policies in which ideology and science combined to selectively breed the human population." By 1924 the State of Virginia had a draft eugenics sterilization act, which called for the sterilizations of patients on the basis of the 5 Ds. The camera moves to a pregnant woman in a blue dress. seely quest performs the story of Carrie Buck's rape by her foster brother and her subsequent pregnancy and state mandated sterilization. The Supreme Court case *Carrie v. Virginia* legalized sterilization in all 50 states in 1927.

In another scene, performer Cara Page walks back and forth on stage as she pulls on long black gloves while a naked black man kneels on the stage floor with a piece of white cloth coming out of his mouth. Page addresses the audience—reflecting on the discriminatory history and prejudice that has dominated the disability community, stating, "Have you been selected for genetic de-selection, have you been used as an argument for abortion, have you been asked not to breathe"—as she looks into the face of the black man continuing to pull the piece of white fabric from his mouth. She continues, "have you been called sick, queer, crazy, have you been called feebleminded, insane deviant, a disease, have you been called needing a cure, genetically inferior, have you been called less than human, a punishment, an impurity, a sin?" Her continuing to pull the long white piece of cloth out of the mouth of the kneeling black man is a gesture that dramatizes the long history behind discourses of disability and their intersection with race, gender, and sexuality.

McRuer (2006) writes about "coming out crip" as a form of talking back and disidentifying with "how bodies and disability have been conceived and materialized in multiple cultural locations, and how they might be understood and imagined as forms of resistance to cultural homogenization" (p. 33). Performing disidentification by disability artists and activists is a direct response to their stigmatization by a culture that cannot or will not accommodate their presence or acknowledge the desire for love and sex of disabled bodies. In the next performance, Rodney Bell is alone playing basketball in his wheelchair. seeley quest approaches Bell and asks to play with him. As the playing continues, quest slaps Bell on his chest, offering her hand to him. Bell takes her hand and suddenly quest slaps Bell's face. A scuffle breaks out and quest pushes Bell's wheelchair to the ground. Bell pulls himself up in his wheelchair as Patty Berne narrates her poem *Fierce*

> Is this desire safe? Is this safe? Are you safe? Are you sufficiently insulated from us, the deviant, the disabled, the non-normative, the cripple, or might you become stained by our leaking needs? Are we the disabled, the unconscious visceral fiend to the able-bodied men of emotional predictability and bodily control? Is that the way you settle most comfortably in your

mental La-Z-Boy, as we labor to shield you to mark our differences? Is that why you contain us in institutions? Police our bodies and movement, abuse us, exterminate us, eliminate us, even before birth? Do we frighten you so, must we frighten you? Living requires risks, as does the hardest of desires. We live in continual risk. And tonight, we are coming home.

Sins' work has become a movement that uses performance as means of performing disidentification to promote their political cause for disability justice. "It's an established venue where queer, racially diverse, gender-variant, and disabled artists create evocative works, touching on themes of love, death, birth, and sex – essentially, the stuff of life" (Pentilla, 2014). They purposefully use the body, cultural ideals, and autobiography to offer counter narratives to two powerful discourses. These discourses relate, first, to the medicalization of disability and the jargon of the scientific community and, second, to the cultural stigma against displaying the disabled body or mind outside authorized settings, which are hospitals, clinics and rehab centers. Through strategies of "self stigmatization" disability performers resist the prevailing histories of such performances as freak shows or as medical theater. They resist the characterization of disability as "frustration, tragedy, tears and struggle" (Kuppers, 2003, p. 55). In particular, Bell (2008) argues that the disabled performer "uses [his or her] body as a weapon to embrace the discomfort—Goffman's 'uneasiness'—that they so often experience in social interactions" (p. 170). Thus the focus of performance groups like Sins Invalid is to complicate Goffman's concept of "spoiled identities," not from a place of disability rights, but rather from that of disability justice. Although the Americans with Disabilities Act of 1990 protects the civil rights of people with disabilities from discrimination, the disability justice movement takes an intersectional approach to challenge the structural oppression experienced by people with disabilities in everyday life. Disability justice challenges the idea that people with disability lack the ability to perform as productive members of society. At the center of the movement are the voices of queer, racially diverse, gender-variant, and disabled artists that advocate for the multidimensionality of disabled bodies and their everyday experiences.

Conclusion

Does identity matter? The projects I have discussed demonstrate the ways in which categories of race, class, gender, sexuality, and disability emerge in the public sphere to create a collective identity politics narrative. The projects not only highlight the significance of identity, but also reframe identity as an important index of analysis. To craft meaningful identities is an important task for disenfranchised people who consistently have to disrupt the stereotypes imposed upon them (Hill Collins & Bilge, 2016). Although scholars differ slightly about the principles of intersectionality, an analysis of power and structural oppression is central to all (Hill Collins & Bilge, 2016; Grzanka, 2014; Zinn & Dill, 1996; Weber, 2001, among others). I use Collins and Bilge's six core principles—social inequity, power, relationality, social context, complexity, and social justice—to contextualize intersectionality in its myriad forms in the above-mentioned projects. A common strategy gleaned from the works discussed is the use of naming, talking back, and disidentification to grapple with issues of social inequity and dimensions of difference. Projects like *Gone But Not Forgotten* and Say Her Name use "naming" to bring attention to the intersection of violence in the context of race, class, gender, and sexuality disproportionately affecting black male, female, straight, gay, trans, and gender non-conforming individuals. The NAMES project brings attention to how the intersection of public policy and lack of access to health care for the gay community cost thousands of people their lives in the 1980s and '90s. The public protest by activists and sanitation workers in 1968 used language and text as a means of talking back to bring attention to the race, class, and gender, thus disturbing the status quo to highlight inhumane working conditions and poor wages; the protest incidentally highlights how an intersectional framework clarifies the roles of race, class, and gender underlying an action for economic equity. Performances by Sins Invalid show how history and representation have continued to reproduce stigmatizing narratives of the disabled body as a homogenous group. Sins' goal is to complicate a unitary concept of disability by interlacing the stories of disability with ones of racism, sexism, and the stigma of shame and silence. Performing disidentification, therefore, is a means of exposing the embodied cultural texts and empowering a politics of identification that is unthinkable by the dominant culture (Muñoz, 1999). By "coming out as crip," people who desire love and sex, Sins' performers challenge the ideas that have been attached to disabled bodies.

Each case offers an example of the power of images, language, and text to evoke emotions and shape the meaning viewers make. The sheer volume of names embroidered on Wallis's quilts in *Gone But Not Forgotten* or the display of 40,000 NAMES project quilts covering the Washington mall, makes the impact of structural oppression almost visceral. In the case of the sanitation workers, their power comes from the visibility of 1300 black, male bodies publically protesting to contest their oppression and make visible the invisible forces that shaped their everyday reality. Hill Collins and Bilge (2016) argue that power is relational. Relationality, they argue, can take on various forms, such as dialogue, collation building, conversations, and I would add protest and performance. Although the community art projects, performances, and activism highlight the relationship between social inequity, power, and relationality, how the projects are received depends on the social context in which they are viewed. The *Gone But Not Forgotten* quilts' naming of victims of police shooting in Chicago are most meaningful to Chicago residents, who intuitively grasp the significance of the unequal distribution of names. The narrative quality and dialectical nature of Sins' performances and the NAMES quilt can speak to a diverse audience. Hill Collins and Bilge (2016) argue that there is no neat way to apply intersectionality. An intersectional analysis is intertwined in elements of complexity. But each project brings a social justice vision. By highlighting the systemic exclusion and the social trauma experienced by marginalized communities, the artists, activists, and performers explored in this chapter, reveal how art, performance, and public projects can play an important role in bringing critical inquiry and praxis together in "doing" intersectionality.

References

African American Policy Forum (2015). Say her name: Resisting police brutality against black women. Retrieved from http://static1.squarespace.com/static/53f20d90e4b0b80451158d8c/t/560c068ee4b0af26f72741df/1443628686535/AAPF_SMN_Brief_Full_singles-min.pdf.

Ahmed, S. (2004). *The cultural politics of emotion*. New York, NY: Routledge.

Anzaldúa, G. (1987). *Borderlands, La Frontera*. San Francisco, CA: Aunt Lute Books.

Bell, E. (2008). *Theories of performance*. Los Angeles, CA: Sage Publications.

Call My Name adds color to the AIDS Quilt, CNN, retrieved from, http://edition.cnn.com/2008/LIVING/05/02/bia.aids.quilt/index.html?eref=rss_latest

Cho, S., Crenshaw, K. W., & McCall, L. (2013). Intersectionality studies: Theory, application, and praxis. Signs: *The Journal of Women in culture and Society*, 38(4), 785–810. doi.10.1086/669608.

Coates, T. (2015). *Between the world and me*. New York, NY: Random House Books.

Cohen, C. J. (2005). Punks, bulldaggers, and welfare queens: The radical potential of queer politics? In E. P. Johnson and M. G. Henderson (Eds.), *Black Queer Studies* (pp. 21–51). Durham, NC: Duke University Press.

Collins, P. H. (1990). *Black feminist thought: Knowledge, consciousness, and the politics of empowerment*. New York, NY: Routledge.

Conquergood, D. (2002). Performance studies: Interventions and radical research. *TDR: The Drama Review*, 46(2), 145–156. doi.10.1162/105420402320980550.

Crenshaw, K. (1989). Demarginalizing the intersection of race and sex: A black feminist critique of antidiscrimination doctrine, feminist theory and antiracist politics. *University of Chicago Legal Forum*, 140, 139–176.

Cvetkovich, A. (2003). *An archive of feelings: Trauma, sexuality and lesbian cultures*. Durham, NC: Duke University Press.

Denzin, N. (2004). *Performance ethnography: Critical pedagogy and the politics of culture*. London, England: Sage Publications.

Foucault, M. (1977). *Discipline and punish*. New York, NY: Vintage Books.

Garland-Thomson, R. (2011). Integrating disability, transforming feminist theory. In K. Q. Hall (Ed.), *Feminist disability theory* (pp. 13–47). Bloomington, IN: Indiana University Press.

Garoian, C. (1999). *Performing pedagogy: Towards an art of politics*. Albany, NY: State University of New York Press.

Goffman, E. (1963). *Stigma: Notes on the management of spoiled identity*. London, England: Penguin Books.

Grzanka, P. R. (Ed.) (2014). *Intersectionality: A foundations and frontier reader*. Boulder, CO: Westview Press.

Hayes, K. (July 29, 2015). Say Her Name: Protesters in Chicago demand justice for Sandra Bland. Retrieved from Truth-out.org.

Hill Collins, P. & Bilge, S. (2016). *Intersectionality*. Malden, MA: Polity Press.

hooks, B. (1998). *Talking back: Thinking feminist, thinking black*. Boston, MA: South End Press.

Huyssen, A. (1995). *Twilight memories: Marking time in a culture of amnesia*. New York, NY: Routledge.

Jones, J. L. (2002). Performance ethnography: The role of embodiment in cultural Authenticity. *Theater Topics, 12*(1), 1–15. doi: 10.1353/tt.2002.0004.

Kuppers, P. (2003). *Disability and contemporary performance: Bodies on edge*. New York, NY: Routledge.

Lamm, N. & Berne, P. (2014). *Sins invalid: An unshamed claim to beauty in the face of invisibility in the darkness*. Blooming Grove, NY: New Day Films.

Mackelprang, R. W. & Salsgiver, R. O. (2009). *Disability: A diversity model approach in human service practice* (2nd Ed.). Chicago, IL: Lyceum.

Madison, D. S. (1998). Performance, personal narrative, and the politics of possibilities. In S. Dailey (Ed.), *The future of performance studies: Visions and revisions* (pp. 276–286). Washington, DC: NCA.

McRuer, R. (2006). *Crip theory: Cultural signs of queerness and disability*. New York, NY: New York University Press

Metzl, E. S. (2009). The role of creative thinking in resilience after Hurricane Katrina. *Psychology of Aesthetics, Creativity, and the Arts, 3*(2), 112–123.

Mitchell, D. T. & Snyder, S. L. (2001). *Narrative prosthesis: Disability and the dependencies of discourse*. Ann Arbor, MI: Michigan University Press.

Muñoz, J. (1999). *Disidentifications: Queers of color and the performance of politics*. Minneapolis, MA: University of Minnesota Press.

Murphy, Y., Hunt, Y., Zajicek, A. M., Norris, A. N., & Hamilton, L. (2009). *Incorporating intersectionality in social work practice, research, policy, and education*. Washington, DC: NASW Press.

Pentilla, A. (October 3, 2014). Embodying our humanity: Sins Invalid promotes disability justice through live performance art. *Tinkkun Daily*. Retrieved from www.tikkun.org/tikkundaily/2014/10/03/embodying-our-humanity-sins-invalid-promotes-disability-justice-through-live-performance-arts/

Saltzman, L. (2006). *Making memory matter: Strategies of remembrance in contemporary art*. Chicago, IL: University of Chicago Press.

Shin, R. Q. (2015). The application of critical consciousness and intersectionality as tools for decolonizing racial/ethnic identity development models in the fields of counseling and psychology. In R. Goodman & R. Groski (Eds.), *Decolonizing "multicultural" counseling through social justice* (pp. 11–22). New York, NY: Springer.

Singh, J. (2015). Religious agency and the limits of intersectionality. *Hypatia, 30*(4), 657–674.

Sins Invalid (2016). Retrieved from www.sinsinvalid.org

Sojourners Truth (1851). Retrieved from www.sojournertruth.com/p/aint-i-woman.html

Struken, M. (1997). *Tangled memories: The Vietnam War, the AIDS epidemic, and the politics of remembering*. Berkeley, CA: University of California Press.

Talwar, S. (2015). Culture, diversity and identity: From margins to center. *Art Therapy: Journal of the American Art Therapy Association, 32*(3), 100–103. doi.10.1080/07421656.2015.1060563.

Talwar, S. (2010). An intersectional framework for race, class, gender, and sexuality in art therapy. *Art Therapy: Journal of the American Art Therapy Association*, 27(1), 11–17. doi. org/10.1080/07421656.2010.10129567.

Taylor, D. (2000). *The archive and the repertoire: Performing cultural memory in the Americas*. Durham, NC: Duke University Press.

Thorton-Dill, B. & Zambrana, R. (2009). *Emerging intersections: Race, class, and gender in theory, policy, and practice*. New Brunswick, NJ: Rutgers University Press.

Weber, L. (2001). *Understanding race, class, gender and sexuality: A conceptual framework*. New York, NY: McGraw-Hill.

Zinn, M. B. & Dill, B. T. (1996). Theorizing difference from multiracial feminism. *Feminist Studies*, 22, 321–331.

4

INTERSECTIONAL REFLEXIVITY

Considering Identities and Accountability for Art Therapists

Savneet K. Talwar, Rumi Clinton, Teresa Sit, and Luisa Ospina

This chapter, using accounts from four art therapists, focuses on examining how a critical art-based inquiry can provide an avenue to explore "intersectional reflexivity" (Jones, 2010). Our goal in telling the stories is to frame the importance of intersectionality and self-reflexivity when conceptualizing a cultural turn in a social model of art therapy. As Madison and Hamera (2005) state, "For many of us performance [of identity] has evolved into ways of comprehending how human beings fundamentally make culture, affect power, and reinvent their ways of being in the world" (p. xii).

As an initial step, whether doing research or preparing to be a therapist, deconstructing our own positions of power and privilege lies at the heart of a social model. Engaging rigorously in understanding intersectionality creates possibilities for not only exploring the complexities of identity, but also building alliances for social change. A social model of art therapy aims for empowerment by resurrecting alternative stories of lived experience. When exploring narratives from personal, social, and political perspectives, we demonstrate that clinical models are not the only therapeutic approaches to trauma arising from oppression (Talwar, 2015). By drawing from social practice, performance, and public art, as discussed in the previous chapter, the work of therapy collapses the distinction between "healing" as a private encounter entailing individual responsibility and one that is collective and political (Cvetkovich, 2003). Visual art becomes a strategy to give "the past a place in the present" (Saltzman, 2006). In this chapter, the authors argue that art making is a powerful tool to explore the complex intersections of identity formation, its performance, and negotiation in the social structures of everyday life. Focusing on the relationships between the personal and political, the private and public, a critical art-based inquiry becomes a meaningful way for art therapists to inquire into the contradictions of lived experience.

Intersectional Reflexivity and Power of Stories

Reflexivity refers to the bidirectional nature of relationships. As a research concept, reflexivity means to use the "self" as a point of reference for an intersectional analysis of one's social position as researcher, therapist, or mental health worker. In order to achieve cultural competence in our everyday lives and practices as mental health workers, art therapists have an ethical obligation to understand how an intersectional analysis that deconstructs concepts of power, privilege, and oppression can contribute to a deeper understanding of issues of health, mental health, and pathology, as well as the body as a site of political struggle (Sajnani, 2013).

Accountability is an important factor in promoting just practices of care. As Hammersley and Atkinson (1983) argue, "reflexivity is an aspect of all social research" (p. 22) and we, the authors, contend, therapeutic practice as well. Reflexivity implies that all researchers are "shaped by their social-historical locations, including the values and interests that these locations confer upon them" (p. 16). This means understanding how culture, society, politics, and institutions work to shape our interactions and understating of cultural difference. Reflexivity allows the researchers, therapists, or mental health workers to explore their assumptions and biases and how they affect their research findings or therapeutic practice. Thus "simply stating the cultural context is not sufficient for understanding the topic" (Thomas, 1993, p. 5); rather, a critical inquiry seeks to represent the "'meanings of meanings' to broader structures of social power and control" (Thomas, 1993, p. 6). In particular, a reflexive approach informed by intersectionality leads to a critique of culture that challenges the arbitrary nature of signs, social arrangements, and their codes to confront the centrality of cultural images, their representation: how they are produced and consumed. Feminist scholars Nagar and Geiger (2007) contend that reflexivity is an act of "radical consciouness of self" (p. 5) produced when researchers are faced with the political dimensions of fieldwork and the construction of knowledge. For them, reflexivity is an analysis of how "knowledge is shaped by the shifting, contextual, and relational contours of the researchers' social *identity* and her social situatedness or *positionality* (in terms of gender, race, class, sexuality, and other axis of difference), with respect to her subjects" (p. 2).

The contributions of feminists of color (Gloria Anzaldúa, Bernadette Calafell, Patricia Hill Collins, Chandra Mohanty, Soyoni D. Madison, and bell hooks, among others) have pushed scholars and researchers to situate the politics of the body—the power of the raced, classed, and gendered body—at the center of research. In naming and problematizing the spaces and places underlying the multiplicity of identities, "they call us to be accountable to ourselves and others in marking the workings of power" (Calafell, 2013, p. 7). By privileging the body, one can theorize not only lived experiences, but also confront the invisible histories of shame and stigma.

A few art and expressive therapists have focused on intersectionality, drawing on critical race feminist theory, black feminism, and antiracism to engage in an inquiry into the body politic and cultural memory as a site of personal and political struggle (George, Green, & Blackwell, 2005; Gipson, 2015; Hogan, 1998; Sajnani, 2012, 2013; Talwar, 2010, among others). By reading images, emotions, memories, and stories through an intersectional lens, therapists are better attuned to the impact of systems and institutions that have produce anxiety and/or "otherness" (Sajnani, 2012). But before undertaking to understand others, we have to first embrace our own "otherness" (Talwar, 2010) within the matrix of domination (Hill Collins & Bilge, 2016) to determine where "we simultaneously exist in spaces of privilege and disadvantage" (Calafell, 2013, p. 7). A reflexive practice resists inflexible conclusions because identity formation over time does not adhere to fixed patterns. It is unpredictable, constantly unfolding. The process of becoming never ceases (Alarcón, 1996), since identity is "a source of value, normativity, ethical aspirations, and political projects" (Singh, 2016, p. 667). Incorporating an intersectional analysis, therefore, can assist art therapists and mental health workers when they collaborate with individuals, groups, and communities that bear the consequences of their essentialized identities. This chapter, therefore, seeks to illustrate the role intersectional reflexivity can play for art therapists in embodying a social justice framework that seeks to make visible oppressive power structures. Exploring reflexivity, art, and principles of intersectionality, the authors of the following narratives illustrate the power of narrative to unpack the relationship between the personal and the political using a critical art-based inquiry.

Critical Art-based Inquiry

The term "art-based inquiry" has come to be recognized as a qualitative method (Denzin, 2000; Finley, 2011; Kapitan, 2014; McNiff, 2013). In recent years, art-based inquiries have gained recognition and are now a popular method of research and inquiry in many art therapy programs across the country. Some art therapists have explored and written about their art-based research (Chilton & Scotti, 2014; McNiff, 2013, among others). Much of the work in this vein has hinged on deconstructing the social-emotional world of the researcher and the personal meaning-making that results from it. Kapitan (2014) argues that art-based inquiry is an emerging paradigm, so there is a "need to more clearly identify its diverse concepts, methodologies, and interpretive methods, such that art-based research may hold its own in art therapy and in the broader field of research" (p. 144).

A critical art-based inquiry hinges on "self-reflexivity" as a cornerstone for research and practice. The focus is on "the blending of cultural and interpersonal experiences of everyday interactions with others, [and] intersectional components of identity" (Boylorn & Orbe, 2014) to investigate what Madison (2012) calls "politics of positionality" (p. 6). Thus, a critical approach to "positionality is vital because it forces us to acknowledge our own power, privilege, and biases just as we are denouncing the power structures that surround our subjects" (Madison, 2012, p. 8). As Denzin (2000) and Thomas (1993) have argued, we need to move beyond "what is" to "what could be" to bring a more holistic approach to investigating the individual and psychological as embedded in the political systems, institutions, social spaces, and practices that define positionality.

A critical art-based inquiry assists in creating spaces for dialogue that embrace diverse discourses and opinions. Exploring the relationship between the artist as researcher and researcher as artist, the goal is to challenge accepted theoretical frameworks to create new understandings that involve communities in self-reflexive practices leading towards meaningful actions. The making of art in such a research practice deliberately initiates a dialogue that can be transformative to the researcher and bring change to the interactions with others. A critical action approach to research and inquiry is based on the "ethics of care in human relationships" (Finley, 2011, p. 531); they embrace and enact a "radical ethical aesthetic" (Denzin, 2000, p. 261).

Denzin (2006) asks that we consider our scholarship, research, teaching and therapeutic practice as "performative, pedagogical and political" (p. 333). By moving qualitative inquiry from the personal (self-reflexive) to the political (reflexive activist), an art practice becomes a form of social critique for creating "a radical ethical aesthetic." For this reason it is important that art therapists consider how art inquiry can be committed to social change and political action, as a means to invoke "critical consciousness" in both the maker and the viewer.

Translating the processes of making and doing is essential for art therapists. A critical art-based inquiry assists in incubation, gathering data, and writing as a way to engage in the process of "stranger making" (Ahmed, 2012), or what ethnographer Rosaldo (1989) calls "the interplay between making the familiar strange and the strange familiar" (p. 39). In order to engage with culture from a critical perspective when analyzing relationships of power, the process of defamiliarization is key to understanding that social norms, laws, identities, culture and politics are "humanly made, and not given in nature" (Rosaldo, 1989, p. 39).

The act of creating, the touch of material, the attention to detail, learning, unlearning, experimenting and reworking tap into what Springgay (2010) terms "pedagogies of touch." For us as authors, creating constantly disrupts and defers knowing. Ahmed (2012) argues that writing helps her to not only get reoriented, but also get in touch with thinking and feeling. We contend that the creative process offers a space for reflection and inquiry on a physical, relational, and social level. Alone, engaging with art materials is a physical form of knowing, but when the creative process turns purposeful, it becomes a form of living inquiry that evokes emotions and feelings. In this sense, bodies are produced through social encounter that are shaped by emotions and feelings that "become sticky, saturated with affect, as sites of personal and social tension" (Ahmed, 2004, p. 11).

Cultural embodiment, knowledge, and the production of bodies, therefore, are not just a private affair; rather, they are ones that are mediated through constant interaction with others in the social world. As authors, we contend that a critical art-based inquiry is a way of coming to know ourselves and the world around us as we explore the social constructedness of our identities in relationship with others.

The narratives that follow offer, through art and personal stories, a cultural analysis that exposes the power and limits of language in defining lived experience. In exploring the intersection of our racialized, gendered, sexual, and classed identities, we complicate the embodiment of language and its performativity through art making to explore the relationship between the personal and the political. As Butler (1990) points out, performativity pays attention to bodies and how speech and communication construct the performance of identity. This does not mean that performativity causes identity or determines it in some quasi-biological manner. It means that the social complexity of everyday life establishes normative boundaries for performativity (Bell, 2008). Boundaries are created in and through language and the institutions that are materially embodied and performed by each of us. Speech acts, therefore, have the power to signify and communicate how identity "is" or "should be" performed (Austin, 1962).

The four narratives offer different self-reflexive strategies to explore citizenship and normativity to question:

1) How can embodied history, social relations, and cultural positioning expose power relations between the embodiment of culture and its performance?
2) What role can art play in creatively challenging and shaping dialogue around normativity and "how things must be?"

What Does an American Citizen Look Like?

Savneet K. Talwar

I have lived in the U.S. for almost 30 years. As an Indian-American, U.S. citizen, a cisgender, middle class woman of color, and university professor, I have choreographed my everyday identity to accommodate both sides of my hyphenated existence. Questions such as "where are you from?" or confused looks when I answer, "I am from Chicago," are an everyday part of my life. That said, I am often caught arguing from both ends of my hyphenated status. Indian-American or Asian-Indian-American, my ethnic identity as the "other" is my most visible trait as I move within spaces in the U.S. or between India and the U.S. Over the years, I have become keenly attuned to the ways in which language signifies and polices normativity, especially discourses of citizenship. The following narrative is an exploration of my reaction to a upsetting event that resulted in crafting a sampler to explore both ends of my hyphenated identity to complicate questions of citizenship.

On September 15, 2013, the winner of the Ms. America contest was Nina Davuluri of Fayetteville, New York (Herbert, 2013). She was the first person of Indian decent to win the contest, and her image was posted on Facebook by my Indian-American friends. Within minutes of her crowning, racist tweeters hit their keypads, calling the 24-year-old Nina Davuluri "Miss 7-11" or "Miss Al-Qaeda" One tweeted "Congratulations Al-Qaeda. Our Miss America is one of you," another responded "#MissAmerica ummm wtf?! Have we forgotten 9/11?"

Reading the tweets evoked a visceral response in me. I tried to shrug off the tweeters as ignorant, misinformed, and racist. But a nagging, uncomfortable feeling persisted. I was reminded of the shooting a year ago in Milwaukee at the Sikh gurudawara (temple). The shooter had mistaken the Sikh community for Muslims on account of their turbans and beards. Similar incidents took place after 9-11. Two Sikh men were gunned down in Arizona and California after the attack on the Twin Towers. There have been over 300 incidences of hate crimes against the Sikh community since 9-11. Often, the message with the crime is "go back home where you belong" or "go back to your country, Bin-Laden."

The news of the Milwaukee shooting spread in Sikh communities across the globe. My nephew, moving from Dubai to attend San Diego State University in the fall of 2012, was instructed by his parents not to go anywhere by himself. Whenever he stepped off campus he was to take along a friend. Sikhs all over the United States began to recount tragedies, highlighting Sikhism's central tenant of peace and affirming that they were not Muslims. Sikh cab drivers in major cities like Chicago, New York, and Los Angeles posted notices in their cabs "I am not a Muslim." While I understood the grief of the Sikh community, I was also bewildered by the contradiction created when Sikhs define their identity as "not Muslim." It is true that Sikhs are not Muslims, nor are Sikhs Hindus, but in clarifying their difference the phrase "not Muslim" added to the perception that there is something wrong with those who are. As Prasad (2000) states, "to be truly critical of multiculturalists, we must be willing to enter domains without safe translations so that we can understand and engage in the complexities that affect the lives of others" (p. ix).

I wanted to avoid becoming entangled in the pitfalls of identity politics, but the above stories collided and grinded against one another. I wanted to trouble the national boundaries, cultures, identities, and histories that defined my everyday hyphenated existence as an Indian-American, Sikh woman, and an American citizen. In order to reflect on the living reality of my brown skinned existence in a post 9-11 era, I decided to embroider a sampler of the racist and sexist tweets following the crowning of Ms. America. In essence, I wanted to experience the concept of "stranger making" (Ahmed, 2012). To be able to think deeply and decenter notions of citizenship, I began to question, how do some bodies become strangers? Why do hatred and fear stick to some bodies? And, finally, which bodies have the right to citizenship?

Ahmed (2012) states that remembering our stories, especially how our identities are constructed and represented, is a way to politically reorient ourselves and to think of the "politics of stranger making" (p. 2). The process of stranger making is about learning to name experiences that are difficult. By taking note of our own strange and difficult experiences we begin to notice what seems incongruous socially, culturally, politically, and personally. A strange experience can teach us about the intimacy of the body and social spaces that we inhabit. We begin to see the oppression of others as one that is linked to ours.

I looked for a piece of cloth long enough to print all the tweets. I spent time deciding what the sampler should look like and what symbols should reflect my concerns, like the American flag and the twitter birds. After transferring the tweets and images onto the fabric, I began to embroider, stitch by stitch, embellishing each word (Figure 4.1).

As I did so, memories emerged of my mother's embroidered fabrics that graced many years of my childhood existence. I remembered being fascinated by the neatly embroidered flowers on dinner napkins, tablecloths, and quilts that my mother had made for her dowry. Learning how to embroider formed an important part of my "domestic" upbringing.

FIGURE 4.1 Savneet K. Talwar, *Sampler 2015*

I stitch, unstitch, and restitch. The repetitive movements make me reflect on the intertwined history of my hyphenated existence. Indian-American—not American—Indian, yes—Indian-American. "Footlong buffalo chicken on whole wheat. Please and thank you," and yes, also, "Miss America? You mean Miss 7-11." Each time the needle goes in and out, forward and backward, the repetition allows me to remember and sort out my entangled thoughts. I begin to think of the politics of cloth: how does cloth contribute to the politics of the body? Why do hatred and fear stick to some kinds of cloth that embody difference? Cloth has been a defining factor all my life. In India, cloth represented our identities, our differences and assumptions of social and cultural history. I grew up witnessing my father, brother, and uncles tie their turbans every day. When opened and unfolded, every turban looks like a long piece of fabric that could be cut into many small scarves. But when worn, the craft, skill, and practice of a lifetime are revealed on their faces. History and politics are carried on the heads of my father, brother, nephews, and uncles owing to the religious and cultural significance of how they

FIGURE 4.2 Baghat Singh Thind

Printed with permission from the South Asian America Digital Archive tie their turbans. In similar ways, cloth defines my gendered existence; Punjabi salwar kamiz or the chunni reveal my social and cultural existence.

It was the politics of cloth that decided the issue of United States citizenship for Baghat Singh Thind (Figure 4.2), a Sikh man who fought for the U.S. army in World War I. In 1923, the Supreme Court, in the decision *United States v. Baghat Singh Thind*, deemed Asian Indians ineligible for citizenship because U.S. law allowed only free whites to become naturalized citizens. When Thind argued that his Aryan descent meant he was white, the court conceded that Indians were "Caucasians" and that anthropologists considered them to be of the same race as white Americans. Justice Sutherland, however, referring specifically to Thind's turban, stated: "It may be true that the blond Scandinavian and the brown Hindu have a common ancestor in the dim reaches of antiquity, but the average man knows perfectly well that there are unmistakable and profound differences between them today" (Lopez, 2006, p. 63). The Thind decision led to successful efforts to denaturalize Indians who had become American citizens before 1923.

In and out, stitch by stitch, I embroidered across the ocean from the United States to India, wanting to delve into "stranger making" though "crafting difference." I continue to stitch and re-stitch, embellishing the words until they could be clearly read on my sampler. An older woman sitting next to me on the Air India flight looked over and said, "back stitch with a single thread looks so beautiful." Taken aback, I glanced back and smiled. She leaned over to see exactly what I am embroidering. I extended my arms so she could read the words. She looked up and shook her head, asking, "Did this really happen?" I shook my head in affirmation, leading us into a conversation about hate speech in India, the media, and the ills brought by new technology. Our conversation ended with Mahatma Gandhi's Swadeshi movement, reminding me about the politics of cloth that, in part, won India its freedom.

The sampler has generated many conversations. Often people encounter the sampler with amusement and then disbelief. On one occasion I was asked to submit a piece of personal art to grace the cover of a conference brochure that would announce a lecture I was going to give. I sent an image of my hands embroidering the text on the sampler (Figure 4.1). One of the sentences revealed was "how the fuck does a foreigner win miss America?" The organizers responded by telling me that the embroidered text was offensive and they could not print the image on the brochure. I had to spell out the irony to the organizers, that indeed the reason to embroider the text was to highlight the offensiveness of the thought embodied. The organizers decided instead to print some student work for the cover of the brochure. I end by questioning therapists' complicity when it comes to images. Images of pain, grief, and trauma are commonly used on art therapy brochures and book covers, so why do we react negatively to text with explicitly vulgar language?

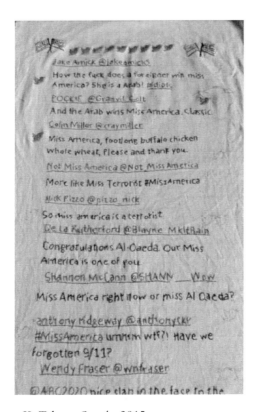

FIGURE 4.3   Savneet K. Talwar, *Sampler 2015*

Subject to Change

Rumi Clinton

I grew up in Princeton, New Jersey, the child of a professor and a psychotherapist. Both my parents were ardent second wave feminists. By the time I was age 10, I considered myself a separatist. By the time I was 15 I came out as a lesbian. At age 20 I identified as genderqueer, and at 22, I lived for a year using only male pronouns. I currently use female pronouns, but as with everything else related to my body, sexuality and gender are subject to change.

By the time I began making art about my experiences as a queer person, I had roughly ten years' experience in handling, or avoiding, the difficult expectations of what my particular body type and gender expression provoked from the world. It started young. You could say I was a tomboy, but really, I had no interest in boys, it was more that I was interested in boy culture. I played baseball on an all-male team, I liked cars and toy guns, and after age ten I refused to wear dresses. That said, I only wanted to be friends with girls. It was also made clear to me that I was somehow not fulfilling some unspoken expectation of what being "female" meant. The most vicious arguments I had as a child were with my mother over clothing choices. My first coming out experience, at age 11, was approaching my parents, full of terror, to ask them if I could get a G.I. Joe for my birthday. The risk of crossing gendered boundaries was deeply ingrained in me.

My first forays into exploring my gender expression and sexuality through art began in high school, when I began drawing a comic strip entitled *Dykalicious and Queer Cat*. Although I did not consider these works art at the time, the foray into comics allowed me to explore gender binaries that I still find terrifying. Using comics as a form of exploration continued to be useful in college, as my identity began to take on a more complex expression.

The first piece created as a part of my undergraduate work was entitled *Boogey Bends Gender*. Originally made as a protest poster and an animation, it was presented, in 2006, as part of a "Gender Awareness" week. The piece expressed the ambivalence I felt toward the gender binary and the ambiguity of my own gender expression. I wanted to evoke the joys of the body coupled with the shame and feeling of entrapment that often come with being gender fluid. Gender, for me and many others, really is a daily undertaking. My experience of being misgendered depends largely on who is doing the misgendering and their response. It can range from "oops, I'm sorry ma'm" to "I'm going to kill you, faggot." This interplay is a form of mutual "outing." Their reaction to me says as much about them as it does about me. Halberstam (2012) speaks to this spectrum of experience in stating that

> we need to think about sex and gender in a more ecological kind of framework, understanding that changes in one environment inevitably impact changes in other environments. Gender here might be thought of more as a climate or ecosystem and less as an identity or discrete bodily location.
>
> *(p. 81)*

As a part of my studies in the graduate Art Therapy department of the School of the Art Institute Chicago, I took some time to revisit this piece ten years after its first iteration. Surprisingly, I found that although much about how I present myself to the world has changed, my feelings and thoughts on my gender have remained very much the same. If anything, the world has taught me how to compartmentalize myself more, as a means of functioning as a professional. I found that once I entered the professional world I had little success if I presented myself as anything other than a woman. Being defined by my sexuality or gender can sometimes only serve to hamper a professional relationship. It can so quickly lead to inappropriate questions about my sex life, or a gender studies lecture. I have a choice in how I present myself—not everyone does—and it has been far easier to flatten or exclude these parts of myself. But this, too, has been difficult. It can feel like being erased. Much like Boogey, I sometimes feel like an amorphous blob, constantly shifting to fit whatever mold will make people most comfortable.

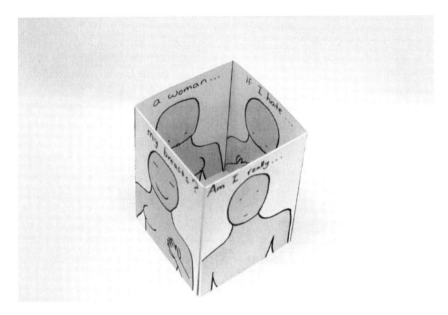

FIGURE 4.4 Rumi Clinton, *Boogey Bends Gender* (2016)

In re-approaching *Boogey Bends Gender* (Figure 4.4), I chose a more sculptural, three-dimensional form, instead of a flat poster, in order to denote inner and outer expression. The outside depicts self-love in the face of ambiguity, the inside self-hatred and internalized body shaming. Much of my recent work has been about outer and inner form. I make boxes that require viewers to open, engage, and unfold the pages of the books resting inside. The process of changing the form of this piece clarified for me that my story is not a linear, but a cyclical one. The piece requires the reader to turn the work and look inside; the inside and outside could easily be reversed, because it is the act of looking inward and recognizing that the inside does not always match the outside that I feel is important. It not only visually demonstrates the feeling of being genderqueer, but also teaches the viewers that they have to look closer.

Where Do I Go? (Figure 4.5) further explores the idea of gender perception and projects it out into the public arena. It explores a typical interaction for transmasculine people like me when entering the "woman" only space of the public restroom. Such spaces straddle the line between public and private. In 2016, North Carolina passed HB 2, the "Public Facilities Privacy and Security Act," which restricted individuals from using public bathrooms that did not correspond to their biological sex. In its wake the public bathroom became a space of controversy for a large number of conservatives projecting their own bathroom discomfort and paternalistic view of sex, sexual orientation, and gender. As is often done, these three separate but overlapping concepts were conflated and mixed with a healthy dose of misogyny, transphobia, and homophobia. Not to mention the wholly paternalistic fear of young women being around "penises."

For many conservatives, unable to contend with their own discomfort, the bathroom became an "unsafe" space for their daughters. For me and for many of the people I know, it was about, and continues to be about, needing to use the goddamn bathroom (and safely). On a personal level the public bathroom is a difficult space. I do not question what bathroom I belong in, but I have often questioned my right to be there because of how I am perceived. As a transmasculine person in a public bathroom I become hypervigilant. I look to others as I walk in to confirm that I have been recognized as a woman. That recognition is what keeps me safe. I am lucky. I have many friends for whom even entering the bathroom means risking a lot more than an uncomfortable moment.

In response to the bathroom crisis I created *Where Do I Go?* (Figure 4.5). I chose a condom dispenser partly for functional reasons, since it allowed me to fit my piece to its specifications, partly for pragmatic reasons, since condom dispensers are found in public bathrooms, and partly for symbolic reasons as condom dispensers connote sex, and are a highly gendered piece of equipment. As one viewer noted to me, I am "dispensing contraception for stupid ideas." This piece was exhibited at Woman Made Gallery in September 2016 as part of their 19th international exhibition. Viewers who inserted a dollar would receive a miniature nontraditional comic book, which also acts as a miniature installation. Once the book is taken from the dispenser it folds out to reveal my personal statement on the outside and, on the inside, a particular incident that sums up my experience of being misgendered in public. The outside is my artist's statement, the inside is a visual depiction of a moment where a woman threatened to call security if I did not leave the bathroom. The use of the dispenser creates a contract with the viewer in which they must trust that by placing money in the slot they will receive something. This process also leaves the piece incomplete unless the viewer is willing to pay. The form of the book also parallels *Boogey Bends Gender*, in that it requires the viewer to "discover" the inside, but it also requires engaging with the impact of laws on real life experience.

The final work presented here relates a memory from childhood—that of being a perpetrator of racism and violence—revealing how the dynamics of otherness begin early (Figure 4.6). If I have been "othered," I cannot deny that I have done the same. For a significant time during my childhood I was taller than all my classmates. This gave me leverage to be an advocate for others, as well as a bully. As a white middle class girl in a conservatively liberal town, I had the power of always being believed, and as a result I got away with a lot. This comic tells the story of one of the few people to call me out during this time. At my school, I was bullying two younger black boys that I carpooled with. I cannot remember my reason for doing so, though the logic of it I'm sure was thin. One of their mothers confronted me and in very simple terms explained to me the damage I was doing to her son. I cannot thank this woman enough for her explanation, because even at that age I could begin to understand its meaning. It was in that moment that I understood that I was white and that this fact held

FIGURE 4.5 Rumi Clinton, *Where Do I Go?* (2016)

Photo credit: Jess Giffen

a dreadful power. This was the first such realization for me, but not the last; it is a lesson I continue to learn over and over again. This piece was very difficult for me to show. I hold a lot of shame about the ways I have perpetrated racism, sexism, homophobia, and other forms of violence on people. That said, I feel the need to be honest about my failings. It is in honoring the truth that I get better in recognizing my short comings and can have hope to effect change.

These three pieces, representing three moments in my life, firmly place me on both sides of the privilege/oppression divide. Lorde (1984) describes the dichotomy as every individual's subconscious response to what she calls the mythical norm.

> It is with this *mythical norm* that the trappings of power reside within this society. Those of us who stand outside that power often identify one way in which we are different, and we assume that to be the primary cause of all oppression, forgetting other distortions around difference, some of which we ourselves may be practicing.
>
> *(p. 446)*

My goal in making these works of art is to be as blunt as possible about my experiences and, I hope, to spark recognition in my viewers. Making the political personal is at the heart of art and art therapy for me.

FIGURE 4.6 Rumi Clinton, *The Bully* (2016)

Photo credit: Jess Giffen

On Questioning a Unified Identity

Teresa Sit

Growing up in the U.S. in the highly segregated city of Chicago, and at a time when Asians were frequently lumped together into a single caricature of pan-ethnicity, I have always been asked to acknowledge and justify the aspects of myself that are Chinese. Because people cannot at first, second, or third glance identify my race, I have been asked to dissect and scrutinize the practices within my family that can be identified as *Chinese*. In contrast, it was not until I began graduate school that I started to wonder how and where I learned to be white. I question whether I have ever felt *white*. I have never been asked to talk about what makes me white, but I have been asked to justify what makes me different racially. I am a tall, middle class woman with olive skin, dark hair, and brown eyes. I wear glasses and frequently carry a camera. I have a Chicago accent. My favorite food is Indian. I have never had the money to travel much and have never been overseas. People confuse me with photographs of my aunt, who is one hundred percent Chinese-American. People also tell me I look like my niece, my half-sister's daughter, who does not have even a drop of Chinese blood in her veins. What is it that defines my difference to others?

I began my piece, *Your Innocence, My Acceptance* (Figure 4.7), with a few questions in mind. People often question me about my race, asking, "what are

FIGURE 4.7 Teresa Sit, *Your Innocence, My Acceptance* (2016)

you?" or "where are you from?" When I explain my biracial heritage as Chinese and white, I am accustomed to the response, "Oh, you are?" While this line of questioning most often feels based in harmless curiosity, and I am sure I have asked others the same thing after they have declared a part of their racial heritage to me, I cannot help but feel a hiccup of hesitation before answering again, "Yes, my father is third-generation Chinese and my mother is white, of primarily Polish and German descent." My art book focuses on the question, "Oh, you are?" in an attempt to express my weariness at confirming and validating my biracial identity to others. Each word was hand-illustrated on a single page of tissue paper and then layered over a painted sheet of watercolor paper. Each letter is filled with cartoon-style drawings of humans who are floating around, balancing and interacting with one another. The first page of the book is primarily green, then comes yellow, then red, echoing a traffic signal as the words take on a layered meaning. "Oh," is an indicator of surprise and the listener is braced for a further remark or question. "You," directs the statement or question at the listener. "Are?" in this case is the conclusion, at which time the listener is asked to answer a question validating a previous declaration about themselves. This question is a common response to many statements, from identifying our musical preferences to sexual orientation to race. *"Oh, You Are?"* (Figure 4.8) is at first innocent; based in a polite curiosity, asking to hear more about an individual. However, having heard this question repeatedly throughout my life, it has become invalidating—as if I should not feel entitled to declare my race without proper justification.

FIGURE 4.8 Teresa Sit, *"Oh, You Are?"* (2016)

While writing my statement of intent for admission to the Master of Arts in Art Therapy program at the School of the Art Institute of Chicago, I reflected deeply upon my intersectionality—racial and ethnic identity, along with class, gender, and familial relationships—which often feels splintered across many social spaces. I am a product of a marriage gone sour; my parents divorced when I was two years old. Half Chinese and half white, I was raised in a lower middle-class community in a south suburb of Chicago where the majority of my peers were black. My older half-sister is white and lived with my mother and me, while my three younger half-brothers grew up with my father and stepmother in a predominantly white, affluent suburb of western Chicago. My father is third-generation Chinese-American, and my mother is white, a self-proclaimed "mutt," whose German and Polish descent is visible in her height, build, and coloring.

I spent most of my weekends with my dad at his parents' home, which was nearby. My grandma and grandpa (whom I affectionately called "Popo") were second-generation Chinese-American, Midwestern artists. Raised in the restaurant business, my grandpa was a prominent Mies Van Der Rohe schooled architect. My grandma graduated from the School of the Art Institute of Chicago with a degree in fashion studies in the 1940s. I spent many Saturdays taking grandma grocery shopping in Chinatown. Sundays were for preparing family dinner in their industrial grade kitchen, folding won ton dumplings, frying shrimp chips, and broiling duck until the skin was browned and crispy.

My dad and I would practice at the Baldwin baby grand piano while my uncles fired up the grill. When our meal was ready, it was spread out onto the round, white dining room table and I was placed in my highchair with a pair of chopsticks and a bowl of rice. Although I shared my grandparents with two cousins and three half-brothers, I was the only one to experience their home in this way. It was important to my father's family for me to learn their customs, not because they were Chinese, but because they were our family customs.

My mother struggled to provide basic needs for my sister and myself. Before earning her degree and going on to work in social services, my mother waited tables at a pizza place, sang in the church choir, performed with the local theatre company, and played co-ed volleyball and softball. I remember holding hands with my mom and sister while my mom prayed for money so that we could eat dinner, but I do not recall feelings of hardship. As a child, it appeared to me that my mother could accomplish anything.

To this day, when I talk about the Asian-American experience with my mother, she tells me that she feels incapable of understanding me. She frequently compares my artistic nature to my Chinese-ness; to her, creativity is a personality trait that I inherited from my father. My mother gets hurt that I do not speak enough about my white experience, *her* experience, and I struggle to explain that I feel like I am living the white experience while grasping onto the remaining pieces of my "cultural heritage." Researchers Xie and Goyette (1997), in a study of the U.S. Census, concluded that biracial individuals with one Asian parent have the *option* of identifying themselves racially, "but the exercise of this option is constrained not only by assimilation and awareness processes, but also by historical, social, and cultural factors unique to the varied racial and ethnic groups living in the United States" (p. 566).

Being raised in close proximity to my grandparents deeply fostered my identification as an Asian-American. My brothers, all born after the death of my grandfather, did not have the same experience, and I was shocked the first time I heard my youngest brother (by nearly 12 years) identify himself as "white." On standardized tests and registration forms, I frequently selected "other" or rebelliously checked more than the one allotted box. When I began my internship at a veterans' hospital, the administrative staff told me that their computer system would not allow them to select more than one race, and when the woman who was running my background check asked me to "choose one," I froze in place. How could I choose just one? To represent only one-half of myself suddenly propelled me backwards to feeling like a child, being forced to choose which parent I wanted to spend the holiday with.

When I was in high school, I volunteered with a non-profit in my community; its mission was to build youth–adult partnerships through use of improvisational theatre, music, and expression. A variety of neighborhood kids participated in activities with the organization, but the theatre group that had formed was comprised of white teens and myself. We had finished a performance at a small gallery space in Chicago and our group leader opened up the space for Q & A. An African-American man dressed in a dashiki and kufi raised his hand and asked how we as a group expected to address social justice issues with "*only half an exception*" in our ensemble. I felt my 16-year-old body go cold and pale with humiliation and fear in this moment, and I froze in place. I was not equipped to have a thoughtful discussion about my race, ethnicity, or how that defined my place within my community. I cannot even remember the words that were shared after that question, and I spent the whole ride home in silence. Experiences such as this one elicit feelings of being "not enough." Not Chinese enough to feel acceptance among one-hundred-percent Asian groups and not white enough to be accepted by one-hundred-percent white groups. The lack of acceptance feels lonely; I have never met another person who shares my race or ethnicity, and I have given up the hope of ever doing so. Instead, I frequently build connections with individuals who share feelings of existing outside of the normative in one way or another: within the LGBT community, other non-white or biracial individuals, artists, people living with illnesses (invisible or otherwise). Developing different ways of presenting ourselves—assimilating to our surroundings—can be a smart and effective coping mechanism, but it does not come without suffering some losses. Eventually, we might find that the personalities we have developed to shield ourselves from being othered are in conflict with one another, and it takes courage and perseverance to forge a unified sense of self.

Even in groups where we typically feel a sense of acceptance, expressing these feelings verbally often leads to further conflict. As with my experience in the theatre, feeling othered can provide a sense of community, but there are still hierarchies being established within subcultures. Conversations frequently devolve into debates over who in the group is *more* "othered" in any given situation, and empathy gets lost in the competition for recognition. In his approach to intersectionality, Grzanka (2014) writes that "intersectionality is foremost about studying multiple dimensions of inequality and developing ways to resist and challenge these various forms of oppression" (p. xv). Visual art has served me throughout my life as a way of processing these experiences, and creating art gives me the freedom to express thoughts and feelings independently of others. It is only after finishing works of art that I make the decision of whether or not to share the work with others. For my piece "*Oh, You Are?*" (Figure 4.8), I pondered deeply a response commonly used in dialogue as a way of examining the micro-aggressions that are considered acceptable in our society; the piece also helped me in viewing my own sensitivity to language that makes questions such as these feel intrusive in the first place. Creating this piece and sharing it revealed my own vulnerability, and therefore set a stage for thoughtful and considerate discussion regarding intersectionality.

Geographies of Loss and Ambiguity

Luisa Ospina

> *so, here you are*
>
> *too foreign for home*
>
> *too foreign for here.*
>
> *never enough for both.*
>
> (Ijeoma Umebinyuo)

As Umebinyuo (2016) states, ambiguous loss is a form of grief that occurs without closure. For me, immigration was a series of ambiguous losses that shaped my bicultural identity. I immigrated to the U.S. from Medellín, Colombia, when I was 12 years old. Moving to the U.S. did not feel like a vacation or a privilege, instead it felt like everything I've ever loved was taken away from me.

When my parents told me about moving to the U.S., I was unaware of their struggles with money and the turbulent political climate in Colombia. As parents do, they attempted to give my sister and me a life without financial and political worries. My mother spoke English well, since she had lived in the U.S. in her 20s; as a result, she was able to get a good paying job in Medellín as a bilingual secretary in the hotel industry. My father had the equivalent of a G.E.D. diploma and had been unemployed since I could remember. He did odd jobs occasionally, but it was my mother who supported the family.

When my mother told me we were moving to the U.S., she said it was because there were many more opportunities for us there. Many years later, she told me that her brother, a U.S. citizen living in Florida, paid our rent in Medellín for six years. I realized then that despite her good job, she was financially unable to support the family. Additionally, my brother, who identified as gay, was a victim of prejudice and threats in Colombia because of his unconventional looks and sexuality. Even my father, my brother's stepfather, did not accept his queer identity. As a result, my brother became homeless and developed a drug addiction. I grew up seeing him come in and out of our home, or on the many visits to various rehabilitation centers. I had no idea how stressful it was for my mother to support our household and keep my brother alive. It wasn't until many years later that I came to understand the reason for our move to the U.S. The more I learned about the reality of our family situation, the less I felt entitled to my anger. As Shire (2013) explains "you have to understand, that no one puts their children in a boat unless the water is safer than the land" (p. xi). With the exception of my mother, brother, and sister, I was physically far away from the rest of my extended family after relocating to Miami. Relationships were severed by distance. I missed my father, my aunts, my grandmother, and my cousins.

I missed *los domingos en la casa de la abuela* (going to my grandmother's house on Sundays), where at least 20 family members would congregate to share a meal. I missed playing with my older cousins, singing *vallenatos*, and playing outside with the neighbors.

Ondaatje (1992) aptly stated "Do you understand the sadness of geography" (p. 314).

In my new geography, family was limited in my new home in Miami. There were a couple of family members who had immigrated before us, but I did not feel connected with them since we hadn't seen much of them in several years. Financial difficulties that were unknown before were far more evident to me now. We no longer lived in a house; we lived in a studio apartment connected to someone else's house. We were isolated and felt even more so since we didn't know the language. We weren't allowed to go outside and play since we didn't know our neighbors and safety in this new country was a concern. My mother continued to work long hours in order to support us, and she spent a majority of her income on lawyers to obtain legal status in the U.S. My sister and I tried to learn English quickly, using a calculator-like machine to translate our essays, writing and re-writing the same words over and over and attempting to integrate ourselves into the new environment that we were part of now. I thought that if we could communicate and have new relationships, it wouldn't be so hard.

The absence of family erased some of our traditions, including Sunday lunches, going to the movies with my mother on the weekends, running around *la cancha* with my dad, and our customary Christmas celebrations, as we knew them. As English became increasingly common in our home, it became more difficult to speak Spanish fluently. We spoke in Spanglish mainly, using both Spanish and English words in the same sentence. Spanish was a connection to home since expressions and feelings didn't have the same depth or humor in English as they did in Spanish, which was my only connection to "home." The loss of language, relationships, and traditions led to a feeling of cultural dissonance and a sort of cultural identity crisis. I felt different from my "American" friends. Even though many of them spoke Spanglish, they were second-generation Latino immigrants or had immigrated so young they could not remember their countries of origin. As a new arrival, I spoke with an accent, I had different values, I danced to Spanish music, and ate *Bandeja Paisa* and *arepas*. Chua (2012) states "Do you know what a foreign accent is? It's a sign of bravery" (p. 64).

I remember feeling flooded with emotions when I visited Medellín ten years later. Everything looked smaller than I remembered. When I tried to speak in Spanish, I knew what I wanted to say, but became tongue-tied and stumbled over my words. "You're so different now," I would hear from my aunts and cousins. "Your English is so good," "You're American now," but my relatives constantly rejected my "Americanness," warning that "It's not good for you to forget Spanish." It was in this moment I realized that I was not "just" Colombian anymore.

Drawing on Vidal- Ortiz's (2004) concept of "On Being a White Person of Color," I complicate concepts of race-making in an attempt to understand my hybridity as a white Latina of Color and a Colombian and American citizen. I face a troubled relationship between the racial privileges I have due to looking white, but my cultural belonging is negated as soon as I speak. I have become familiar with everyday comments such as "You don't look Hispanic," "You are so light skinned," "No way, you speak Spanish?" "Where are you *from?*" "But, you're white," "You don't look Colombian" "What is that accent?" and the most distressing one, "Are you Pablo Escobar's daughter?" (referring to the Colombian drug lord).

Calafell (2013), a feminist scholar of color, proposes that we problematize the homogenous categories that are imposed on people of color to consolidate ethnic and racial difference. Following Calafell's line of thought, I questioned the way racial privilege, especially privilege in passing as white, have both dominated and contradicted my experiences of space and place in the U.S. My experiences make me question how race/ethnicity and language have determined my experiences of nationhood: Who am I? and, did I leave my Colombian childhood at the border? In order to explore the "hybridization" and "multiplicity" of my identity, I took up an art-based project (*Identity 2015*) to deconstruct and analyze my experience of race, gender, and transnationalism that underlies the ambiguousness of my cultural identity.

Scholars of contemporary transnationalism have argued that migrants live in a duality, or between place of origin and place of residence (Appadurai, 1996; Basch, Schiller & Blanc, 1994). Transnationalism is a process by which immigrants forge and sustain multi-stranded social relations that link their countries of origin and places of resettlement. Transnationalism recognizes that today many immigrants build social fields that cross geographic, cultural, and political borders. As a conceptual framework, transnationalism allows us to analyze the lived and fluid experiences of individuals who act in ways that challenge our previous conflation of geographic space and social identity (Basch, Schiller & Blanc, 1994).

Do you understand the sadness of geography?

(Ondaatje, 1992: 296)

Identity 2015, represented in three parts, explores aspects of my transnational narrative as a white Latina of color. Each piece, framed within an embroidery hoop, offers a context for the social and cultural construction of my identity. One (Figure 4.9) is a cross-stitch of a light-skinned figure framed within a black and white background. Feeling split between two worlds, this sense of "in-betweenness" or "not belonging" has permeated my life. Engaging in the process of making, I am reminded of growing up in Medellín and my mother teaching me the step-by-step process of cross-stitching. As I made the piece, I found myself reflecting on the sense of pride I feel from speaking English well.

I also remembered the sadness and anger I have experienced whenever my Latina identity is denied, either because of the color of my skin or when I sometimes stumble over my Spanish words. I also consider the irony of my white skin and the colonial heritage of Colombia. Passing as white has not really protected me in the U.S.; it has only highlighted the ambiguousness caused by the loss of home, culture, and nation, further begging the question, "Where do I belong?"

Geography, place, and space have directly impacted my cultural identity everywhere I have lived: Medellín, Miami, and now Chicago. In Chicago, my ethnic and racial identity as a Colombian seems to raise more questions than in Miami. In Miami, other Latinos with various skin tones always surrounded me. Although my identity has been questioned in similar ways in both cities, in Miami almost everyone is an immigrant or is related to immigrants. On the one hand, I encounter many more Latinos in Miami who speak Spanglish with ease; code switching is a common strategy that we use to remain connected to our ethnic identities. On the other hand, Chicago, although a diverse city, is much more segregated. There are Spanish speakers in my community, but when I encounter Latino clients or acquaintances, my accent, Spanish, and white skin become a riddle to solve. In Chicago, I am constantly defending my Latina identity.

FIGURE 4.9 Luisa Ospina, *Identity 2015*

FIGURE 4.10   Luisa Ospina, *Identity 2015*

Questioning my identity further, I began to explore objects that give me legal status in the U.S. and Colombia. *Identity 2015* (Figure 4.10) was made using the layering capability of an inkjet printer to overlap the scanned identification pages of my Colombian and American passports, both concrete evidence of belonging and legal status. Surrounding the images, I repeated the microaggressions I've experienced. The written words emphasize the contradiction of my racial/ethnic and national representation. In repeatedly inscribing contradictory phrases such as "Why do you get tongue tied?" "Where is your accent from?" "You're very white," and "You're American?" I tried to deepen my feelings of cultural ambiguity. Yet, I realize the tremendous privilege I have as a Latina who can pass as a white person. I am often able to move freely between spaces without being racially targeted, which many of my friends of color—Latino, Asian, and African American—cannot take for granted. But it is language, my spoken words that highlight the politics and performance of my body.

The process of making *Identity 2015* evoked anger, shame, and guilt for not acknowledging the influence American culture has had on my life and body, superseding my Colombian heritage. In my effort to integrate myself into American culture, I had allowed other people to question who I was. This was the first time I had looked at my identity through a tangible object with images of myself as multidimensional. Although I wanted to preserve being Colombian, my American identity appeared just as important as my Colombian identity within the hoop. By superimposing the colors of the passport images, I could see the interconnectedness and intersections of my identity. The process of making the piece became a way to reconstruct my immigration experience, especially the loss and ambiguity that defined my identity as a first-generation immigrant, both a Colombian and an American citizen, and a white Latina of color.

In the third part of *Identity 2015* (Figure 4.11), I combine my Illinois driver's license and a mirrored image of my Colombian identity card. The images intentionally overlap to signify that both my cultural identities, Colombian and American, coexist within me. I came to further understand my immigration experience, my ambiguous losses, and the feelings associated with experiences of racism, ethnocentrism, and privilege.

In retrospect, reflecting on my identity through art-making allowed me, with time, intimacy, and creative space, to deconstruct the social, cultural, and personal experiences that shaped my development as a young adult. I was compelled to repurpose the images with my identity cards, which became the last installment

FIGURE 4.11 Luisa Ospina, *Identity 2015*

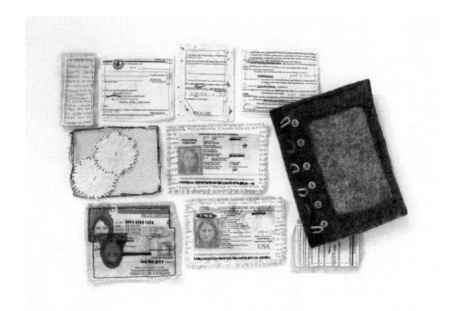

FIGURE 4.12   Luisa Ospina, *Wallet 2015*

of the *Identity* series, entitled *Wallet* (Figure 4.12). Wallets are carried everywhere and contain convenient identifiers. *Wallet* was constructed from many non-traditional materials that represented memories of my childhood in Colombia and of my grandmother's house: miniature Colombian coffee bags, tea bags, and flowers from tablecloths. Other pieces (Figures 4.9–11) were repurposed to create *Wallet*. The documents inside the wallet contain cutouts of the images of my bi-cultural identity, the covert aggressions, identification images, and immigration documents highlighting the language used to describe immigrants, such as "aliens," and the requirements to attain political asylum in this country. A piece composed of a white flower sewn on a piece of copper wire is also included in the *Wallet* to memorialize my losses.

This final work, *Wallet* (Figure 4.12), became a way to integrate aspects of an identity shaped by loss and memories of my immigrant experience. Wallet, in this sense, becomes a metaphor for how I carry with me everyday memories of my past. As Alcoff et al. (2006) argue,

> Our social realities are not just imposed upon us by society; rather we create positive meaningful identities that enable us to better understand and negotiate the social world. They enable us to engage with the social world and in the process discover how it really works. They also make it possible for us to change the world and ourselves in valuable ways.
>
> *(p. 7)*

Using art to reflexively explore my intersectionality has been a valuable tool for me to confront my own prejudices, values, beliefs, and feelings. Through my art practice, I have developed the capacity to be an introspective and self-reflexive art therapist, who is more attuned to the social, cultural, and political forces that impact my life and the lives of my clients. Approaching my work through an intersectional reflexivity lens has helped me to empathically understand my clients, as well as encourage my clients to explore their essentialized identities through art. Such a stance allows for clients to feel empowered, to explore the many forms of oppression, historical systems, and power structures that affect their everyday lives.

Conclusion

The above narratives explore, in diverse ways, the relationship between the social and structural frameworks of personal meaning making; in other words, how society shapes our everyday experiences. By examining the multiple cultural dimensions of intersectionality the narratives demonstrate how the personal, social, and political dimensions intersect in shaping stories. An intersectional reflexivity methodology allows the examination of experiences of difference. By rethinking the value of experience oriented narratives rooted in life experiences, art therapists can begin to realize the full potential of an intersectional approach.

For art therapy or mental health counseling, an intersectional approach asks that identity and difference be approached from the following:

1. On an individual level, intersectionality invites an investigation of the race, class, gender, sexuality, religion, and ability as intersecting principles and to consider identity as fluid, rather than fixed.
2. Analyzing identity, the body politic or the "self" as embedded in systems of relationships of power. As Hill Collins and Bilge (2016) argue, power is not a thing, it is a relationship. Thus, decoding the cultural, historical, and political forces that have created systems of inequality, power, privilege, and oppression, means analyzing how such relationships of power persist in personal relationships as well on an institutional level.
3. Deconstructing cultural memory to understand the embodiment of shame, fear, trauma, and stigma on the body as a consequence of structural forces This means exploring the psychological impact of trauma and stigma in relationship to the structural forces and relationships of power.
4. Working towards increasing critical consciousness in therapists and clients to make visible the everyday encounters with oppression as "an interconnected invisible web of power and privilege" (Sajnani, 2013, p, 384)
5. Challenging the power of language and the homogenous notion of difference (all women, all men, all gays, all lesbians are the same), referred in mental health language as "populations" (Sajnani, 2013).

An intersectional analysis, therefore,

> does not seek to rank the dimensions of inequality that individuals may experience or determine who has suffered the most; rather, it helps people achieve understanding in a way that empowers them to advance the cause of social and economic justice.
>
> *(Weber, 2001 as cited in Talwar, 2010, p. 13)*

References

Ahmed, S. (2004). *The cultural politics of emotion.* New York, NY: Routledge.

Ahmed, S. (2012). *On being included.* Durham, NC: Duke University Press.

Alarcón, N. (1996). Conjugating subjects in the age of multiculturalism. In A. F. Gordon & C. Newfield (Eds.), *Mapping multiculturalism* (pp. 127–148). Minneapolis, MN: University of Minnesota Press.

Alcoff, L., Hames-Garcia, M., Mohanty, S., & Moya, P. (Eds. 2006). *Identity politics reconsidered.* Basingstoke, England: Palgrave Macmillan.

Appadurai, A. (1996) *Modernity at large: Cultural dimensions of globalization.* Minneapolis, MN: University of Minnesota Press.

Austin, J. L. (1962). *How to do thing with words.* Cambridge, MA: Harvard University Press.

Basch, L., Schiller, N. G., & Blanc, C. S. (1994) *Nations unbound: Transnational politics, post-colonial predicaments, and deterritorialized nation-states.* New York, NY: Taylor & Francis.

Bell, E. (2008). *Theories of performance.* Thousand Oaks, CA: Sage Publications.

Boylorn, R. M. & Orbe, M. P. (Eds. 2014). *Critical autoethnography: Intersecting cultural identities in everyday life.* New York, NY: Routledge.

Butler, J. (1990). *Gender trouble.* New York, NY: Routledge.

Calafell, B. (2013). (I)dentities: Considering accountability, reflexivity, and intersectionality in the I and We. *Liminalities: A Journal of Performance Studies, 9*(2), 6–13.

Chilton, G. & Scotti, V. (2014). Snipping, gluing, writing: The properties of collage as an arts-based research practice. *Art Therapy: Journal of the American Art Therapy Association, 31*(4), 163–171.

Chua, A. (2012). *Battle hymn of the tiger mother.* London: Bloomsbury.

Cvetkovich, A. (2003). *An archive of feelings: Trauma, sexuality and lesbian cultures.* Durham, NC: Duke University Press.

Denzin, N. K. (2000). Aesthetics and the practices of qualitative inquiry. *Qualitative Inquiry, 6,* 256–265.

Denzin, N. K. (2006). Pedagogy, performance and autoethnography. *Text and Performance Quarterly, 26*(4), 333–338.

Finley, S. (2011). Critical arts-based inquiry: The pedagogy and performance of a radical ethical aesthetic. In N. Denzin & Y. Lincoln (Eds.), *Handbook of qualitative research* (4th ed., pp. 435–450). Thousand Oaks, CA: Sage.

George, J., Greene, B., & Blackwell, M. (2005). Three voices on multiculturalism from the art therapy classroom. *Art Therapy: Journal of the American Art Therapy Association, 22*(3), 132–138.

Gipson, L. (2015). Is cultural competence enough? Deepening social justice pedagogy in art therapy. *Art Therapy: Journal of the American Art Therapy Association, 32*(3), 142–145. doi: 10.1080/07421656.2015.1060835.

Grzanka, P. R. (2014). *Intersectionality: A foundations and frontiers reader* (p. xv). Boulder, Colorado: Westview Press.

Halberstam, J. J. (2012). *Gaga feminism: Sex, gender, and the end of normal* (Vol. 7). Boston, MA: Beacon Press.

Hammersley, M. & Atkinson, P. (1983). *Ethnography: Principles in practice*. New York, NY: Routledge.

Herbert, G. (September 16, 2013). Nina Davuluri, Miss America's first Indian-American winner, shrugs off racist backlash. Retrieved from www.syracuse.com/news/index.ssf/2013/09/nina_davuluri_miss_america_indian_racist_backlash.html

Hill Collins, P. & Bilge, S. (2016). *Intersectionality*. Malden, MA: Polity Press.

Hogan, S. (1998). *Feminist approaches to art therapy*. London: Jessica Kingsley Publishers.

Jones, R. G. (2010). Putting privilege into practice through "intersectional reflexivity": Ruminations, interventions, and possibilities. *Faculty Research and Creative Activity, 3* (Winter), 122–125.

Kapitan, L. (2014). *Introduction to art therapy research*. New York, NY: Routledge.

Lopez, H. (2006). *White by law: The legal construction of race*. New York, NY: New York University Press.

Lorde, A. (1984). *Sister outsider: Essays and speeches*. New York, NY: Crossing Press.

Madison, S. D. (2012). *Critical ethnography: Method, ethics, and performance* (2nd ed.). Los Angeles, CA: Sage Publications.

Madison, S. D. & Hamera, J. (Eds. 2005). *Sage handbook of performance studies*. Thousand Oaks, CA: Sage Publications.

McNiff, S. (2013). *Art as research: Opportunities and challenges*. Chicago, IL: University of Chicago Press.

Nagar, R. & Geiger, S. (2007). Reflexivity, positionality and identity in feminist fieldwork revisited. In A. Tickell, E. Sheppard, J. Peck, & T. Barnes (Eds.), *Politics and practice in economic geography* (pp. 267–278). London, UK: Sage Publishers.

Ondaatje, M. (1992). *The English patient: A novel*. New York, NY: Knopf.

Prasad, V. (2000). *Karma of brown folks*. Minneapolis, MI: University of Minnesota Press.

Rosaldo, R. (1989). *Culture and truth: The remaking of social analysis*. Boston, MA: Beacon Press.

Sajnani, N. (2012). Response/ability: Imagining a critical race feminist paradigm for the creative arts therapies. *Arts in Psychotherapy, 3*(3), 186–191.

Sajnani, N. (2013). The body politic: The relevance of an intersectional framework for therapeutic performance research in drama therapy. *Arts in Psychotherapy, 40*(4), 382–385.

Saltzman, L. (2006). *Making memory matter: Strategies of remembrance in contemporary art*. Chicago, IL: University of Chicago Press.

Shire, W. (2013). Home. In A. Triulzi & R. L. McKenzie (Eds.), *Long journeys. African migrants on the road* (pp. xi–xii). Leiden, The Netherlands: Brill.

Singh, J. (2016). Religious agency and the limits of intersectionality. *Hypatia, 30*(4), 657–674. doi. 10.1111/hypa.12182.

Springgay, S. (2010). Knitting as an aesthetic of civic engagement: Re-conceptualizing feminist pedagogy through touch. *Feminist Teacher, 20*(2), 111–123.

Talwar, S. (2010). An intersectional framework for race, class, gender, and sexuality in art therapy. *Art Therapy: Journal of the American Art Therapy Association, 4*(1), 11–17, doi, org/10.1080/07421656.2010.10129307.

Talwar, S. (2015). Culture, diversity and identity: From margins to center. *Art Therapy: Journal of the American Art Therapy Association, 32*(3), 100–103. doi.10.1080/07421656.2015.1060563.

Thomas, J. (1993). *Doing critical ethnography*. London, England: Sage.

Umebinyuo, I. (2016). *Questions for Ida*. Self published.

Vidal-Ortiz, S. (2004). On being a white person of color: Using autoethnography to understand Puerto Rican's racialization. *Qualitative Sociology, 27*(2), 179–203.

Xie, Y. & Goyette, K. (1997). The racial identification of biracial children with one Asian parent: Evidence from the 1990 census. *Social Forces, 76*(2), 547–570.

5

ENVISIONING BLACK WOMEN'S CONSCIOUSNESS IN ART THERAPY

Leah Gipson

> There is a strong need for intellectual and philosophical viewpoints, as well
> as practice, which reflect the understanding that personal problems, particu-
> larly in poor Black communities, are the results of the social pathology of
> this society.
>
> *(Lucille Venture 1977, pp. 80–81)*

> I am committed to exploring the oppressions, the insanities, the loyalties, and
> the triumphs of black women . . . the most fascinating creations in the world.
> *(Alice Walker 1983, pp. 250–251)*

I have been on the verge of leaving the profession of art therapy many times.
Students, art therapy participants, and colleagues have challenged me to question the norms of the profession and shift its culture instead. Still, I often think
about leaving, although I cannot escape or prevent the institutional problems that
I encounter in art therapy by leaving the field. I am a Black woman. Locating a
place for my history and values in my professional and personal life is essential to
my survival. This process of naming, analyzing, and working to create the changes
that are necessary for me to thrive as a Black woman in multiple communities is
a practice of *place making* (McKittrick, 2011). On the occasion of an expanding
social justice framework in art therapy, I draw on the opening quotes by Venture
(1977) and Walker (1983) to ask what ideas and strategies from Black women can
help to analyze professional norms that maintain the violent outcomes of systemic
oppression in the everyday lives of people of color. This question is entangled
with my life experiences, and so I begin, in Part I of this essay, with stories from
my life: first, to illustrate how I came to womanism and, second, to conceptualize

Black women's corrective responses to invisibility in the profession of art therapy. I examine the contributions of three Black art therapists, all deceased: Georgette Seabrooke Powell (1916–2011), Sarah Pollard McGee (1930–2002), and Lucille D. Venture (1919–2006). I offer a brief historical analysis of their work in Part II, where I also explore ideas of womanism, place making, and the role of multiculturalism in art therapy.

Part I

Black Women's Corrective Responses to Invisibility

1993

My mama's library was a place of creativity and responsibility. Behind the circulation desk, new children's books awaited a catalogue number and fresh barcode sticker. Stacks of returned books to be scanned and re-shelved rested inside a wooden mechanical bin with springs that would squeak each time the weight of its contents was lifted. Once in a while a new piece of hardware or technology appeared and my mama would teach me how to use it. The smell of the laminator filled the back workroom; its plates warmed and ready to make library cards or the slick sheen on graphics for the library bulletin boards. In the classrooms, it was my mama's voice that came over the PA system, in sweet songs about literacy and life, "A you're adorable, B you're so beautiful . . ."

By the time I was ten, my mama made three corrective decisions concerning my education. She enrolled me at the elementary school where she worked, a public school in a white, middle class neighborhood that was outside of the zoning guidelines for our residence. She later decided to postpone my placement in a third-grade *gifted* class so I would have a Black woman, Mrs. Parker, as my teacher. My mama was perceptive enough to know that throughout my education I would have few opportunities to gain valuable life lessons from Black women educators, and she believed that I needed these experiences to prepare for the discrimination I would face as a Black girl in advanced level classes. Finally, when my mama learned that I had been feeling ignored in my fourth-grade classroom, she decided to confront my teacher, a young white woman who admitted to her that she was *unfamiliar* and *unsure* of how to teach a Black student. This teacher was surprised to learn from my mama that I had noticed her discomfort. I remember noticing her tears and flushed face, when she apologized to me in the school library at my mama's request. That day I learned something new about myself. I would carry this particular knowledge of a racialized self every day, from that point forward, especially in the moments in classrooms with white teachers and white students who were surprised to see color over and over again.

1995

In what must have been my childhood idea of God's wrath, I dreamt a reoccurring dream of my Daddy's church engulfed in raging flames. In these nightmare visions, I was captured between two real worlds of knowledge, one spiritual and one physical. My dream felt like a warning, but how could this place, a spiritual home for my family and community, be in the path of God's eternal condemning judgment? My step-grandfather, Deacon Sconiers, and members of the community built this church. He and Grandma Sconiers lived in a house just a few feet away. My mama was raised in this church. She and Grandma Pruitt were the ones to convince my Daddy to become the pastor. This church was a place where I could escape the normalization of white-only spaces in the South, spaces that were always becoming "whiter" in spite of the histories that were still present. In my church, the only white people in sight hung in the center of the wall above the pulpit and choir stand at the highest point in the sanctuary—white Jesus and his disciples in a tapestry of the Last Supper.

My friends memorized lines from the plays I wrote, and we performed them before an attentive and affirming audience. Women placed money in my hands to give in church offerings or to buy Sister Dawson's miniature sweet potato and pecan pies after service. There were unspoken codes about worship. I danced in church. Wary of my hips, I moved so that my body's gestures could be viewed as *holy*. Only boys played the drums (except for the girls who dared). After the soprano section, then the altos, the boys sang their tenor parts, and at that precise moment, praise and worship really *got good*. But, it was the protégé preacher boys that were seen as a true gift, a fulfillment of prophecy. Girls emptied each other's purses, sat with closed legs, crossed always at the ankles. I wore stockings, no nail polish and certainly not lipstick. But just outside the church walls, I used my body to break these gendered expectations. I sat with my elbows to my knees on the church's front steps. I raced from the corner of East Second Street near the railroad crossing to the point between the shade tree and the power pole. I gripped my fingers tightly around the rocks from the tracks and slowly drew back my arm.

I was in the fifth grade, one of three girls and the only Black student in a *gifted* class. Far from the neighborhood of my church, the only expectations I could see were racial ones. When O. J. Simpson's final verdict was to be announced, my teacher turned on the television mounted above her desk. We awaited the results of the trial as a class. Three moments in public memory taught me about my body and place in society after that day. They were the murder of Nicole Brown Simpson, in 1994; the testimony of Anita Hill during the confirmation hearings of the Supreme Court nominee Clarence Thomas, in 1991; and the murder of four Black girls in the 1963 bombing of 16th Street Baptist Church in Birmingham, Alabama. I was not Nicole Simpson, though I would become a woman. I was not Anita Hill, though I was Black. I was, however, a Black girl, who attended Sunday school each week at a Black church in the South and in these spiritual, physical worlds in which I lived, judgment came down.

A Womanist Method

Surviving racism meant that my mother constantly made ethical decisions to promote the wellbeing of her family. In the vignette *1993*, I describe my mother's strategy for dealing with institutional racism during my childhood education. My mother often used her class privilege and position as an educator and elementary school librarian to access resources and protection against racism. Ultimately, her interventions made space for me to use my voice and visibility in the political arenas of girlhood and education. My mother's corrective responses to the impacts of racism in her children's lives relate to the opening portion of Alice Walker's (1983) definition of womanism, "From the black folk expression of mothers to female children" (p. xi) (Table 5.1). Moving between my story and a womanist analysis of Black women's responses to invisibility, I have chosen to work with an everyday expression addressed to children. "Stay in your *place*." Among the number of cautionary sayings for children who make their presence known or attempt to engage in adult conversations, I read the phrase in the voice of a Black woman as author and as caregiver.

TABLE 5.1 Alice Walker's definition of womanism (1983)

Womanist
1. From womanish. (Opp. of "girlish," i.e. frivolous, irresponsible, not serious.) A black feminist or feminist of color. From the black folk expression of mothers to female children, "you acting womanish," i.e., like a woman. Usually referring to outrageous, audacious, courageous or willful behavior. Wanting to know more and in greater depth than is considered "good" for one. Interested in grown up doings. Acting grown up. Being grown up. Interchangeable with another black folk expression: "You trying to be grown." Responsible. In charge. Serious.
2. Also: A woman who loves other women, sexually and/or nonsexually. Appreciates and prefers women's culture, women's emotional flexibility (values tears as natural counterbalance of laughter), and women's strength. Sometimes loves individual men, sexually and/or nonsexually. Committed to survival and wholeness of entire people, male and female. Not a separatist, except periodically, for health. Traditionally a universalist, as in: "Mama, why are we brown, pink, and yellow, and our cousins are white, beige and black?" Ans. "Well, you know the colored race is just like a flower garden, with every color flower represented." Traditionally capable, as in: "Mama, I'm walking to Canada and I'm taking you and a bunch of other slaves with me." Reply: "It wouldn't be the first time."
3. Loves music. Loves dance. Loves the moon. Loves the Spirit. Loves love and food and roundness. Loves struggle. Loves the Folk. Loves herself. *Regardless.*
4. Womanist is to feminist as purple is to lavender.

(Walker, 1983, p. xi)

The first section of Walker's literary definition describes a necessary community orientation for determining one's *place*. In a dialogue between Black women and Black girls, this process of *knowing* involves moments of tension and negotiation. Walker's Black girl is "acting womanish," and signaling her social power. She is performing and locating her work by deciding what is "good for one" (p. xi). Often communicated through everyday experiences and the "speech culture of black women" (Allan, 1995, p. 69), womanism is informed by the knowledge of Black women and other women of color. Womanism values Black women's experiences of problem solving in the face of racism, cis-hetero-sexism, classism, and other forms of compound oppression (Floyd-Thomas, 2006a, 2006b; Phillips, 2006; Marparyan, 2012). To be seen and not heard, a point which I highlight in *1993*, is a particular problem of Black women's and girl's experiences of multi-layered oppression. My womanist exploration reinterprets the idea of staying in one's *place* as a type of epistemology and labor for social change. To restate this, the concept of *place making* is action-oriented, similar to the idea of "making a way out of no way" in womanist theology, which "articulates black women's relationships with God as they navigate the reality of their lives in the pursuit of wholeness and justice" (Coleman, 2008, p. 12). To explain my concept of place making, I will show how my experiences with education and religion have led me to question art therapy in a particular way. I build on a portion of Walker's (1983) classical womanist text *In Search of Our Mothers' Gardens* to analyze the contributions of Black women in art therapy, ones whose practices included advocacy and activism in art therapy. I am suggesting an original conception of *place making* that allows me to introduce a womanist methodology to art therapy. A womanist method asserts an ethical authority granted by Black women's humanity and experiences of histories of marginalization and violence. I use a womanist analysis to offer a corrective response to Black women's invisibility in art therapy.

The command or expectation to "stay in one's *place*" seemingly contradicts goals of liberation. If understood in relation to a liberal notion of freedom, which invites independent self-expression, exploration, and property ownership, the phrase can suggest coercive limits to personal freedom. If the phrase is understood in terms of one's survival under oppressive conditions, it can suggest a strategy of survival. Viewed from the latter perspective, the expression offers a counter response to an individualistic idea of freedom. Such a perspective assumes that there are histories and knowledges that are tied to one's place; therefore, the existence of dominant ideological forces complicate place making as a survival strategy. I will later raise the contradictions within the strategy of *place making* to draw a parallel with the conflicting role of multiculturalism in Black women's historical experiences of the art therapy profession. My emphasis on the word *place* from the expression, "stay in your *place*" is meant to distinguish harmful attitudes toward others, rooted in a desire to dominate, from an altogether different purpose and motivation. As a survival strategy, *place making* aims to establish safety among a Black communal network based on historically shared or lived experience of oppression. This aspirational safety aims to keep people who are vulnerable out of harm's way in response to the profound distortions of dominant views and constant erasure. In the story *1995*, I show contradictions within my communal safety network where I experienced mixed messages about personal empowerment in my father's church. I compare this environment to that of the public school in my mother's library. In both places, my early race consciousness conflicted with my ideas about gender and sexuality. The stories demonstrate that place making is not foolproof. There must be interventions that call for a paradigm shift that questions prevailing knowledge. My mother's position at her school could not prevent my encounters with racism. Instead, my feelings of being ignored and her experience of school segregation were a part of a shared history, to which she responded. Using her knowledge to question my teacher's actions, she challenged the hegemonic status of power. In a different way, the imagery from my childhood nightmare illustrates the fallacies of safety and the need to examine work from a critical theoretical lens. Higginbotham's (1993) historical example of Black women's radical leadership in the Black Baptist church is a description of Black women's "multiple consciousness and multiple positioning" (p. 14), which informed their organizational efforts to transform the Black church into an institution for social change despite its sexist traditions. The two personal stories that I offer are meant to convey a womanist complexity that allows for bold contradictions in navigating oppressive and hierarchical structures. Therefore, I view the request to stay in one's place as a womanist call and response, to which Walker's (1983) womanist definition answers with willfulness. Black women's corrective response to invisibility is one that looks for the opportunities to be "Responsible. In Charge. Serious" (p. xi).

The term "womanist" arose within the context of Black women's invisibility in mainstream feminist discourse. Scholars have attributed the term to three originators, Alice Walker (1981, 1983), Chikwenye Okonjo Ogunyemi (1985), and Clenora Hudson-Weems (1993). Womanism suggests a "humanist vision" (Coleman, 2008, p. 46) that is based on women of color's intimate knowledge of the historical conditions they have navigated for hundreds of years. Walker (1983) defined a womanist as a Black feminist or a feminist of color who is, ". . . Committed to survival and wholeness of entire people, male and female. Not a separatist, except periodically, for health" (p. xi). Womanism also critiques claims that deny Black women's particular struggles, especially noting that Black women have been forced into submission and death by means of silencing and marginalization. I highlight the womanist notion that links the health of Black women to the liberation of others, but first to her own liberation (Coleman, 2008).

I use my stories as examples to introduce some of the considerations of womanism that will be important in Part II, a womanist review of the history of art therapy. Yet, there is more to these stories than their telling. I am still and always on the verge of leaving the profession of art therapy. I am a womanist.

Although I cannot independently escape or prevent the social issues arising from oppression, I refuse to stay in a *place* where the layers of invisibility for Black girls and Black women are not taken seriously as an ethical issue. As a womanist, I am concerned with the lives of Black girls, who are still increasingly vulnerable to overt forms of institutional violence (Richie, 2012). A womanist way of being relates to the kind of *place making* that is acutely necessary for Black life. When Walker (1983) wrote the lines in her womanist definition— "Traditionally capable, as in: 'Mama, I'm walking to Canada and I'm taking you and a bunch of other slaves with me.' Reply: 'It wouldn't be the first time'" (p. xi)—she captured a historical reality for Black women who have needed to determine the right time and place for their participation, and how to approach leaving if it becomes a viable option. Womanism asserts the epistemological value of Black women's experiences (Cannon, 1995; Floyd-Thomas, 2006a). If a professional turn toward social justice is meant to effect a positive change for people of color, art therapists must develop critical practices that can confront the discursive problems woven into the discipline (Talwar, 2015a; Sajnani, Marxen & Zarate, 2017). An emerging emphasis on social justice (Gipson, 2015; 2017; Karcher, 2017; Talwar, 2015a; 2015b) offers an opportunity to develop a counter-disciplinary inquiry, which questions assumptions in art therapy that are taken for granted, including Euro–American ethnocentric values that prioritize individual psychological change, independence, and freedom of expression. It is time for art therapy to deal with difference in gender struggles that have long been a source of debate and a place for active transformation led by Black feminists and womanists.

Part II

Becoming Art Therapy

Following World War II economic expansion, a number of white and Jewish women began to practice art therapy in the Eastern and Midwestern parts of the U.S. (Gerity, 2000; Junge, 2010; Naumburg, 1966; Ulman, 1970; Wix, 2000). Postwar conditions led to the professional growth of psychology (Pickren, 2007), setting the stage for the future professionalization of art therapy. What has not been plainly stated or explored is how the founding women of art therapy were able to forge a discipline during a time in which many people of color, Jews, poor whites, and women could not benefit from the opportunities reserved for a predominantly white, middle class America. A discussion of the social dynamics that allowed white and Jewish art therapists to gain acceptance among an initial community of professional insiders could offer insight into the current values and norms of art therapy. Founding art therapy professionals of color (Dye, 1901; Lomoc-Smith, 1979; McGee, S., 1979; McGee, S. E., 1981; Venture, 1977) recognized that both the benefits and pitfalls of the professionalization of art therapy hinged on social injustice, and that to advance their position through greater exclusivity also meant to embrace the opportunities that arose from the injustice of war, racism, poverty, ableism and other forms of oppression. What, then, would it mean to approach an emerging social justice interest in art therapy not as a sign of a new trend, but as a tradition begun by people of color in the discipline to develop corrective responses to the ways in which art therapy has mirrored a wider historical refusal of social change? Art therapists of color began raising consciousness through their organizational leadership during the early formation of the field (Potash & Ramirez, 2013; Venture, 1977). Black founding professionals expressed their political attitudes in art therapy, giving close attention to the impact of social forces. They proposed practical ideas for the work that art therapists might do in response to the violence of oppression, but their contributions have been made invisible. Uncovering the histories of a few Black women in art therapy could lead to theorizing from a place that values the knowledge of people of color, including their ideas that have given rise to larger historical movements for change.

Georgette Seabrooke Powell (1916–2011)

The Harlem Renaissance is well documented for its significance in American cultural life of the late 1910s to mid 30s. Georgette Seabrooke (later Powell) migrated North with her family from Charleston, South Carolina, to Harlem between the ages of four and six (Black Smith, 2014; Hayden & Sterns, 2006). Thousands of other Blacks from the U.S. South and the Caribbean colonies would seek opportunities in Harlem during the Great Migration. As a young woman and an artist, Powell would have found herself in the midst of a gendered *New Negro* revolution, where an ideology of Black subjectivity and self-determination flourished in a post-Reconstruction, international Harlem (Stephens, 2005). Powell's battle for her education at Cooper Union in the mid 1930s prefigured the later struggles of the Civil Rights Movement, which led Black art therapist Cliff Joseph to the profession (Riley-Hiscox, 1997).

Georgette Seabrooke Powell would not begin studying art therapy in New York City until 1958, but her opportunities to major in art at a predominantly white high school and complete a Works Progress Administration (WPA) mural commission in Harlem placed her among a young, educated African American elite in the 1930s. Powell attended Cooper Union for the Advancement of Science and Art from 1933 to 1937 (Black Smith, 2014). At the Harlem Art Workshop and the Harlem Community Center, she worked with her contemporaries, Romare Beardon and Jacob Lawrence, and teachers James Lesesne Wells, Gwendolyn Bennett, and Augusta Savage (Hayden & Sterns, 2006). In 1937, Powell completed the mural *Recreation in Harlem* at Harlem Hospital and another mural at Queens General Hospital after an extensive struggle between city and hospital officials, the WPA, and a community of artists in Harlem.

FIGURE 5.1   Georgette Seabrooke Powell, *Recreation in Harlem* (Detail), 1937. Harlem Hospital Center – New York City, New York, Restored in 2012

Recreation in Harlem, 1938
Artist: Georgette Seabrooke Powell
©Harlem Hospital Center, New York City, permission granted.

She and other renowned Black artists worked with Charles Alston, the first African American supervisor of a New Deal mural project (Linden & Greene, 2001). Powell's *Recreation in Harlem* depicted interracial scenes and a noticeably high ratio of Black women engaging with others in activities of everyday community life (http://iraas.columbia.edu/wpa/). Local white administrative officials refused Powell's and three other murals for the project. Alston accused Superintendent Lawrence T. Dermody of discrimination and gave the hospital official's reasons for rejecting the mural sketches by Powell, Vertis Hayes, Sarah Murell, and himself when he stated that:

> [according to Dermody] the murals contained too much Negro subject matter; . . . Negros may not form the greater part of the community 25 years hence; . . . Negroes in the community would object to the emphasis on Negro subject matter in the murals, . . . [Harlem] hospital is not a Negro hospital, therefore it should not be singled out for Negro subject matter.
>
> *(Discrimination Charges Hurled, 1936, p. 3)*

Linden and Greene (2001) explained that in addition to neighborhood ghettos, Black workers and middle-class professionals saw the development of an "institutional ghetto that segregated nearly every aspect of life, from employment and education to housing and health care" (p. 409). Harlem Hospital was a site of political and ideological struggle, especially since it was one of few hospitals where Black doctors and nurses could undergo training and find employment. Located in a neighborhood where half of the Black people in the entire city resided, Harlem Hospital's majority patient population was also Black. Alston, with the help of the Artists' Union and the Harlem Artists' Guild, viewed the local administrative opposition to the murals as a product of institutional racism, including segregationist practices in the WPA. The artists joined a wider campaign against employment discrimination in Harlem, where the riots of March 19th and 20th 1935 had recently brought the severity of the economic situation to public attention. Powell joined the protests and won, but the political pushback against the project caused a delay to the mural's completion and Cooper Union considered her work-study credit for the mural incomplete. The school would deny her a certificate of graduation until 1980 (Linden & Greene, 2001).

The New York Age, a historically influential Black newspaper, featured excerpts from Powell's early art practice, including the story of the Harlem Hospital murals. An issue dated Saturday, October 7, 1933, provided a glimpse into the political significance of art and community in Harlem in the 1930s: "there is a collection of some ninety odd paintings, drawings and prints that will certainly offer a few moments of pleasure to the wide awake Negro who finds realism in the cultural advancement of his race" (Brandford, 1933, p. 7). The article described Powell's block print *Tropical Scene* and pencil drawing *Catherine* as examples of a "natural racial style" in an exhibition of "some forty-nine young men, women and children" at the 135th Street Public Library, further adding that "this exhibition deserves more than ordinary scrutiny, for it bespeaks the hope and redemption of Negro Art" (p. 7).

Powell spent the next two decades caring for her three children and supporting her husband Dr. George Wesley Powell, who had difficulty working in his field of podiatry due to racial segregation and the status of the young profession. Owing to her domestic responsibilities, Powell placed her practice of painting and printmaking on hold, but soon began to develop ideas and projects that would build on her previous public art experiences to form a multidisciplinary, community art practice. She read about an art therapy course with Edith Kramer at the Turtle Bay Music School in New York City. Deciding that it would be a way to return to her work, Powell took the course (Boston & Short, 2006). She subsequently established her art therapy career in medical settings after moving to Washington, D.C., in the early 1960s. She worked with Elinor Ulman and Bernard Levy at D.C. General Hospital (Boston & Short, 2006). Throughout her involvement with the profession, Powell remained engaged in education, curatorial projects, exhibitions, and organizations that she established, including the Powell Art Studio (Hayden & Sterns, 2006), Tomorrow's World Art Center and Art in the Park (Boston & Short, 2006; Hurtibise, 2008). Curator and cultural historian Black Smith (2014) described Powell as an active leader in the Black Arts Movement and noted her involvement in the annual Art in the Park held at Meridian Hill Park, commonly known as Malcolm X Park. Powell initially organized community members to exhibit work and make art in a grocery store parking lot on Sundays, when the store was closed (Hurtibise, 2008). Collins (2008) argued that one of the commonalities between the Black Arts and Feminist Art Movement was a vision that challenged the Western ideal of a singular artist with one who was "immersed in community," in an art practice that "honored and empowered his or her new and non-elite audience for art through validation and consciousness-raising" (p. 283). It is difficult to situate Powell in one specific movement, but worth noting that her ideas can be captured in the ways in which her experiences as a Black woman unfolded in multiple and overlapping spheres of professional practice.

Powell's early influences and ideas have likely not been recognized in contemporary art therapy history because her art practice, running parallel with her professional career, has not been considered a significant factor in her contribution to art therapy. Even when compared to one art therapist, Mary Huntoon, whose influence before the founding of the AATA has received the recent attention of art therapy scholars (Junge, 2010; Wix, 2000; Wix, 2010), Powell's ideas continue to be overlooked. Huntoon returned to the U.S. from an art career in Europe and became Director of the WPA in Topeka until 1938, when Powell's art education and WPA mural work took place. Junge (2010) credited Huntoon as an "artist/social activist," whose "WPA social awareness" (p. 56) would later inform her community oriented art therapy practice. In New York, social awareness would cost Powell her certificate of graduation from Cooper Union for more than 40 years.

Accounts of art therapists such as Naumburg, Kramer, Ulman, and Rubin describe their education at elite schools, art practices, international travel, and professional innovation, as providing important context for the ideas that they would bring to art therapy. Arnheim (1984) lauded Naumburg for being self-taught in an emerging discipline in which she would teach others. Kramer wrote of her path to art therapy, "Instead of undergoing formal training, I could build upon ideas and information that came to me in the late 1920s and 1930s in my native Vienna" (Gerity, 2000, pp. 20–21). Kramer's description of an environment of influential artists, political, and psychoanalytical ideas might well be compared to Powell's community in Harlem. Although Powell's community art practice was innovative, it stands in contrast with the accounts of Naumburg, Kramer, and Ulman and speaks to the unique historical experiences of Black women in the US. The impact of racism on Powell's art therapy career can be seen not only in the failure to recognize her work, but also the inattention to the potential ways in which education, employment, family, and community informed her ideas.

Social justice might have been integral to the field had her experiences and those of other art therapists of color been valued equally with those of their contemporaries. In an interview (Hayden & Sterns, 2006), Powell described how she became an art therapist. Powell's reflections on meeting Ulman in New York and later working with her in D.C. captured the discrimination she encountered, in 1963, in the fledgling field of art therapy:

> . . . actually, it was sort of a new ground . . . artists . . . were working not with a title but just working with patients and hospitals and so forth . . . since I didn't know about civil service and the kinds of jobs that they were giving black people and white people. And they gave me a low [civil service] grade and as her [assistant] to help her . . . She was a woman who had been a product of Wellesley . . . I think she was a Jewish lady and her father was the first Jewish judge in Baltimore . . . she had a very good background and she was a very good writer, too. But then as far as . . . taking the job, she did not make the job. She only told them that she needed someone.
>
> *(Hayden & Sterns, 2006)*

Powell described how she was unfairly assigned to Ulman as her assistant at D.C. General Hospital. She cited Ulman's summer trips to Maine that left her in charge—although Ulman had given her a low-ranking pay level—as a reason to question how she had been positioned as a student of art therapy. Powell's assertion that Ulman "did not make the job," refuted the diminished status she was given in developing art therapy practice at the time. Boston and Short (2006) stated that Powell did not believe her contributions to the *American Journal of Art Therapy*, started by Ulman and Levy, were included. A womanist perspective in art therapy would explore the political realities for women of color in the profession to uncover the ideas that were lost through censorship and exclusion.

I have revisited some of the prominent art therapy figures in relation to Powell's story to shift who is acknowledged and centered in art therapy literature and its history. Art therapy has not explored the Harlem Renaissance as a traditional source for understanding a connection between art and human well-being. Scholars in the discipline have preferred to study European *Outsider Art* and the controversial Prinzhorn Collection of the same period (Junge, 2010; Rubin, 1986; Vick, 2003). Unfortunately, the art that has been a part of global resistance movements led by people of color has been largely overlooked by the art therapy community.

Sarah Pollard McGee (1930–2002)

Sarah P. McGee's early art therapy practice was a part of the Asbury Park Riots in New Jersey in 1970. The Asbury Park Riots were among hundreds occurring across the U.S. President Lyndon B. Johnson's response to the crisis had been an executive order to form the National Advisory Commission on Civil Disorders. The Report of the National Advisory Commission on Civil Disorders (1968) described the racial scene in Newark three summers prior to the Asbury Park Riots:

> Between 1960 and 1967, the city lost a net total of more than 70,000 white residents. Replacing them in vast areas of dilapidated housing where living conditions . . . so bad that "people would be kinder to their pets," were Negro migrants, Cubans, and Puerto Ricans.
>
> *(p. 30)*

Prior to the Great Depression and World War II, Asbury Park was a summer resort community. When economic changes altered the vacation industry, the few job opportunities to accommodate short-term, weekend visitors were given to white youths from the suburbs, instead of the local African-American youth. A response to racism, economic inequality, and unacceptable living conditions for African Americans, the riots spanned four days, resulting in nearly two hundred people injured and an estimated 5.6 million dollars in damage and clean-up costs (Martin, 2016). According to Peyser (1989), McGee's decision to bring art supplies to the riots, "to try to replace non-communicative anger with order and understanding" was successful (p. 7). McGee curated an exhibition of "charcoal, pen and ink drawings, pastels, watercolors and one oil painting by 13 black artists from Asbury Park" in early October of 1970 (Asbury Park Riots, 1970, p. 69). The show was titled *Artistry in Black from the Riots in Asbury Park* and took place at Rutgers Graduate School of Education.

Only days prior to the exhibition, on September 25th, the first AATA Conference, held in Virginia, came to an intense close, when Wayne Ramirez and others from the Wisconsin Art Therapy Association were unsuccessful in an attempt to prevent the executive board from establishing restrictive criteria for art therapy certification (Potash & Ramirez, 2013). Far beyond the boundaries that were being established at this initial conference to define practice, McGee's art therapy interventions surrounding the Asbury Park Riots were focused on finding ordinary solutions to pervasive community trauma resulting from structural violence. McGee learned to incorporate a therapeutic practice into art educational workshops that she led at Sarah's Shangrala, her personal studio located behind her home (Peyser, 1989). What began for her as drop in visits from children who were clients of her husband, a Black psychologist (Scuddie Eugene McGee), soon became a new way of thinking about art. McGee was also interested in cultural work for social uplift, and although there is no record of her use of the term, her practice centered on Afrocentric philosophy (Boston & Short, 1998). McGee traveled to Nigeria with Chuck Davis, who did research toward creating the DanceAfrica festival in 1977. On the 20th anniversary of this festival, she recalled, "We both felt it was important for people in America to know more about the real things of Africa, not the negative images that most people associated with Africa" (Collins, 1997, p. 55). Doby-Copeland's (2006) experience with McGee offers a window into her ideas, which integrated West African traditional spirituality into art therapy. McGee became known as Mama Sarah (Figdore, 2001) and Nam Samay Ndiya, a priestess of Ndepp (Harness, 2002). She traveled regularly to Senegal where she likely cultivated her ideas about family-based art therapy.

The reform of public education pressured farm owners to allow children to attend school, and McGee began working with families from the "Eastern Migrant Stream" in a crib-preschool program in the South Brunswick School District in 1977 (McGee, 1981, p. 33). The work with "teenage mothers," "field mothers," and "surrogate mothers" provided education, child care, and an "avenue for emotional ventilation and creative expression for both child and adult participation through the use of art" (McGee, 1981, p. 33). McGee's ideas of art therapy explored the cultural relevance of materials and media. In her early work with migrant women, she used potatoes for printmaking and wild blueberries for dyes, materials that were familiar to the women she was working with. By the late '80s, she was encouraging students at Rugby School to create film, drama, and dance performances in art therapy (Peyser, 1989). McGee, whose granddaddy was a musician and drummer, used African drumming and dance in addition to traditional practices of drawing and sculpture with children at Amanda's Easel, an art therapy program for families impacted by domestic violence (Figdore, 2001; Harness, 2002).

McGee earned a Bachelor's degree in art and psychology from Thomas Edison State College and a Certificate Pratique de Médecine Traditionnelle from the University of Dakar, Senegal, West Africa (the equivalent of a doctoral degree in art therapy) in 1986 (Harness, 1986; Snell, 2002). Short's (2014) recollection of the early years of art therapy and existing research on art therapists of color reveals the hegemony of whiteness in art therapy. She stated:

> Cheryl Doby-Copeland researched Sarah McGee. Ahead of her time, Sarah worked with migrant workers. Often her presentations were not accepted by the AATA conference, so she would present them and her videos in her hotel room.
>
> *(p. 189)*

Like Powell's, McGee's practice extended outside of a mainstream approach to art therapy. Her visibility and accomplishments in professional and civic communities are compelling reasons to evaluate the politics of art therapy and ask why it has failed to consider her work as a source when theorizing the practice of art therapy. McGee's use of art therapy as a way to resist violence and oppression—through communal work and a global consciousness that reclaimed African culture—is related to womanist ideas on spirituality, community, and self-care. As Walker (1983) described, a womanist is:

Committed to survival and wholeness of entire people, male and female. Not a separatist, except periodically, for health. Traditionally a universalist, as in: "Mama, why are we brown, pink, and yellow, and our cousins are white, beige and black?" Ans. "Well, you know the colored race is just like a flower garden, with every color flower represented." . . . Loves music. Loves dance. Loves the moon. Loves the Spirit. Loves love and food and roundness. Loves struggle. Loves the Folk. Loves herself. Regardless.

(p. xi)

Lucille D. Venture (1919–2006)

Lucille Venture is best known as an early advocate of diversity in art therapy and for being the first person to obtain a Ph.D. in the field, in 1977. Years prior to earning her doctoral degree, Venture assembled a committee of four Black professional AATA members to serve on the Ad Hoc Committee to Investigate Encouraging Minority Groups to Enter and Study in the Field of Art Therapy (Correspondence 1973–1974, L. Venture to F. Cohen, March 6, 1974, p. 6). She also worked independently with four Black students at Antioch, Homestead Montebello Center. Venture, like other art therapy founding professionals of color, actively brought perspectives that advanced social consciousness in response to the increasing value of professionalization during the 1970s. Venture's leadership is shown in the Association correspondence, which provides some of the history associated with the ad hoc committee. In a letter dated November 19, 1973, former AATA President Felice W. Cohen wrote to Venture:

Hopefully, you and the committee members you choose to work with will "come up" with some definitive findings, so that we may inquire more knowledgeably into the question of why we have so few members of minorities exploring and studying Art Therapy.

(p. 1)

The letters document Venture's efforts to organize a committee of three additional members, Lemuel Joyner, Cliff Joseph, and Georgette Seabrooke Powell. The group had not only worked with other founding professionals in the field, but also formulated responses to the increasing value of professionalization during the 1970s that were rooted in a global social consciousness and a vision of liberation art therapy (Venture, 1977). Venture stated in a report that the "committee recognized the need for job opportunities for everyone . . . but our commitment is to . . . Third World People," who shared common experiences and culture, "with the community in which the need for help is ever present and where they (more or less) will be employed" (Correspondence 1973–1974, L. Venture to F. Cohen, March 6, 1974, p. 7). The report indicated the committee's decision to change its name to Third World People. The concept of the Third World in the 1970s was attached to the worldwide revolutionary movements of the 1960s, which was a radical shift from Western conceptions of the world and the self. In the U.S. the Third World paradigm for activists was deeply intertwined with the Black Power Movement. Organizations and individuals used the phrase *Third World* in solidarity with liberation struggles that were now part of an international community (Christiansen & Scarlett, 2015). Venture explained, "The term 'Third World' refers to the less economically developed groups and communities of the world, including Black, Hispanic, American Indian, and Asian" (Correspondence 1973–1974, L. Venture to F. Cohen, March 6, 1974, p. 9). The action to rename the committee by the early group of four Black art therapists was met with resistance from the AATA Board of Directors. Then President-Elect Don Jones wrote to Venture:

> I am pleased that this is an area that you and Lem Joyner are working on in another context. It is bound to carry over into art therapy. Obviously, our Ad Hoc committee must continue to focus on minority groups in the broadest sense as well as specific Third World individuals who need special emphasis. My advice is that we not limit the exploration nor the name of the committee to the Third World Area, but be more inclusive. I think the committee might also think in the area of males, and people who are aging and retired.
>
> *(Correspondence 1973–1974, D. Jones to L. Venture,*
> *April 29, 1974, p. 10)*

Venture's organizational leadership was as much an effort to shape the profession as it was a cultural viewpoint that explained her theoretical orientation in art therapy with children. Later, Venture would use graduate research as a place to challenge the discriminatory ideas of the profession. The title of her dissertation, *The Black Beat in Art Therapy Experiences*, alluded that she would call into question the history of art therapy using the knowledge of Black experience. Not only do the connections to the Black Power Movement seem to be present in Venture's work with the *Third World Committee*, but her analysis of the case examples in her dissertation also points to a sustained relationship to cultural and political ideas of the period. Venture (1977), wrote in her dissertation, "It is my feeling that art therapy, if it is to be effective, must be approached in a manner which enables the poor to become actively involved on their own terms in the struggle against racism and poverty" (p. 81). Venture referred to the slogan "Black is Beautiful" and singer James Brown's song "Say It Loud—I'm Black and I'm Proud." She questioned whether the consciousness of the time was reaching the youngest of Black children. Venture conceptualized children's problems within the cultural context of their family and community systems. She included an institutional analysis in her work with clients in art therapy. Venture explained that advocating for the support of a multidisciplinary team of administrators, faculty, and staff was integral to her role as the "art teacher-therapist" and to her Crisis Art Therapy (CAT) program at a "special school for behavior problem and emotional handicapped youth on the grounds of a State hospital" (1977, pp. 84–86). In one case, "Bret's Bus," she described ten-year-old Bobby, a Black male student, whose teacher brought him to the art room after his display of aggressive behavior toward other children in the classroom. Bobby drew two buses, his older white male classmate Bret's and his own. Venture reflected on her observations of the student's drawings and described her interactions with the student. Her verbal interventions responded to the student's language and ideas (i.e., she repeated words the client used to describe the bus, "the biggest" and "the best"), encouraging the student's technique (i.e., color, representation, quality), and affirmed Bobby's desire to show his teacher the drawing of his bus. Here, Venture referred to Carl Jung's assertion that patients should be responsible for interpretation of their symbolic imagery. After the student returned to class, he shared with his teacher that he was being bullied by Bret on the bus. Venture described her approach within the school system:

> I requested Mrs. A to explore the bus issue with him [Bobby] and Bret . . . I believed that she his beloved teacher with whom he was in the classroom all day, would be the natural one to explore the bus in his drawing and work out Bobby's problem.
>
> *(p. 96)*

She discussed their collaborative work with Bobby, which included Mrs. A's acknowledgment of the possibility of a racial problem between Bret and Bobby. The teacher spoke to Bret, alerted the bus driver, and gave Bobby himself a note for the driver. They notified the faculty to support change in both students. This intervention represents the type of systemic thinking and community focus that Venture promoted through her art therapy practice.

Multiculturalism as Place Making for Black Women's Ideas in Art Therapy

As a Black woman in art therapy, the challenges of staying in the profession are linked to the two vital institutions that have shaped my own consciousness—predominantly white educational institutions and the Black church. Each of these spaces yield multiple and conflicting dimensions of place for my visibility and voice. Similarly, my historical reflections on Powell, McGee, and Venture highlight the complexities of place making for Black women's visibility and influence in the profession of art therapy. Revisiting the three Black women layers the discussion about a social justice approach with the recognition that Black women in art therapy have historically provided their corrective responses to invisibility as a strategy for wider social change. A social justice approach in the profession of art therapy is, therefore, not new; in earlier times the profession resisted it. The interventions of Black women in the 1970s to find a place for Black people in the field of art therapy resembled those of Black feminists who addressed problems with contemporary feminism, which centered the values and experiences of middle class white women. Black women's practices of correcting institutions involve both perceiving safe and unsafe spaces for Black people and correcting those in close proximity to Black communities, their spaces of learning, creativity, and responsibility. In some cases, Black women have felt compelled to temporarily leave dominant spaces and begin their own projects. Examples of these responses can be seen in the work of each of the three women. Powell was a member of the National Alliance of Third World Creative Therapists (NATWCT), founded in 1978, and founded her own organizations and projects while practicing art therapy in a more traditional setting in Washington, D.C. (Boston & Short, 2006). McGee gave art therapy presentations in her hotel room at AATA conferences when her papers were rejected (Short, 2014). Venture led the Ad Hoc Third World Committee and initiated independent work with Black art therapy graduate students at Antioch. Each of these women traveled internationally, although little is written on their respective work in Venezuela, Nigeria, Senegal, and other countries. Throughout its history, the institution of art therapy has not been receptive to corrective responses from Black women. Their ideas about art, therapy, and social change have yet to be widely explored. In some ways, the professional organization has functioned as a structure that has set the terms for how people of color can be visible, keeping them in a marginal capacity in the association's literature and leadership. Black women have remained engaged in resisting such trends from the formation of the field to the present.

We might understand Venture's leadership of the first ad hoc committee addressing "minorities" in the AATA as a form of place making. Lorde (1984) wrote:

> Within this country where racial difference creates a constant, if unspoken, distortion of vision, black women have on the one hand always been highly visible, and so, on the other hand, have been rendered invisible through the depersonalization of racism.
>
> *(p. 42)*

Similar to other fields, the "depersonalization of racism" permeated the profession at its formation, from the AATA Board of Director's decision to ignore the Ad Hoc Third World Committee's self-naming to the consistent invisibility of Black art therapists through token representation by merely listing their names without exploring their ideas. Tokenism is the result of the contradictions of multiculturalism in art therapy. Tokens are "made aware of their differences . . . but then must often pretend that the differences do not exist, or have no implications," and they are, "among the most visible and dramatized of performers, noticeably on stage, yet they are often kept away from the organizational backstage where the dramas are cast" (Kanter, 1977, p. 258). Black women have *always been visible* at the forefront of issues framing diversity in art therapy (Boston, 2015; Potash, Doby-Copeland, Stepney, Washington, Vance, Short, Boston, & Ballbé ter Maat, 2015; Talwar, Iyer, & Doby-Copeland, 2004). The naming of the Mosaic Committee in 1990 related to the early consciousness of people of color in the profession and their visibility in the field, but it was "de-named" by the AATA board and changed to the Multicultural Committee in 1995. From its inception as the Mosaic Committee in 1990 to the present Multicultural Committee in 2017, eight of the thirteen chairpersons for the AATA Multicultural Committee have been Black women: Anna Riley Hiscox, Charlotte Boston, Cheryl Doby-Copeland, Gwendolyn Short, Stella Stepney, Lindsey Vance, Brittney Washington, and Delora Putnam Barnes (current chairperson). Black women have needed to develop their ideas both within the spaces of the discipline and beyond the profession (Lumpkin, 2006; Farris, 2006). The actions of some individual art therapists reveal the history of Black art therapy professionals, yet there are no contemporary theories in art therapy that are formed on the basis of their history and ideas. Multiculturalism in art therapy appears paradoxically connected with the marginalization of Black history and culture, and that of other people of color in the profession (George, 2006; Talwar, 2006). What seems implicit in the culture of art therapy is that white art therapists have largely accommodated multiculturalism, while continuing to view "contributions of different cultural strands" as passé (Kaplan, 2002, p. 138; Iyer, Talwar, & Doby-Copeland, 2003). The documentary film *The Wheels of Diversity* was probably the only substantial study to highlight the work of Powell and Venture, and other art therapists of color (Short, 2014). The film, which was once offered as part of the continuing education program of AATA (2011), could not be located at the time of writing this essay.

Viewing a history of the three Black women—Georgette Seabrooke Powell, Sarah Pollard McGee, and Lucille D. Venture—in art therapy provides an opportunity to remember that simply changing the rules and terminologies does not automatically mean that cultural environments hostile to people of color will be transformed. A new use of the term social justice in art therapy will not change the dynamic. Thus, an analysis of the term multiculturalism, a term with considerable history in art therapy has a particular relevance to the current use of the term social justice. To this end, multiculturalism in art therapy viewed through womanism offers what I call *womanist authoritative strategies of survival* and liberation in relation to the notion of "staying in one's place."

It was not until the late 1990s that students and those mentored by Venture, Powell, McGee, and Joseph, began to introduce their work through the strategy and emerging rhetoric of "multiculturalism." Multiculturalism for Black women in art therapy has been a survival strategy of place making. Black women's corrective response as a womanist survival strategy was to find a place in art therapy through the professional language of multiculturalism. Riley-Hiscox (1999) described multiculturalism as the consequence of an unwillingness to include

African Americans in American society and challenged art therapists to examine the type of multiculturalism they supported. Building on this work, I argue, through the historical narratives of Powell, McGee, and Venture, that the strategy of multiculturalism in art therapy since the 1990s has been both empowering and problematic. The narrative of professionalization in art therapy is in part a story of the refusal to accept the corrective responses of Black women in the 1970s. It is what places their experiences in the margins of the profession. The institutionalization of multiculturalism has not adequately fostered a paradigm shift to question accepted knowledge, rather it has moved into the realm of that which is acceptable or the norm (Gorski & Goodman, 2015). It points to homogeneity in the discipline and the problems with a race-only analysis.

An intersectionality that is built into a womanist analysis makes it possible to respond to the survival strategy of staying in your place with being "responsible, in charge, and serious" about layered oppression. As a womanist liberation strategy, to be responsible is to embrace the contradictions in Black women's experiences, in this case Black women's conflicting experience of multiculturalism. Although multiculturalism has led to recognition for Black women in art therapy, highlighting their impact on educational programs and AATA as an organization, the conversation for liberation has yet to begin. Conversation about multiculturalism must move further still, beyond naming the -isms to confront the established knowledge of whiteness that has limited the dialogue about racism and structural oppression in the field of art therapy (Hamrick & Byma, 2017). There is a need to look deeper and learn from the Third World global consciousness that was present for early Black art therapists.

Considering the historical realities of Black women in the U.S., one can suggest new methods for developing contextualized understandings of social justice within art therapy. My personal reflections on the particular experiences of Black womanhood reveal potential ways to interpret some of the ideas that Black women have offered throughout the development of the profession. Art therapists must strive to employ deconstructive and generative responses to the pervasive violence in our culture by rethinking the disciplinary boundaries that shape the profession, and advocating for the structural inclusion of people *along with* their social histories. More specifically, professional ethics must center the moral agency and strategies of people within groups that have struggled against oppression, including Black women and children from poor and working-class communities. The expansion of current concepts and methods of inquiry, diversity, and cultural competence in art therapy might be reexamined through a womanist lens.

Conclusion

Art therapy has, as an institution, a white supremacist history that has dismissed ideas that appear unrecognizable from a dominant place of inquiry (Hamrick and Byma, 2017). Art therapy education has not gone far enough to take advantage of the ideas of Black women and other people of color in the profession. Understanding

Black women's corrective response to invisibility is a way to begin addressing problems in art therapy if it is to develop a social justice framework. Art therapists have been willing to address issues of diversity and cultural competence as long as these ideas have not fundamentally changed the structural and intellectual makeup of the profession. Relevant here are the professional practices of knowledge that have driven the field into greater popularity while the white women who position themselves as the professional healers are complicit in marginalizing and dehumanizing people of color. The conversation about social justice has accompanied an expansion among people in the field categorized as "special populations," ones faced with poverty, violence, and mental illness. Yet, the growth in the profession in this direction has seldom reflected knowledge of those who have been disenfranchised. As a result, the dominant discourse about violence and trauma has little pushback from within the profession that would challenge the status quo. The move toward a social justice lens is a positive one. This transition is an opportunity for art therapy as a profession to reframe trauma as the impact of violence and systemic oppression. To do so, however, the shift must continue to criticality examine the discipline of art therapy.

References

Allan, T. J. (1995). *Womanist and feminist aesthetics: A comparative review.* Athens, OH: Ohio University Press.

American Art Therapy Association (AATA) (2011). Wheels of diversity: Pioneers of color course materials for students of art therapy. Retrieved from https://arttherapy.org/upload/wheels.pdf.

Arnheim, R. (1984). For Margaret Naumburg. *The Arts in Psychotherapy, 11,* 3–5.

Asbury park riots art exhibit theme (1970, September 27). *The Central New Jersey Home News.* Retrieved from www.newspapers.com/image/316092262.

Black Smith, M. (2014). At the feet of a master: What Georgette Seabrooke Powell taught me about art, activism, and the creative sisterhood. *The Hampton Institute.* Retrieved from www.hamptoninstitution.org/georgette-seabrooke-powell.html#.WlXws1Q-fR3.

Boston, C. (2015). Art therapy and multiculturalism. In D. Gussak & M. Rosal (Eds.), *The Wiley-Blackwell handbook of art therapy* (pp. 822–828). Oxford, England: Wiley Blackwell.

Boston, C., & Short, G. (1998). Art therapy: An Afrocentric approach. In A. Hiscox & A. C. Calisch (Eds.), *Tapestry of cultural issues in art therapy* (pp. 36–48). London, England: Jessica Kingsley.

Boston, C., & Short, G. (2006). Notes: Georgette Seabrooke Powell. *Art Therapy: Journal of the American Art Therapy Association, 23*(2), 89–90. doi: 10.1080/07421656.2006.10129649.

Brandford, E. J. (1933, October 7). Art exhibit at library. *The New York Age.* Retrieved from www.newspapers.com/image/40876854.

Cannon, K. (1995). *Katie's canon: Womanism and the soul of the black community.* New York, NY: The Continuum Publishing Company.

Christiansen, S., & Scarlett, Z. A. (2015). In *The third world in the global 1960s. Protest, culture and society.* New York, NY: Berghahn Books.

Cohen, F. W. (1973, November 19). Correspondence 1973–74. [Letters from AATA to Lucille Venture]. Retrieved from www.arttherapy.org/aata-archives-historicfigures founders.html.

Coleman, M. (2008). *Making a way out of no way: A womanist theology.* Minneapolis, MN: Fortress Press.

Collins, K. D. (1997, May 18). Festival of African dance, culture celebrates 20 years. *The Central New Jersey Home News*, p. 65. Retrieved from www.newspapers.com/image/318725567.

Collins, L. G. (2008). The art of transformation: Parallels in the Black arts and feminist art movements. In L. G. Collins & M. N. Crawford (Eds.), *New thoughts on the Black arts movement* (pp. 273–296). New Brunswick, NJ: Rutgers.

Discrimination charges hurled at Supt. of Harlem Hospital for rejecting negro artists' murals. (1936, February 29). *The New York Age*. Retrieved from www.newspapers.com/image/40821147.

Doby-Copeland, C. (2006). Things come to me: Reflections from an art therapist of color. *Art Therapy: Journal of the American Art Therapy Association, 23*(2), 81–85, doi: 10.1080/07421656.2006.10129646.

Dye, S. K. (1981). The Native American: Developing cultural foundations as a tool for problem solving and expression. In A. D. Maria (Ed.), *Art therapy: A bridge between worlds. Proceedings of the 12th Annual Conference of the American Art Therapy Conference* (pp. 32–33). New York, NY.

Farris, P. (2006). Mentors of diversity: A tribute. *Art Therapy: Journal of the American Art Therapy Association, 23*(2), 86–88. doi: 10.1080/07421656.2006.10129645.

Figdore, S. (2001, December 25). Therapist helps kids heal through art: Eatontown 'pioneer' cited for her work. *Asbury Park Press*. Retrieved from www.newspapers.com/image/145007226.

Floyd-Thomas, S. M. (2006a). Writing for our lives: Womanism as an epistemological revolution. In S. Floyd-Thomas (Ed.), *Deeper shades of purple: Women in religion and society* (pp. 1–17). New York, NY: New York University Press.

Floyd-Thomas, S. M. (2006b). *Mining the motherlode: Methods in womanist ethics.* Cleveland, OH: Pilgrim Press.

George, J. (2006). Commentaries. *Art Therapy: Journal of the American Art Therapy Association, 23*(1), 5.

Gerity, L. A. (Ed.) (2000). *Art as therapy: Collected papers, Edith Kramer.* London, England: Jessica Kingsley.

Gipson, L. (2015). Is cultural competence enough? Deepening social justice pedagogy in art therapy. *Art Therapy: Journal of the American Art Therapy Association, 32*(3), 142–145. doi: 10.1080/07421656.2015.1060835.

Gipson, L. (2017). Challenging neoliberalism and multicultural love in art therapy. *Art Therapy: Journal of the American Art Therapy Association, 34*(3), 112–117. doi: 10.1080/07421656.2017.1353326.

Gorski, P. C., & Goodman, R. D. (2015). Introduction: Towards a decolonized multicultural counseling and psychology. In R. D. Goodman & P. C. Gorski (Eds.), *Decolonizing "multicultural" counseling through social justice* (pp. 1–10). New York, NY: Springer.

Hamrick, C., & Byma, C. (2017). Know history, know self: Art therapists' responsibility to dismantle white supremacy. *Art Therapy: Journal of the American Art Therapy Association, 34*(3), 106–111.

Harness, J. A. (1986, October 22). Teacher brings word of thanks from Senegal. Asbury Park Press. Retrieved from www.newspapers.com/image/145081991/.

Harness, J. A. (2002, July 12). Art therapist's legacy of healing: Sarah McGee, 72, aided troubled children. *Asbury Park Press*. Retrieved from www.newspapers.com/image/145890165

Hayden, C. (Interviewer), & Stearns, S. (Videographer) (2006). Georgette Seabrooke Powell remembers the Harlem arts workshop [Video file]. Chicago, IL: The HistoryMakers Digital Archive.

Higginbotham, E. B. (1993). *Righteous discontent: The women's movement in the Black Baptist Church, 1880–1920.* Cambridge, MA: Harvard University Press.

Hudson-Weems, C. M. (1993). *African womanism: Reclaiming ourselves.* Troy, MI: Bedford Press.

Hurtibise, R. (2008). Daytona beach news. Retrieved from www.youtube.com/watch?v=4sgaaZ-I6eU.

Iyer, J., Talwar, S., & Doby-Copeland, C. (2003). Deconstructing Kaplan's views on multiculturalism. *Art Therapy: Journal of the American Art Therapy Association, 20*(2), 65–66.

Junge, M. (2010). *The modern history of art therapy in the United States.* Springfield, IL: Charles C. Thomas.

Kanter, R. M. (1977). *Men and women of corporation.* New York, NY: Basic Books Publishers

Kaplan, F. (2002). Cross-cultural art therapy: A now and future therapy. *Art Therapy: Journal of the American Art Therapy Association, 19*(4), 138–138, doi: 10.1080/07421656.2002.10129679.

Karcher, O. P. (2017). Sociopolitical oppression, trauma, and healing: Moving towards a social justice art therapy framework. *Art Therapy: Journal of the American Art Therapy Association, 34*(3), 123–128.

Linden, D. L., & Greene, L. A. (2001). Charles Alston's Harlem hospital murals: Cultural politics in depression era Harlem. *Prospects, 26*, 391–421.

Lomoe-Smith, J. (1979). Cultural influences in art therapy with Hispanic patients. In L. Gantt (Ed.), *Focus on the future: The next ten years, Proceedings of the 10th Annual Conference of the American Art Therapy Conference* (pp. 17–22). Washington, D.C.

Lorde, A. (1984). *Sister outsider.* Freedom, CA: Crossing Press.

Lumpkin, C. (2006). Relating cultural identity and identity as art therapist. *Art Therapy: Journal of the American Art Therapy Association, 23*(1), 34–38.

Marparyan, L. (2012). *The womanist idea: Contemporary sociological perspectives.* New York, NY: Routledge.

Martin, K. (2016). The Asbury Park July 1970 Riots. Retrieved from https://blogs.library.duke.edu/rubenstein/2016/06/28/asbury-park-july-1970-riots/.

McGee, S. E. (1979). Art therapy as a means of fostering parental closeness in a migrant preschool. In L. Gantt (Ed.), *Focus on the future: The next ten years. Proceedings of the 10th Annual Conference of the American Art Therapy Conference* (pp. 32–35). Washington, D.C.

McGee, S. E. (1981). The Black family: Culture specific therapeutic needs. In A. D. Maria (Ed.), *Art therapy: A bridge between worlds, Proceedings of the 12th Annual Conference of the American Art Therapy Conference* (pp. 34–36). New York, NY.

McKittrick, K. (2011). On plantations, prisons, and a black sense of place. *Social & Cultural Geography, 12*(8), 947–963. doi: 10.1080/14649365.2011.624280.

Naumburg, M. (1966). *Dynamically oriented art therapy: Its principles and practice.* New York, NY. Grune & Stratton. [Reprinted in 1987, Chicago, IL: Magnolia Street]

Ogunyemi, C. O. (1985). Womanism: The dynamics of the contemporary black female novel in English. *Signs: Journal of Women and Culture in Society, 11*(1), 63–80.

Peyser, M. N. (1989, June 7). Eatontown educator to receive arts award. *The Register*. Retrieved from http://209.212.22.88/Data/RBR/1980-1989/1989/1989.06.07.pdf.

Phillips, L. (2006). *The womanist reader: The first quarter of a century of womanist thought*. New York, NY: Routledge.

Pickren, W. (2007). Tension and opportunity in post-world War II American psychology. *History of Psychology, 10*(3), 279–299.

Potash, J., & Ramirez, W. (2013). Broadening history, expanding possibilities: Contributions of Wayne Ramirez to art therapy. *Art Therapy: Journal of the American Art Therapy Association, 30*(4), 169–176.

Potash, J., Doby-Copeland, C., Stepney, S, Washington, B., Vance, L., Short, G., Boston, C., & Ballbé ter Maat, M. (2015). Advancing multicultural and diversity competence in art therapy: American art therapy association multicultural committee 1990–2015. *Art Therapy: Journal of the American Art Therapy Association, 32*(3), 146–150.

Report of the National Advisory Commission on Civil Disorders (1968). Washington, D.C.: Government Printing Office. Retrieved from www.ncjrs.gov/pdffiles1/Digitization/8073NCJRS.pdf.

Richie, B. (2012). *Arrested justice black women, violence, and America's prison nation*. New York, NY: New York University Press.

Riley-Hiscox. A. (1997). Interview—Cliff Joseph: Art therapist, pioneer, artist. *Art Therapy: Journal of the American Art Therapy, 14*(4), 273–278. doi: 10.1080/07421656. 1987.10759297.

Riley-Hiscox, A. (1999). Critical multiculturalism: A response to "questioning multi-culturalism." *Art Therapy Journal of the American Art Therapy Association, 16*(3), 145–149. doi: 10.1080/07421656.1999.10129651.

Rubin, J. (1986). From psychopathology to psychotherapy through art expression: A focus on Hanz Prinzhorn and others. *Art Therapy: Journal of the American Art Therapy Association, 3*(1), 27–33.

Sajnani, N., Marxen, E., & Zarate, R. (2017). Critical perspectives in the arts thera-pies: Response/ability across a continuum of practice. *The Arts in Psychotherapy, 54*, 28–37.

Short, G. M. (2014). Art therapy and identity. In M. B. Junge (Ed.), *Identity and art therapy: Personal and professional perspectives* (pp. 187–197). Springfield, IL: Charles C. Thomas.

Snell, R. (2002). *Sarah Eliza Pallard McGee*. Retrieved from www.findagrave.com/memorial/6602795/sarah-eliza-mcgee.

Stephens, M. A. (2005). *Black empire: The masculine global imaginary of Caribbean intellectuals in the United States, 1914–1962*. Durham, NC: Duke University Press.

Talwar, S. (2006). Commentaries. *Art Therapy: Journal of the American Art Therapy Association, 23*(1), 4.

Talwar, S. (2015a). Culture, diversity, and identity: From margins to center. *Art Therapy: Journal of the American Art Therapy Association, 32*(3), 100–103 doi.10.1080/07421656. 2015.1060563.

Talwar, S. (2015b). Creating alternative public spaces: Community-based art practice, critical consciousness and social justice. In D. Gussak & M. Rosal (Eds.), *The Wiley-Blackwell handbook of art therapy* (pp. 840–847). Oxford, UK: Wiley Blackwell.

Talwar, S., Iyer, J., & Doby-Copeland, C. (2004). The invisible veil: Changing paradigms in the art therapy profession. *Art Therapy: Journal of the American Art Therapy Association, 21*(1) 44–48. doi.org/10.1080/07421656.2004.10129325.

The murals: Recreation in Harlem. Columbia University Institute for Research in African-American Studies. Retrieved from http://iraas.columbia.edu/wpa/.

Ulman, E. (1970). First annual conference of the American Art Therapy Association. *American Journal of Art Therapy, 10*(1), 30–31.

Vick, R. (2003). A brief history of art therapy. In C. A. Malchiodi (Ed.), *Handbook of art therapy* (pp. 5–15). New York, NY: Guilford Press.

Venture, L. (1977). *The Black beat in art therapy experiences.* Unpublished dissertation, Union Institute (formerly Union Graduate School), Cincinnati, OH.

Walker, A. (1981). *You can't keep a good woman down.* Orlando, FL: Harcourt.

Walker, A. (1983). *In search of our mothers' gardens: Womanist prose.* New York, NY: Houghton Mifflin Harcourt.

Wix, L. (2000). Looking for what's lost: The artistic roots of art therapy: Mary Huntoon. *Art Therapy: Journal of the American Art Therapy Association, 17*(3), 168–176. doi.org/10.1080/07421656.2000.10129699.

Wix, L. (2010). Studios as locations of possibility: Remembering a history. *Art Therapy: Journal of the American Art Therapy Association, 27*(4), 178–183. doi.org/10.1080/07421656.2010.10129388.

PART II

Praxis

Public Therapeutics and Art Therapy

6

"YOU WANT TO BE WELL?"

Self-Care as a Black Feminist Intervention in Art Therapy

Salamishah Tillet and Scheherazade Tillet

> Are you sure, sweetheart, that you want to be well? (p. 3) . . . Just so's you're sure, sweetheart, and ready to be healed, cause wholeness is no trifling matter. A lot of weight when you're well.
>
> *(Bambara, 1992, p. 10)*

Last July, as we sat in our small, well-lit classroom at the School of the Art Institute of Chicago, a group of African-American teen girls enrolled in the Girl/Friends Leadership Institute at A Long Walk Home began to prep for the daily closing self-care ritual. They were tired. The group had just spent the weekend in their first artist-activist training and on this Monday afternoon, the girls were restless, dragging their feet and chairs to the conference table. Outside, a few blocks away, the streets were abuzz; hundreds of teens under the banner of Black Lives Matter were gathered at Millennium Park to protest police violence in the city of Chicago (Chang, 2016). That this massive sit-in was led by four African-American teen girls was not lost on the Girl/Friends; distracted and slightly disengaged, one of the girls, a 15-year-old named Danielle, said, "I think we should join the protest as our self-care today."

The term self-care is now ubiquitous, yet as Minnie Ransom asks in Toni Cade Bambara's *The Salt Eaters*, "Are you sure, sweetheart, that you want to be well? (p. 3). . . Just so's you're sure, sweetheart, and ready to be healed, cause wholeness is no trifling matter. A lot of weight when you're well" (1992, p. 10). This past June, NPR's Christianna Silva (2017) reported, in "The Millennial Obsession with Self-Care," that this generation "has been consistently defined by its obsessions: avocado toast, memes, Harry Potter . . . and self-care. They are often perceived as entitled snowflakes, but millennials might be the generation of emotional intelligence" (para 1). And yet, Silva is quick to point out that despite its currency today, the idea of self-care has ancient roots. In fact, as philosopher Michel Foucault (2005) notes in *The Hermeneutics of the Subject*, self-care was foundational to Western thought:

> In Plato's too well-known but still fundamental text, the *Apology*, Socrates appears as the person whose essential, fundamental, and original function, job, and position is to encourage others to attend to themselves, take care of themselves, and not neglect themselves.
>
> *(p. 5)*

Foucault's main question was why Socrates' philosophy of self-care went so under-appreciated in the canonization of his theory of self-knowledge. "Why did Western thought and philosophy neglect the notion of *epimeleia heautou* (care of the self) in its reconstruction of its own history?" (p. 12), Foucault asks.

> How did it come about that we accorded so much privilege, value, and intensity to the "know yourself" and omitted, or at least, left in the shadow, this notion of care of the self that, in actual fact, historically, when we look at the documents and texts, seems to have framed the principle of "know yourself" from the start.
>
> *(p. 12)*

Ultimately, this de-emphasis of self-care relative to self-knowledge has been quite costly as individuals, and more importantly, Western societies, interpolated an understanding of care devoid of morality or in Foucault's estimation, ethics.

Danielle's definition of self-care, however, directly takes up Foucault's concerns. Rather than exclusively consider self-care as an individual act for herself, she tied hers to others and a sense of collaboration and community. Her suggestion that we join the protest as self-care was even more compelling because she had just learned the term a few days before in her orientation at our Girl/Friends Leadership Institute, a yearlong artist-activist program that A Long Walk Home created in 2009 to empower teen girls in Chicago to advocate for gender and racial equality in their communities, city, and the country-at-large. Starting in the North Lawndale section of the Westside of Chicago, Girl/Friends originally served a community that is 92 percent black, where the homicide rate is 45 per 100,000—triple the rate of the city as a whole. The infant-mortality rate is 14 per 1,000—more than twice the national average. Forty-three percent of the people in North Lawndale live below the poverty line—double Chicago's overall rate. Forty-five percent of all households are on food stamps—nearly three times the rate of the city at large (Coates, 2014). In addition, despite the fact that North Lawndale has one of the highest incidents of sexual assault in Chicago, and is one of only five neighborhoods in which the reported number of sexual assaults has not decreased within the last decade, there was no declared rape crisis from 2011 to 2016. During that time, Girl/Friends acted as the first responder for the majority of the affected girls and their families.

Over the past couple of years, Chicago's Westside has also been plagued by a string of law enforcement controversies: in 2012 an off-duty detective was acquitted of manslaughter for the murder of 22-year-old Rekia Boyd (Goldstein, 2013), who was killed near Douglas Park in North Lawndale, and the federal investigation of Homan Square in North Lawndale, a secret detention site where for over a decade 7,000 citizens, of whom 6,000 were African-American, were interrogated without access to attorneys or a public notice of their whereabouts (Ackerman, 2015). Tragically, community violence is occurring at levels unseen for years. In the first quarter of 2016, 141 people were killed, up from 82 last year, according to police department data. The number of shootings surged to 677 from 359 a year earlier. The city is on track to have more than 500 killings this year, which would make this just the third year since 2004 that Chicago topped that figure. According to a *Washington Post* article about this phenomenon, there was major concern that 2016 would far outpace the number of killings in 2015, which was "particularly worrisome considering that Chicago had more murders that year than any other city in the United States" (Berman, 2016, para 3). Three quarters of all homicide victims are African American.

African-American girls like Danielle live at the intersections of acts of violence. Not only are they, as high school girls, part of a national demographic that is four times more likely than any other group of Americans to be victims of sexual assault or domestic violence, but also, as African-American working-class girls, they have significantly fewer resources to address or alleviate the trauma that they experience. More specifically, in our Girl/Friends Leadership Institute report (2015–2016), 95 percent of Girl/Friends reported a family income at or below the poverty line, and 75 percent have one or more incarcerated parent. Their exposure to violence is even more disturbing: 47 percent have witnessed or experienced a hate crime, 63 percent are the child of a parent or guardian who has experienced sexual assault, and 26 percent have experienced sexual assault or abuse themselves. Seventy-four percent have experienced and witnessed domestic violence in the home, and 31 percent have experienced violence in their own intimate relationships. In response to their trauma, Danielle and other Girl/Friends revealed that they primarily relied on coping mechanisms such as journaling, or in her case writing poetry, rather than seeking formal counseling or therapy. There are several reasons for their reticence: the lack of services in their neighborhood, the social stigma attached to mental health, and the absence of culturally relevant and age-appropriate models of therapy in their schools or the local anti-violence agencies.

As an organization that is founded and staffed by African-American women art therapists, art therapy remains a foundational component to all A Long Walk Home programming. Searching for the models of psychotherapy that might be most welcomed by the Girl/Friends youth leaders, we embraced feminist approaches to art therapy like that of Hogan (1997), who argued for alternatives that begin with a deep understanding of the cultural and historical context of artistic production, ones that consider identity and difference as categories that shape client and therapist alike. But, as African-American women working with mainly African-American girls, we understood the limits of even feminist art therapy. Gender mattered but so did race, and if the girls were to be fully empowered the design of the program needed to reflect the multidimensionality of the Girl/Friends individually and as a group. In order to destigmatize therapy and make counseling more affordable and accessible to the Girl/Friends' communities, it is practiced under the black feminist rubric of "self-care," a Long Walk Home's blend of art therapy, social justice, and community development. Turning to black feminism—a theoretical and political tradition that views racism, sexism, classism and other forms of oppression as mutually dependent and coterminous—seemed most relevant to the Girl/Friends project. To alleviate the suffering that can be caused by multiple forms of discrimination, we draw from the work of black feminists—like Kimberle Crenshaw's (1989) "intersectionality," Barbara Smith's (1983) "simultaneity," Francis Beale's (1969) "double jeopardy"—to advocate for a holistic understanding of oppression itself. As a black feminist intervention into the field of art therapy, the methodology of self-care is about individual and communal healing, enabling girls like Danielle to link their own stories of trauma *and* health to those of their neighborhood and a larger community of young people in Chicago. During their tenure in Girl/Friends, the teen girls engage with their own stories of trauma and invisibility in order to heal, raise awareness about the violence plaguing them, and advocate for themselves and other girls and women. By the end, the Girl/Friend's practice provides the ultimate rejoinder to Foucault's concerns: black feminist self-care is not only about individual transformation, but in fact the foundation of community care.

Part I

A Black Feminist Ode: Stigmas and Self-Care

Solange Knowles (2016) in "Borderline (An Ode to Self Care)" speaks of the duality of her existence as an African-American woman and the violence against black bodies. She points to the need for self-preservation to deal with her everyday disparities she faces. As research shows, African Americans have had a long and complicated history with American medicine. Despite sharing the same mental health issues as the rest of the population, with arguably even greater stressors due to racism, prejudice, and economic disparities, African Americans received 50 percent less mental health treatment or counseling than whites in 2008 and half the prescription medication for mental health-related issues (2010 National Healthcare Disparities Report). This is partly due to a greater distrust of medical professions, especially after the Tuskegee experiment in which the U.S. Public Health Service knowingly withheld syphilis treatment from black men to observe the disease run its course over the period from 1932 to 1972. But it also results from a skepticism towards mental health care facilities themselves: the poor quality of black hospitals during segregation and the high rate of involuntary commitment of African Americans into institutions. Today, while African Americans might be underrepresented in outpatient therapy, they are still committed to inpatient care at twice the rate of whites, sometimes against their will. Fueled by suspicion that they are less likely to be treated well by a health professional of a different racial or cultural background (Blanchard & Lurie, 2004), many African Americans continue to resist seeking traditional treatment, and in many cases, cultivate alternative spaces for counseling, such as church and community settings. As a result, there continues to be huge racial disparities in treatment.

Moreover, for many African Americans their ongoing resistance is often exacerbated by the feelings of shame or stigma that comes with seeking treatment. According to the qualitative study "The Experience of Stigma among Black Mental Health Consumers" by Alvidrez, Snowden, and Kaiser (2008), one-third of African Americans who were already mental health consumers felt that mild depression or anxiety would be considered "crazy" among their peers and that talking about problems with a therapist might be viewed as airing one's "dirty laundry." Strikingly, over a quarter of respondents felt that discussions about mental illness would not be appropriate even within the family. For African-American teen girls, who have even fewer financial resources or services targeting their specific age, the use of professional mental health care is even less likely than for adults.

And yet, according to research published by Sanders-Thompson, Bazile, and Akbar (2004) in *Professional Psychology*, many African Americans prefer the term "counseling" over "psychotherapy," viewing the typical psychologist as an older, white male, who would be insensitive to the social and economic realities of their lives. The authors argue that the result is a reluctance to turn to psychology, which, we argue, would include art therapy, for treatment. At A Long Walk Home, we have found that self-care is an even less alienating term than counseling and is much more easily embraced as a healing practice by the Girl/Friends and their families. This is perhaps because Girl/Friends' self-care dissolves the boundaries between the personal and political, and builds on a practice that civil rights and feminist activists in the 1960s used in their own battles for social equality. Self-care was a claiming of "autonomy over the body," said Mehlman Petrzela, an associate professor of history at the New School in New York, who writes about the history of American fitness culture (as cited in Harris, 2017). Harris (2017), in her article "A History of Self-care," argues that attending to and controlling one's emotional and mental health, alongside physical illnesses, was considered, as Petrzela notes, to be "a political act against institutional, technocratic, very racist, and sexist medicine" (para 4). The legacy of self-care as political resistance and psychological healing has gained even more momentum in the last few years of social justice organizing.

In February 2016, philosopher and social activist Angela Davis told *Yes* magazine, "I think our notions of what counts as radical have changed over time" (van Gelder, 2016). Reflecting on her own organizing in the 1960s and 1970s, Davis in an interview with Sarah van Gelder (2016) noted that contemporary social movements like Black Lives Matter put more emphasis on the interior lives of the activists and those for whom they are advocating. "Self-care and healing and attention to the body and the spiritual dimension," she revealed, are "now a part of radical social justice struggles" (van Gelder, 2016). Davis's emphasis on self-care and healing as twin actions in the racial and gender justice movements of today is not hers alone; her insights build upon the proliferation of Black Lives Matter chapters that use the language of health, wellness, grief, and trauma in order to prevent burn-out and encourage organizational efficiency and sustainability.

Likewise, in an interview with *Religion Dispatches* in July 2015, Black Lives Matter co-founder Patrisse Cullors sees the turn to self-care and healing crucial in her fight for justice. Talking about hiring a paid director of health and wellness at Dignity and Power Now (DPN), a grassroots organization that she started with other Black Lives Matter-affiliated groups to advocate for incarcerated people, their families, and communities, Cullors describes the establishment of such a position, which typically would be associated with the church rather than a nonprofit, as "a political choice to try to build a new way of fighting" (Farrag, 2015, para 13). She continues,

> It's not just about changing policies. It's not just about changing lives. It's about changing our culture and changing how we fight. We can change policies all day but if the fight to get there was full of trauma, was replicating oppressive dynamics, abusive dynamics, then what is the point?
>
> *(Farrag, 2015, para. 14)*

In the remainder of the conversation, Cullors notes a trend in "healing justice networks" that is aligned with the racial justice groups, like Harriet's Apothecary in New York, Social Transformation Project, and Black Organizing for Leadership & Dignity (Farrag, 2015).

While Davis and Cullors are right to point out that the focus on self-care in social justice movements is in many ways new, as we have already noted it is in fact part of a longer tradition of black feminist writing, healing, therapy, and recovery that has been theorized as forms of activism. Poet and activist Audre Lorde (1988) published a series of journal entries in the essay, "A Burst of Light: Living with Cancer." A follow-up to her 1980 memoir on surviving breast cancer, *The Cancer Journals*, the later essay begins with her fatal diagnosis of liver cancer while living in Berlin. Divided into journal entries in which she describes her attempts to seek alternative treatments as her medical condition worsens *and* to continue her political organizing of women of color in Germany, the essay first reads like a split self; we move in and out of Lorde's despair about racism as a social cancer and her recognition that she will shortly die from a disease that is both inoperable and quickly spreading.

But, near the end of the essay, the reader realizes that taking caring of herself and her political activity were not two strands of Lorde's identity, but in fact ones feeding off each other, her activism giving her a will to live and her quest for mental and physical wellbeing essential to honing her political vision. "My aim is to move more easily between the two," she confesses. "Make transcriptions the least costly, approach a student's complete manuscript and the medical reports and house estimates in some open-hearted way, with a sense of proportion. I order a perfume from Grenada called 'Jump Up and Kiss Me'" (p. 130). Lorde's synthesis here underscores a struggle that defines much of her political and poetic work and is a central tenet of black feminist self-care: how does one learn to care deeply for oneself, while also advocating for others? Lorde (1988) concludes that there can be no separation between one's inner life, such as emotions and mental health, and his/her commitment to justice, stating, "Caring for myself is not self-indulgence, it is self-preservation, and that is an act of political warfare" (p. 130).

Extending the argument, bell hooks (1993) turns Lorde's personal narrative into a political prescription in *Sisters of the Yam: Black Women and Self-Recovery*; published a year after Lorde's death, hooks goes to great lengths to distinguish her project from other women's self-help books of the time—like Melody Beattie's *Codependent No More* (1986) or Susan Powter's *Stop the Insanity!* (1993)—by detailing the link between self-recovery and political change. In the opening pages of the book, she lays out her theory: "When we choose to heal, when we choose to love, we are choosing liberation. This is where all authentic activism begins" (hooks, 1993, p. 147). Here hooks points out that authentic or real activism requires a reciprocity, not a division, between practices of wellbeing and pursuits of justice. But, she notes, despite the urgency the challenges for African-American women to cultivate their own self-care rituals are multifold. According to hooks (1993),

> Black women have not focused sufficiently on our need for contemplative spaces. We are often "too busy" to find time for solitude. And yet it is in the stillness that we also learn how to be with ourselves in a spirit of acceptance and peace.
>
> *(p. 186)*

It is only after these periods of reflection and respite can change occur and be sustained. hooks goes on, "Then when we re-enter community, we are able to extend this acceptance to others. Without knowing how to be alone, we cannot know how to be with others and sustain the necessary autonomy" (p. 186). In other words, self-care is a series of individual acts that must be engaged before African-American women can fully enter or even attempt to heal a larger racial or gendered collective.

By building on this long tradition of black feminism in which self-care has emerged over time as integral to social justice, Girl/Friends not only opens and closes each day of its program with "self-care" rituals led by art therapists, social workers, or healing experts, but also it has integrated its definitive feature into its social justice campaigns. By the end of the program, self-care is so indistinguishable from their social action—be it a sit-in against police violence, a march against domestic violence, or a public awareness campaign about street harassment—that political organizing is seen as a form of "community care."

Part II

What Is Self-Care? Pre-Counseling and Self-Care Plans

Before the Girl/Friends Leadership Institute officially begins its five-week artist-activist training, girls participate in several activities that demystify art therapy and promote holistic healing practices of self-care. The first is the selection of the girls by the A Long Walk Home staff; each potential Girl/Friend submits an art portfolio along with her application and interview. In order to reflect the various forms of self-expressions that are present in their homes and community, such as hair braiding, rapping, and stepping, as well as creative writing, photography, dance, and visual art, Girl/Friends embraces a more expansive definition of art than many other youth art programs. And "because we actively target young artists," says Marline Johnson, art therapist and Girl/Friends program coordinator, "art therapy becomes an accessible and somewhat more familiar way for the girls to share their stories and begin the journey of healing" (personal communication, July 3, 2017).

In that early stage of selection, the Girl/Friends staff members identify girls who are suitable for pre-counseling, a three-week session with an art therapist that happens before the launch of the summer program at the School of the Art Institute of Chicago. Typically, the staff will suggest the pre-counseling services, which are free to about 70 percent of those admitted based on the information in their application essays or their interview. Oftentimes, after we go through our discussion about Girl/Friends' emphasis on ending both racial injustice and gender violence, the girls disclose their individual or familial trauma, such as being a child of an incarcerated parent, sexual assault, or the loss of a parent. "In traditional classroom settings, these experiences might be 'red-flagged' as potential problems for these girls successfully completing school," says Johnson. "However, in Girl/Friends, we see them as barriers that the girls need to work through in order to become their full selves to themselves and in their communities" (personal communication, July 3, 2017). Once the girls are accepted into and committed to the program, they are provided with a therapist with whom they meet before and during the life of the program and whose sole purpose is to give psychological support during the summer and throughout the school year. While therapy is not mandatory, because it takes place within an art-based social justice program and the youth leaders see their peers also receiving traditional help, they admit to feeling little or no stigma in seeking these services. This is a substantial change in their understanding of therapy within a very short time span, and more than 75 percent of those to whom we recommend pre-counseling attend individual sessions.

The next phase of Girl/Friends is a three-day overnight orientation retreat in which the youth leaders attend a number of workshops dedicated to the concept of self-care. In the beginning, staff members ask the girls the simple question, "What is self-care?" Initially, the girls have a very narrow view of self-care and exclusively focus on occasional activities like pedicures and facials, or going to the movies with friends. During orientation, however, they participate in a diverse set of workshops that highlight other forms of self-care, for example, a workshop on intersectional feminism and social justice, a spa night led by

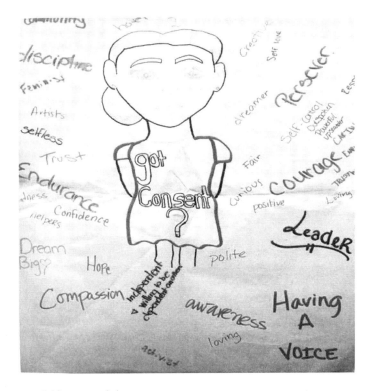

FIGURE 6.1 Self-care workshop

Girl/Friends alumnae, meditation and yoga, and individual meetings with their therapist. By the end of the orientation, the girls are again asked "What is self-care?" as a prompt to help them draft their self-care plan for the program. Now, their answers range from "respect yourself," "self-love," "dreaming," "being an artist," to "finding your voice" (Figure 6.1). Here, a central theme emerges that not only represents their broader understanding of self-care, but also marks an important step for them to move to the next phase of the program: the expression of "critical consciousness." Self-care, including attending one-on-one sessions with an art therapist, marks an important turning point for the youth leaders as they learn to value their own experiences, point-of view, and leadership potential.

Part III

Girl/Me: Critical Consciousness

> I enjoyed being in a space, of shared lived experiences of what it means to be a black girl. I didn't realize how rare those spaces are. I was able to talk about things that I have never told anyone. I felt safe enough to talk about all the things I keep locked away.
>
> *(Girl/Friend Youth Leader, age 15)*

The term "critical consciousness" originated with Brazilian educator Paulo Freire's ground-breaking book *Pedagogy of the Oppressed* in which he defined "conscienti-zaçao" as a form of personal awakening and development of critical consciousness (Freire, 1970). Applying Freire's theory to the relationship between art therapist and client, Talwar (2015), in "Creating Alternative Public Spaces: Community-based Art Practice, Critical Consciousness and Social Justice," adds that critical consciousness is "an understanding of race, class, gender, and sexuality as reflections of the systems of power and subordination within which we all function" (p. 841). Talwar notes that while all members of American society are impacted by these systems, people of color are particularly disadvantaged systemically and do not shed their experiences when they enter a therapeutic relationship. As such it is important for art therapists to understand the "link between trauma, oppression, power, privilege and the historical inequities embedded in social relationships" (p. 843), "recognize the prevailing power structures" in order to reduce their client's "entrapment in systems of domination and dependence" (p. 842). Not only is this an essential step of helping clients work through their trauma, but it is also, as Talwar, much like Freire, sees it, an integral step to a more just society. In other words, for those most oppressed by inequity to liberate themselves and by extension the larger society, they must eventually transform their awakening into political action.

The Girl/Friends' curriculum identifies the evolution of the youth leaders' critical consciousness in three phases: (1) Girl/Me, (2) Girl/Culture, and

(3) Girl/Power. The first stage, Girl/Me, is inward-looking and addresses identity and self-awareness. It is centered on helping the youth leaders understand their individual social identities, thoughts, feelings, emotions, and the major influences of their behaviors. In order to promote self-reflection, Girl/Me activities include workshops on reproductive justice and women's health, as well as yoga and meditation. Artistically, the youth leaders are given art journals and digital cameras so they can document and express their sense of self through monologues and self-portraits. By practicing the critical process of self-awareness, the Girl/Friends learn that building a healthy sense of self is integral to strengthening their relationships with their peers and advocating for themselves, their families, and other girls in their community.

In Girl/Me, the youth leaders attend a series of art therapy workshops led by social documentary photographer and executive director of A Long Walk Home, Scheherazade Tillet, in which she presents self-portraits by visual artists like Frida Kahlo and Adrian Piper and female photographers like Carrie Mae Weems, Nan Goldin, Renee Cox, along with her own self-portraits from the multimedia performance, "Story of a Rape Survivor," and past Girl/Friends images. Self-portraits are introduced to the participants for several reasons: first, to familiarize the participants with different photographic genres as well as to hone in on fine art techniques; second, to give the young girls an opportunity to tell their stories on their own terms; and third, to give them an opportunity, an object, and process through which they could identify sites of trauma, reflect on their inner lives, and share their experiences with each other. "My understanding of the phototherapy section of Girl/Me," says Leah Gipson, A Long Walk Home board member and the first Girl/Friends art therapy intern,

> is to teach the girls to practice seeing themselves. What makes it different from simply art education is the safe space that we have created for them to share and sit with these photographs. Once they begin to look at and look back at themselves in this private space and through their own eyes, art takes on a new meaning.

She concludes, "It enables them to value an integrated self, a step that needs to take place before joining any collective" (personal communication, July 2, 2017).

Perhaps there is no better example of this than the series of self-portraits that came out of the Girl/Me art therapy workshops in which the girls were given the directive: "Share an image that represents you." In July 2015, a 16-year old African-American girl Datavia, in her first year of Girl/Friends, using charcoal and colored pencils, drew an image of herself with a sprawling mane of brown hair framed by a red headband, eyes shut, and mouth taped by the words "I Am Not Heard" (Figure 6.2). Datavia said that before attending Girl/Friends, she would get in trouble for "being too quiet" and "not speaking up enough" at home and in school. She would spend hours in her bedroom becoming more and more reclusive, eventually feeling alienated from her mother. While many African-American girls are stereotyped for being "too loud" (Brown 2013), Datavia's discipline for being the opposite reveals the ways in which African-American girls are held to higher, and sometimes contradictory standards, compared to their peers. Nationwide, black girls are 16 percent of girls in schools, but 42 percent of girls receiving corporal punishment, 42 percent of girls expelled with or without educational services, 45 percent of girls with at least one out-of-school suspension, 31 percent of girls referred to law enforcement, and 34 percent of girls arrested on campus (Morris, 2016). Before they are punished and forced out of school, however, many of these girls have already experienced forms of racial discrimination, harassment, and sexual violence in schools that fail to recognize and address these traumas. Kayla Patrick (2017) of the National Women's Law Center has reported on "Let Her Learn – What About Girls?", a survey of 1,003 girls ages 14–18, which included interviews with the Long Walk Home Girl/Friends; according to the survey, one-third to more than two in five girls had experienced a racial slur, and almost one in three girls (31 percent) reported experiencing sexual assault or other violence.

While in Girl/Friends, Datavia began connecting her personal experiences with the larger black feminist themes of intersectional oppression that she had been introduced to in the program; she states,

> I started noticing the things that I had felt, but didn't quite have the words to describe. I knew girls like me were being shunned or shamed for the things they were wearing, like tight clothing or short skirts and dresses.

She went on, "And I used to believe some of these stereotypes, too, but then I realized this was just another way to make girls feel small and stay silent when they were sexually assaulted or harassed" (personal communication, July 28, 2017). Armed with her own history of feeling silenced, as well as similar stories from her fellow Girl/Friends, Datavia's image of herself reflects her critical consciousness and growing awareness of invisibility as a political condition that impacts black girls and women. The image of the taped mouth "I Am Not Heard" (Figure 6.2) then is both anecdotal and allegorical, reflecting a fate that Datavia believes her work in Girl/Friends can transform.

In the summer of 2016, Zilah, a 16 year-old girl who had just joined Girl/Friends, came across Datavia's image in a phototherapy workshop. Inspired by the sentiment, Zilah adapted it for her own self-portrait. Pulling the camera close to her face, Zilah, sits in her bedroom with closed eyes and the word "ANXIETY" taped on her mouth (Figure 6.3), thereby creating an image that sought to counter stereotypes of black girls as being too loud, disruptive, or uncontrollable (Morris, 2007). But, unlike Datavia, who challenged her invisibility, Zilah's photograph raised the issues of depression and anxiety. A mere two years before, she lived in Atlanta as an only child. Near her fourteenth birthday,

FIGURE 6.2 Datavia—*I Am Not Heard*

FIGURE 6.3 Zilah—*ANXIETY*

Zilah's mother gave birth to Zilah's siblings, a pair of twins, afterward suffering a severe case of postpartum depression. Feeling unable to take care of all her children by herself, Zilah's mom sent her oldest daughter to Chicago to live with her parents in the middle of Zilah's first year of high school. Displaced and alienated,

Zilah began to suffer from anxiety, for which she received no formal counseling or treatment until she entered Girl/Friends. Instead, she dealt with her symptoms by turning inward; "This photo is personal to me because it reflects the stereotype of me being a black girl," writes Zilah in her caption. "Of having a bad attitude instead of me being a black girl with a mental illness" (personal communication, July 10, 2016).

Part IV

Girl/Culture: Advocacy

> I initially joined Girl/friends for my grandmother who was a victim of domestic violence. Domestic violence ultimately took her life. But by the end of the program I was doing the program not only for my grandmother, I was doing it for myself, because I am a childhood survivor of sexual abuse and did not identify as that before this program.
>
> *(Girl/Friend, age 13)*

The next section of the Girl/Friends' curriculum is Girl/Culture, a unit that focuses on racial and gender socialization in which the girls reflect on how their shared experiences of being girls impact how they relate to each other and the outside world. Girl/Culture builds on Girl/Me by moving from introspection to building empathy between participants with shared experiences, as well as with others of different backgrounds. In the Girl/Culture workshops, the Girl/Friends learn about reproductive justice, healthy and unhealthy relationships, and peer to peer support; they also discuss how broader social issues like sexual assault and harassment, racial profiling, and police violence impact girls and their larger community.

Two years after her original illustration, an 18-year-old Datavia drew another self-portrait that resembled her earlier one (Figure 6.4), but with some differences: her eyes now open with tears pouring out, her arms are bare, framed by heart shaped halter top. The key distinction, though, is the dark brown hand holding a bright red lollipop, covering her mouth with the words, "IF YOU TELL ANYONE . . ." This image is in response to learning that her mother's brothers and sisters were all victims of sexual assault as children. "They should have been protected," says Datavia. "And now I have all these little cousins who could experience the same thing. I drew this image so they could know the truth." Datavia reflected on the hand replacing the tape of the earlier image; "I want to show the strategies of manipulation that adults use when they assault children: both the lollipop and the threats that they use" (Personal communication, July 28, 2017).

As part of the "The Visibility Project: A Celebration of 100 Black Girls," the Girl/Friends culminating summer public performance and exhibition in July

FIGURE 6.4 Datavia—*IF YOU TELL ANYONE*

2017 at the School of the Art Institute of Chicago, Datavia's self-portrait became part of a tapestry of images and installations that actively centered their art, experiences, and stories. The audience was not only made up of their parents, friends, teachers, and partner organizations, but also consisted of over a hundred African-American girls, ranging in age from one to 19. Alongside "Dear Sister" letters written by Girl/Friends addressed to female survivors of sexual assault, Datavia's image marked an important shift that all the Girl/Friends went through during their summer intensive: the transformation from being an individual actor who experiences or witnesses sexual and racial trauma, through then gaining critical consciousness about the personal and societal impact of those events, to finally becoming an activist who advocates for *herself* and other girls and young women. "By sharing their art in this very public way, the Girl/Friends have reached another stage in their artist–activist identity," says Leah Gipson. "They have taken what they focused on in therapy, in their workshops, and in their conversations with each other and turned it into a collective experience for others. By doing so, they are now 'talking back' to those powers that have silenced them *and* teaching others how to see black girls through their own eyes" (Personal communication, July 3, 2017).

Part V

Girl/Power: Agents of Change

> Because of the Girl/friends program, I now consider myself a feminist.
>
> *(Girl/Friend, age 17)*

After the summer intensive, Girl/Friends enter the yearlong program, a series of weekly meetings in which they launch Girl/Power and develop and implement their own social action projects and racial and gender justice campaigns. Building on the previous stages, Girl/Me and Girl/Culture, Girl/Power is a direct engagement with the community. The individual youth leaders not only reflect on their own experiences and use their stories to advocate for themselves and other girls, but also create a collective "counter public space" (Fraser 1990). They thereby challenge the invisibility and structural inequities into which they are born, while working with each other and other citizens to stage alternatives. Theoretically, as Girl/Power focuses on merging the individual actor and the collective group, the concept of self-care, too, evolves from psycho-social support for specific Girl/Friends to Girl/Friends artist-activists engaging in a form of what we are calling "community care," an ethical and political commitment to the wellbeing and spiritual health of their neighborhoods and the city of Chicago.

As in our descriptions of Girl/Me and Girl/Culture in which Ziliah referenced Datavia's self-portrait and Datavia deliberately expanded on her own original image, Girl/Power exemplifies how those same images can be used as a form of awareness and resistance within the dominant public sphere. As a poster used in A Long Walk Home street protests against domestic violence and police violence against black girls and women, Datavia's self-portrait about "being silenced" sat alongside other Girl/Friends' portraits of Rekia Boyd and Jessica Hampton. Each October, A Long Walk Home hosts a community march in North Lawndale to acknowledge Domestic Violence Awareness and Prevention Month. In October 2015, the march was dedicated to Rekia Boyd; it took place in North Lawndale, a few blocks away from where she, as an unarmed 22-year-old, was fatally shot in the back of the head by the off-duty police officer Dante Servin, who was acquitted by a jury in April 2015 (Sweeny, 2015). In June 2016, the Girl/Friends again took up the voice of Jessica Hampton, a 25-year-old woman who was fatally stabbed by an ex-boyfriend on Chicago's CTA-Red Line as onlookers recorded the event on Facebook (Hussain, 2016). Beginning in the community, the Girl/Friends' protests took place on the train, and ended at the 47th Street stop of the Red Line, the site of Hampton's death.

Taken together, these protests serve as a form of memory resistance against black women's political invisibility to themselves, to their communities, and to the state. They function as a willful remembering to counter the social forgetting of Boyd's and Hampton's deaths as a result of racialized gender-based violence. While Hampton's, and to a much larger degree Boyd's, death garnered some public attention and outrage, the vast majority of African-American girls like Datavia and Zilah, who experience multiple forms of oppression, get none. During the marches to celebrate the lives and lament the deaths of Boyd and Hampton, Girl/Friends youth leaders hold and hand out posters that they make in the program. They do not simply dedicate their images to call attention to those who are dead, but by including images of themselves like Datavia's self-portraits, the posters become a form of protest art (Figure 6.5). By dissolving the boundaries between politicized violence and personal trauma, between icon and individual subject, and between public suffering and personal experiences, the presence of the Girl/Friends' portraits of themselves alongside the images of other black girls and women symbolizes their own understanding of and connection to a larger collective. The self-portraits now function as the ultimate form of protest and protection, for they are not only publicly stating that their lives as black girls matter, but also interrupting the very cycle of violence that makes them hyper-vulnerable in the first place.

Part VI

Conclusion: Self-Care as Community Care

> Each time a woman stands up for herself, without knowing it possibly, without claiming it, she stands up for all women.
>
> *(Maya Angelou, n.d.)*

Last July, political scientist, media personality, and frequent supporter of A Long Walk Home, Melissa Harris-Perry (2017) penned a piece entitled "How #SquadCare Saved My Life" in which she critiqued the self-care model currently marketed to mass culture. She writes, "whether it's through selling bath soaps or encouraging activists to take mental health breaks, celebrating individual self-reliance elides the fact that ultimately care is not something we do for ourselves" (para 7). Her concern is that self-care is inherently anti-feminist for it "encourages women to rely solely on themselves rather than to make demands on anyone or anything else" (para 8) as well as racist:

> Self-care validates as good and noble all of those women with sufficient resources to "take a break" from the hustle and bustle while it censures those who seek relief from the collective care of the state—through child care subsidies, food assistance, low-income or subsidized housing, or health care. In so much of our political language, the black, brown, and poor women who seek care in these ways are still represented as bad, fraudulent, lazy, and wasteful.
>
> *(para 8)*

In its place, Harris-Perry argues for "squad care," which is "a way of under-standing our needs as humans that acknowledges how we lean on one another, that we are not alone in the world, but rather enmeshed in webs of mutual and symbiotic relationships" (para 9). This shift in emphasis from focusing exclusively on oneself to recognizing that one's individual needs for health, safety, and in many cases justice are an integral component of the black feminist tradition in which Harris-Perry, as well as our Girl/Friends, belong. But one crucial differ-ence between Harris-Perry's critique and A Long Walk Home's embracing of self-care is our commitment to art therapy and belief that through multiple forms of creative expression the girls and young women with whom we work can be seen, heard, and valued.

Perhaps, no image encapsulates this merging of art therapy, social action, and collective consciousness than that of Danielle, the 15-year-old Girl/Friend who wanted to attend the sit-in as a form of self-care in July 2016. In the group por-trait, Danielle, stands in the middle, her long braids, parted into two, flowing down her head and framing her ID from the School of the Art Institute. Her black braids, name tag, and her black v-neck t-shirt only highlight the dominance of the color black, one that is intensified by the shiny tape that covers her lips.

FIGURE 6.5 Danielle—*Self Portrait*

FIGURE 6.6 Protest march 2016

Although the masked mouth nods to the silence that Datavia and Zilah capture in their self-portraits, Danielle further expands their narratives by putting them front and center at a youth-led city-wide Black Lives Matter protest. Her chosen silence merely amplifies the fact that the condition of invisibility is one that is imposed on her, while her defiant, straightforward look at the camera and her occupying of Millennium Park, one of Chicago's most sacrosanct public spaces, opposes those systems and individuals that devalue the experiences and contributions African-American girls give to their communities and city. Through the adaptations of this singular form, an illustrated self-portrait, to a photograph, to a group portrait, Girl/Friends offers a small glimpse into their collective power to engage, redefine, and radicalize self-care as a tool of individual and community transformation and healing.

References

2010 National healthcare quality and disparities reports. U.S. Department of Health and Human Services Department. Retrieved from https://archive.ahrq.gov/research/findings/nhqrdr/nhqrdr10/qrdr10.html

Ackerman, S. (2015). "I sat in that place for three days, man": Chicagoans detail abusive confinement inside police "black site." *The Guardian.* Retrieved from www.theguardian.com/us-news/2015/feb/27/chicago-abusive-confinement homan-square

Alvidrez, J., Snowden, L. R. & Kaiser, D. M. (2008). The experience of stigma among Black mental health consumers. *Journal of Health Care Poor Underserved,* 19(3), 874–893.

Angelou, M. (n.d.) www.mayaangelouquotes.org/each-time-a-woman-stands-up-for-herself-without-knowing-it-possibly-without-claiming-it-she-stands-up-for-all-women/

Bambara, T. C. (1992). *The salt eaters.* New York, NY: Vintage Books.

Beal, F. (1969). Black women's manifesto; Double jeopardy: To be Black and female. Retrieved from www.hartford-hwp.com/archives/45a/196.html

Beattie, M. (1986). *Codependent no more: How to stop controlling others and start caring for yourself.* Center City, MN: Hazelden Foundation.

Berman, M. (2016, April 2). Chicago's staggering rise in gun violence and killings. *The Washington Post.* Retrieved from www.washingtonpost.com/news/post-nation/wp/2016/04/02/chicagos-staggering-rise-in-gun-violence-and-killings/?utm_term=.c5b88e63131c

Blanchard, J. & Lurie, N. (2004). R-E-S-P-E-C-T: Patient reports of disrespect in the health care setting and its impact on care. *Journal of Family Practice, 53* (9), 721–730.

Brown, R. N. (2013). *Hear our truths: The creative potential of Black girlhood.* Chicago, IL: University of Illinois Press.

Chang, B. (2016, July 14). How four teenage girls organized this week's huge silent protest. *Politics and City Life.* Retrieved from www.chicagomag.com/city-life/July2016/Black-Lives-Matter-Chi-Youth-Sit-In-Rally/

Coates, T. (2014, June). The case for reparations. *The Atlantic.* Retrieved from www.theatlantic.com/magazine/archive/2014/06/the-case-for-reparations/361631/

Crenshaw, K. (1989). Demarginalizing the intersection of race and sex: A Black feminist critique of antidiscrimination doctrine, feminist theory and antiracist politics. *University of Chicago Legal Forum,* 1989, 139–176.

Farrag, H. H. (2015, June 24). The role of spirit in the #BlackLivesMatter movement: A conversation with activist and artist Patrisse Cullors. *Religious Dispatches.* Retrieved from http://religiondispatches.org/the-role-of-spirit-in-the-blacklivesmatter-movement-a conversation-with-activist-and-artist-patrisse-cullors/

Foucault, M. (2005). *The hermeneutics of the subject: Lectures at the college de France 1981–1982.* New York, NY: Palgrave Macmillian.

Fraser, N. (1990). Rethinking the public sphere: A contribution to the critique of actually existing democracy. *Social Text, 25/26,* 56–80.

Freire, P. (1970). *Pedagogy of the oppressed.* New York, NY: Continuum.

Goldstein, S. (2013, November 25). Chicago cop charged with killing unarmed young woman during off-duty confrontation. *New York Daily News.* Retrieved from www.nydailynews.com/news/crime/chicago-charged-killing-unarmed-young woman-article-1.1529041

Harris, A. (2017, April 5). A history of self-care: From its radical roots to its yuppie-driven middle age to its election-inspired resurgence. *Slate.* Retrieved from www.slate.com/articles/arts/culturebox/2017/04/the_history_of_self_care.html

Harris-Perry, M. (2017, July 24). How #SquadCare saved my life. *Elle.* Retrieved from www.elle.com/culture/career-politics/news/a46797/squad-care-melissa-harris-perry/

Hogan, S. (Ed.) (1997). *Feminist approaches to art therapy.* London: Jessica Kingsley.

hooks, b. (1993). *Sisters of the yam: Black women and self-recovery.* Cambridge, MA: Southend Press.

Hussain, R. (2016, June 30). Public defender; Man accused of stabbing Jessica Hampton on Red Line train suffers from paranoid schizophrenia. *Chicago Sun-Times.* Retrieved from http://homicides.suntimes.com/2016/06/30/public-defender-says-man-accused-of-stabbing-jessica-hampton-on-red-line-train-suffers-from-paranoid-schizophrenia/

Knowles, S. (2016). Borderline (an ode to self care). *YouTube*. Retrieved from www.youtube.com/watch?v=kAyVT6h1Gjk

Lorde, A. (1988). *A burst of light: Living with cancer*. Ithaca, NY: Firebrand Books.

Morris, E. W. (2007). "Ladies" or "loudies"? Perceptions and experiences of Black girls in classrooms. *Youth & Society*, *38*(4), 490–515. doi.10.1177/0044118X06296778

Morris, M. (2016). The black girl pushout. *The Atlantic*. Retrieved from www.theatlantic.com/education/archive/2016/03/the-criminalization-of-black girls-in-schools/473718/

Patrick, K. (2017). Let her learn—What about girls? *National Women's Law Center*. Retrieved from https://nwlc.org/blog/let-her-learn-what-about-girls/

Powter, S. (1993). *Stop the insanity!* New York, NY: Simon & Schuster.

Sanders-Thompson, V., Bazile, A. & Akbar, M. (2004). African-Americans' perceptions of psychotherapy and psychotherapists. *Professional Psychology: Research and Practice*, *35*(1), 19–26.

Silva, C. (2017). The millennial obsession with self-care. *National Public Radio, Health*. Retrieved from www.npr.org/2017/06/04/531051473/the-millennial-obsession with-self-care

Smith, B. (Ed.) (1983). *Home girls: A Black feminist anthology*. New Brunswick, NJ: Rutgers University Press.

Sweeny, A. (2015, July 3). Inside the failed prosecution of Chicago detective Dante Servin. *Chicago Tribune*. Retrieved from www.chicagotribune.com/news/ct-dante-servin-acquittal-met-20150626-story.html

Talwar, S. (2015). Creating alternative public spaces: Community-based art practice, critical consciousness and social justice. In D. Gussak & M. Rosal (Eds.), *The Wiley handbook of art therapy* (pp. 840–847). Oxford, UK: Wiley Blackwell.

van Gelder, S. (2016). The radical work of healing: Fania and Angela Davis on a new kind of civil rights activism. *Yes! Magazine: Powerful Ideas, Powerful Actions*. Retrieved from www.yesmagazine.org/issues/life-after-oil/the-radical-work-of-healing-fania-and-angela-davis-on-a-new-kind-of-civil-rights-activism-20160218

7

RADICAL CARING AND ART THERAPY

Decolonizing Immigration and Gender Violence Services

Sangeetha (Sangi) Ravichandran

On May 23, 2016, fifteen Chicago activists boarded a bus to Indianapolis and the Supreme Court of Indiana to hear the appeal in *Purvi Patel v. State of Indiana*. Purvi Patel, a woman of South Asian descent and an American citizen, was sentenced to 20 years in prison for feticide and child neglect after miscarrying her fetus in March 2015. Her sentencing caused international outcry for the criminalization of her abortion. She was also the first woman in the U.S. to be convicted and sentenced on feticide charges (Bazelon, 2015).

As we rode together, my fellow activists and I were nervous. Our excitement, conversations, and anxiety became a way to cultivate camaraderie. As we got closer to the court, other activists from the National Asian Pacific Women's Forum, Indiana Religious Coalition for Reproductive Justice, and the Korean American Resource & Cultural Center greeted us. About 100 people had gathered at the courthouse to hold a vigil for Purvi as a demonstration of solidarity. As we entered the courtroom, we were told that the hearing had been moved to a larger room to accommodate more people. Hearing this made it feel like it was the first victory. The courtroom was filled with Purvi's supporters. The appeal in *Patel v. State of Indiana* was presented and a strong conservative political agenda became apparent.

Briefly, Purvi Patel, a 33-year-old woman living in Indiana, was accused of feticide for inducing an abortion and killing her fetus. According to Purvi's statement, she went to the emergency room in South Bend, Indiana, to receive medical care after her miscarriage. When asked what she had done with the fetal remains, she told the doctor she had put them in a bag and left them in a dumpster. Purvi was charged with felony child neglect and feticide and sentenced to 20 years. Indiana's feticide law were intended to "protect pregnant women against unscrupulous abortion providers or abusive partners" (Bazelon, 2015, para 14), especially in cases of domestic violence.

Purvi Patel was not the first person of color to be tried under the feticide laws of the state of Indiana. In 2011, a Chinese immigrant, Bei Bei Shuai, was charged with intentionally ending her pregnancy when she attempted suicide. Although she survived, her fetus did not. Instead of assisting Bei Bei with mental health counseling to deal with her depression, the state charged her with attempted feticide and she was incarcerated. Bhattacharjee and Silliman (2002), in their book *Policing the National Body*, illustrate the impact of aggressive law enforcement on the reproductive rights of women, especially those of women of color. They argue that the reproductive justice movement, led by white feminists, is rooted in neoliberalism; the sole interest, they argue, is protecting women's right to abortion and power over their bodies. The narrow focus on reproductive justice ignores a host of factors affecting women of color: access to medical care, safe birth control, and "economic and political resources to maintain healthy children" (Silliman, Fried, Ross, & Gutierrez, 2004, p. xii). Historically, we have seen the impact of eugenic laws, immigration restriction, forced sterilization, and family planning played out on the bodies of women of color (Silliman et al., 2004). More recently, the negative impact of birth control choices such as Depo-Provera on black and Latino communities has been devastating (Mintzes, Hardon, & Hanhart, 1993). The Indiana feticide laws were enacted to protect pregnant women from violence; instead, the law is now being used against women's choice. Furthermore, laws guided by religious values overlook the impact of poverty, racism, lack of access to healthcare, and the social environment in which many women live (Iyer, 2015).

The cases of Purvi Patel and Bei Bei Shuai raise questions about reproductive justice, the rights of women over their bodies, and how women of color, citizens or immigrants, are viewed. In both cases the focus of the State of Indiana has been on criminalizing abortion and doing so in ways that treat women of color unjustly. These cases raise questions about western notions that consistently represent women of color across the globe as helpless "victims" or "criminals." To break down colonial structures (Mohanty, 2003; Narayan, 1998), it is necessary to re-contextualize social change within the framework of transformative justice, steering away from abolitionary practices in order to rebuild communities and raise awareness from the grassroots. In order to create a movement for transforming the culture of gender violence we need to incorporate "critical consciousness" (Talwar, 2015), cultural humility (Young, 2015), and "radical caring" (Rudrappa, 2004). We need to envision a new paradigm of care to end gender violence.

This chapter is divided into two parts. In the first part, I critique how gender violence has been traditionally defined. Drawing on intersectionality, I argue for the importance of understanding gender violence from a systemic perspective, critiquing the existing patriarchal power structures that have further colonized discourses of gender violence. In the second part of the chapter, I draw from my experience of working as an art therapist at Apna Ghar (Our Home), an organization that works to "conduct outreach and advocacy across immigrant communities to end gender violence" (www.apnaghar.org/). I explore the role art therapy can play in building a critical mass to create a movement for decolonizing the culture of gender violence using the "radical caring" methodology of Apna Ghar. Radical caring in this context is defined as embracing a social justice vision "at both individual and larger social level" (Rudrappa, 2004, p. 589). That is, it is focused on the individual client seeking help and the staff's ability to assist their growth as an autonomous individual, while also focusing on organizational structures that work towards collective gender justice.

Part I

Overview of Gender Violence: Troubling Language

Historically, gender violence has been viewed as a normal part of life that has been rationalized by a biological determinism based on the correlation between testosterone and aggression in men (Archer, 1991; Ehrenkranz, Bliss, & Sheard, 1974). Walker (1979) coined the term "the battered woman syndrome," to characterize the domestic violence "victim" as a woman who is "compliant, passive, and submissive" (p. 46). Walker's (1977) article "Battered Women and Learned Helplessness" proposes a psychological rationale for the victimization and entrapment of women in domestic violence. She argues that as a result of the "psychological paralysis" women are often unable to leave abusive relationships. Rothenberg (2003) critiques the concept of battered "women's syndrome" and the stereotype of women as "helpless victims." She argues that such stereotypes are inadequate and asks that scholars begin to examine the systemic inequalities that perpetuate gendered violence.

Richie (2012) traces the beginning of a movement against male violence to the mid 1960s, when women started publicly disclosing and publishing their experiences of horrific abuse. One of the important aspects of the early grassroots activity was that the published accounts of violence "described women's experiences as strikingly similar across racial, ethnic and class lines" (p 69). The movement began with women gathering in spaces such as day care centers and around kitchen tables to discuss their stories of abuse. It is not until the early 1970s that an informal movement became formalized through the emergence of shelters and crisis centers, as feminists began organizing around issues of domestic violence (Richie, 2012; Rothenberg, 2003). Grassroots activism led to coalitions at the local, state, and national levels to advance public education and influence policy reform. The movement to end male violence against women, which demanded legal and criminal recognition for cases of domestic violence, followed a course similar to that of the civil rights movement. The 1980s saw the implementation of the rape shield laws and, in 1994, the passing of Violence Against Women Act (VAWA). Richie (2012) contends that by 2004 the anti-violence movement had become an institutionalized reality with over 1500 rape crisis centers and over 2000 domestic violence shelters. But staffing by white, middle-class women who had little or no experience with gender violence created a sterile, clinical, and hierarchical climate when providing services for battered women. A robust movement that was led by survivors to end violence against women began to lose its footing. Richie's (2012) historical overview offers a mournful account of how white, middle class women won by streamlining the movement, leaving out women of color, immigrants, lesbians, sex workers, trans women, and other marginalized women who had been on the frontlines when the movement began.

Incite!, a national network of feminists of color, works to "end violence against women, gender non-conforming, and trans people of color" (www.incite-national.org/home). In their book, *Color of Violence: The Incite! Anthology* (2006), the authors argue for repositioning the anti-violence movement by centering the voices of people of color. Their goal is to build a movement that actually addresses concerns beyond domestic violence or sexual assault by mapping strategies of resistance used by women of color around the world. The model is not focused on a prescribed program, but rather on an intersectional analysis since the issues facing women are constantly shifting and changing.

Intersectionality and Discourse on Gender

In order to build a decentralized movement to end violence against women, many activists and academics have turned to intersectionality. Crenshaw (1991) proposed intersectionality, not as a new, totalizing theory of identity, but rather as a way to examine the intersecting role of various social categories (age, race/ethnicity, class, gender, sexuality, nationality, religion, and disability, among other markers of difference). It is a way, she argued, to understand the experiences of power, privilege, and marginalization within a particular society, when "race and gender intersect in shaping structural, political and representational aspects of violence against women of color" (1991, p. 1244). Talwar (2010), brings this idea into the epistemology of art therapy in not only theory but also praxis. She questions an art therapy that focuses on clinical paradigms of "normal vs abnormal," and urges art therapists to produce and engage in counter-hegemonic discourses in order to operate within an anti-oppression framework from an intersectional perspective. According to Talwar (2010), "intersectionality as it is integrated into our discourse will offer art therapists a means to identify and deal with cultural complexity and issues of power from personal, national, and global perspectives" (p. 16).

When art therapists grapple with intersectionality as one way to help understand identity, they must also confront the colonial perspective that sees people as indistinguishable masses (Fanon, 1967). To conceptualize an anti-hegemonic art therapy practice means to understand the notion of decolonization. In *Postcolonial Theory*, Gandhi (1998) gives an account of the collision and collusion of postcolonial theory and feminism, the "double colonisation" of being a "third world woman." Mohanty (1988) critiques the "double colonisation" that occurs when white feminists in the social sciences benefit from the creation of the "third world woman," a reductive construct that views its subject as ignorant, poor, uneducated, tradition-bound, religious, family-oriented, victimized, and universally dependent upon others (Harasym, 1990; Narayan, 2013). This view leads to the creation of a specific Third World feminism in which, the term "'third world' refers not only to underdeveloped and over exploited geographical areas, but also and perhaps more importantly to oppressed minorities living in the First World countries" (Talwar, 2002, p. 186). A parallel issue in the counseling professions providing gender violence services is the use of the term "multicultural," which has become an all-encompassing label for every culture other than a static "white" or European one. Grzanka (2014), an intersectionality scholar, critiques the term multiculturalism as it is "produced, practiced and elaborated" (p. xix), including terms such as "diversity," "cross-cultural," and "culturally sensitive" that are used by those who see service to the poor as an act of rescuing (Gorski & Goodman, 2015). Implementing an intersectional framework means critically examining the dichotomous "us vs. them" thinking to include the multiple identities of third world women (Mohanty, 2003; Talwar, 2002). Furthermore, trauma-informed practices that are truly decolonizing require that clinicians take an active role in the process of decolonizing themselves. This requires health providers to enter into the process of advocacy and activism, especially social justice action (Goodman, 2015).

In this context, the notion of "radical care" means questioning the nature of gender violence from a lifetime spiral of abuse, patriarchal, and hegemonic structures that have been normalized. The Asian Pacific Institute of Violence sees domestic violence as only one form of violence against women. For them, gender violence and abuse is spread over the life cycle and is more than just

> physical, sexual, economic and emotional abuses; violence is about living in a climate of fear, shame, coercive control, and devaluation. It is often experienced in the context of additional oppressions based on race, ethnicity, age, sexual orientation, gender identity, type of labor performed, level of education, class position, disability, and immigration or refugee status. Raising awareness about the historical nature of gender violence confronts victim-blaming, informs advocacy, and empowers survivors.
>
> *(www.api-gbv.org/about-gbv/our-analysis/lifetime-spiral/)*

In the next section, I elaborate on how an intersectional analysis informed by notions of radical care informs services at Apna Ghar.

Part II

Apna Ghar

History and Context

Apna Ghar ("Our Home" in Urdu and Hindi) is a non-profit organization that was founded, in 1990, by five Asian women to address gender violence within immigrant communities. At Apna Ghar, gender violence is broadly understood as violence impacting women and girls who live on the margins of society. Often, they have been stripped of their personal power by an individual, a group, and/or systems of oppression, and become victims of domestic and family violence, forced marriage, human trafficking, and honor killing (www.apnaghar. org). Prem Sharma, one of the founders of Apna Ghar, states that one of the biggest challenges faced at the start was that mainstream services failed to understand the eating habits, religious practices, language, dress, and other. basic aspects of Asian culture. After five years of operating the crisis hotline, a shelter for survivors of domestic violence was founded (Incite! Women of Color Against, 2006). What began as a crisis hotline is now a prominent social service agency in the Chicago metropolitan area. The mission of Apna Ghar is to end gender violence by providing holistic services, education, and advocacy across immigrant communities. Apna Ghar addresses gender violence using a radical care methodology that focuses on a client-centered, trauma-focused, and empowerment-based approach that promotes radical caring. The concept of radical caring means to empower survivors to be self-sufficient. At Apna Ghar this entails a full spectrum of programming, such as education and outreach, art therapy and counseling, legal advocacy and emergency housing in the Chicago area. Additionally, the organization offers consultation and referrals across the U. S. and abroad.

Historically, Apna Ghar, like many other non-profit organizations, has functioned using a top-down structure, which only proved to marginalize survivors even further. Rudrappa (2004) argues that disciplining an immigrant survivor within institutional structures that exert power and control and use victim blaming further isolates the survivor from her community, reducing her to yet another colonized body. Specifically, she referred to Apna Ghar's compulsory nature of its counseling services, which included art therapy. Over the years, careful staff restructuring and evaluation from a radical care perspective meant asking "who is serving" (staff) and "who is being served" (client) in order to alleviate some of the clients' isolation. The institutional structure at Apna Ghar is similar to that of other domestic violence service providers in the area, although its services are decentralized to serve the needs of immigrant survivors using a Third World feminist perspective that considers the "multi-dimensional nature of power" (George & Stith, 2014) rather than taking a "one size fits all" approach.

At Apna Ghar, moving clients from "victim" to "survivor" has meant paying special attention to cultural competence through staffing suited to working with a large immigrant population. The intersectional nature of programming allows for a strength-based approach; staff members are required to provide advocacy services using the trauma-informed and crisis intervention model mandated by the Illinois Domestic Violence Act (IDVA). Specifically, Apna Ghar's counseling services enable survivors to heal from trauma and regain the confidence needed to rebuild their lives and achieve safety, stability, and self-sufficiency.

Art Therapy: Advocacy and Social Justice

My first experience with Apna Ghar was as an art therapy intern in 2010. As an intern, I was less interested in convening weekly mandatory art therapy groups than in creating an accessible space that was welcoming and supportive. I organized a weekly fiber arts group that allowed the women to freely engage with textiles, yarn, and other fiber materials. The goal of the group was to provide a safe space where anyone could drop in to learn or teach or create fabric art. Women from various ethnic backgrounds attended the group to create small or large works using materials that they could intimately relate to. One of the participants, S, a survivor of gender violence of South Asian origin, had suffered severe physical abuse and struggled with pain. Most days, the pain caused her to lie in bed for much of the day. She, however, made a great effort to stitch a *kurta* (Indian tunic) with the block printed fabric she had found in the studio. She spent four months in completing the *kurta*. When she was finished, S wore it to the group, proud of her accomplishment as an artist and a creator. For her, sewing the *kurta* became a way to deal with her history and the pain of physical violence. The knowledge that emerged from creating it, using fabric that connected her back to her homeland, and finally wearing it became a metaphor of the resilience and strength she was building by being part of the program.

Another survivor, X, was a teenager from China who had survived labor trafficking, and could converse only in Mandarin. She was often quiet and rarely engaged with other group members. Before the Christmas holidays, I brought balls of yarn and saw X's eyes light up. She immediately grabbed three big balls of yarn and started finger knitting. In that moment, all of the participants in the studio stopped to observe her intently and with awe as she created a scarf on her fingers. Another Arabic speaking participant in the group, signaled to X to teach her finger knitting (Figure 7.1). Before we knew it, all eight members of the group had gathered around X to learn how to finger knit a scarf. Communication happened through gestures, laughing at one another's mistakes and frustrations, but knitting colorful scarves that everyone wore to the Apna Ghar holiday party.

X was proud every time she saw one of us knitting or wearing a finger-knitted scarf. Mostly, X took great pride in sharing her knowledge and skill. Soon, everyone at Apna Ghar, including students in the art therapy graduate program, was finger knitting, and I was able to share with X that she had taught more than 50 people how to knit in one month. These two experiences had a lasting impact on my early learning as an art therapist, for they demonstrated the power of art in community development and fostering empowerment and leadership among survivors. Rather than a clinician, advocate, or helper approaching healing through a one-dimensional rescue model, I became interested in creating spaces that were shared, meaningful, and led to positive actions.

In 2013, after working for three years as an art therapist and program coordinator at A Long Walk Home's (ALWH) Girl/Friends Leadership Institute, I returned to Apna Ghar as Manager of Counseling Services. My experience using arts-based activism to end gender-based violence at ALWH took on a new form at Apna Ghar, where I was encouraged to incorporate art therapy into the various levels of programming. Having interned there, I was familiar with the individual and structural challenges survivors faced when seeking support. Most survivors were usually dependent on their husband's visa, had little to no job

FIGURE 7.1   Finger knitting

prospects (it is illegal to work without a work permit), and lacked a family and support network. Employing an intersectional approach informed by radical care methodology to understand the power structures and markers of interpersonal and systemic oppression became central to developing a program that had social justice at its center and relied on culturally sensitive healing practices. Thus, the focus at Apna Ghar as part of its radical care approach was less on creating a strict mental health regime focused on diagnoses and prescribed remedies than on creating a program that offered the resources the larger community needed and created leadership positions for its members. The overall plan not only included the arts and expressive therapies as central to healing, but also threaded them into every aspect of a program that centered on social justice practice.

Counseling Team

The counseling team consisted of a talk therapist working with adult survivors and their families, a full-time art therapist who worked with children and their families, a part-time art therapist who worked with all of the participants in the safe house shelter, an art therapy intern, and myself, as the manager of the counseling program. Typically, clients who received counseling services came to Apna Ghar through the 24-hour crisis hot line or when needing the services of the safe home, the Apna Ghar shelter. This meant that people who were reaching out to Apna Ghar had heard about the services through word of mouth, the National Domestic Violence Hotline, or the Internet. A majority of the clients were women immigrants between 23 and 45 years of age with young children. Another important focus was the outreach program for the young people and older adults who had little access to information. Raising awareness of gender violence through outreach programming, therefore, became an important focus of the counseling programming at Apna Ghar.

Youth Program

One of the first programs established as part of Apna Ghar outreach was for young people experiencing or witnessing violence in immigrant homes. By building partnerships with several schools that served immigrant communities in the Chicago area, specifically with the schools' counseling or social work departments, an art therapist began two weekly groups.

Many models for school youth programs are prevention focused and do not have room to address trauma that is already present in the lives of young people. By providing arts-based therapeutic services within schools, the youth program helped decentralize services and decolonize models of care within gender violence services. The partnerships helped the art therapist to build relationships with teachers, who ultimately became the primary source of referral of students who might best fit the program. Initially, the referral process was more difficult than anticipated since the teachers lacked the language and information on how to identify and understand gender-based violence among their students. A significant part of the art therapist's time was spent on training teachers and social workers about gender violence, microaggressions, and the confidentiality issues that affected students of color. The teacher training helped to maximize the referral process for students who could most benefit from the youth program. In addition, the art therapist created a referral form that was designed to identify participants who might best benefit from the program.

The art therapist formulated an arts based curriculum that aimed to create a safe space for students to process their experience, learn more about gender violence, ways to address it and help each other, and gain access to resources for themselves and their families. The curriculum, designed for an 11-week program, helped the participants first to explore their personal identity and then to examine themselves in relation to their immediate community, and finally to understand their place in larger society. The art therapist established an open studio that the youth participants could access once they had completed the 11-week curriculum. The open studio became a valuable space for the youth participants to continue to build strong bonds and sense of community.

The program's effectiveness was measured through pre and post surveys that the students completed to measure the impact of the group on them. Teachers and social workers were also surveyed to assess the program's impact on the students' performance in school, as well as relationships with peers and families. For young people who had witnessed violence at home, the art therapist met with the family to offer resources and connect them to Apna Ghar or another appropriate service in the community. The result was an action oriented and sustainable program that identified young people who would benefit from the arts based curriculum and raised awareness of gender based violence in the immigrant community.

Self-Care Sundays

Another element of the arts-based programming at Apna Ghar was Self-Care Sundays. The stigma surrounding gender-based violence, therapy, and other health and safety issues, often prohibits individuals from reaching out to Apna Ghar for services. To reduce the stigma Self-Care Sundays were introduced as a drop in, healing space for women in the community. Centered on principles of radical caring (Rudrappa, 2004) , the program prioritized the idea of community care, in which the entire community agrees to assume responsibility for creating a healing space (as opposed to individuals responsible for their own healing). While radical healing justice can take place in individual spaces, it is the shared responsibility that removes shame from the idea of caring for your mind, body, and soul (Loewe, 2012; Padamsee, 2011).

The program took place every first and third Sunday for two hours in the afternoon. Lunch and childcare were provided to reduce some of the obstacles faced by the women who wished to attend. Self-Care Sundays made a huge impact within the community. Women who were already receiving services became regulars. Several women brought friends or other community members who would benefit from the program.

Apna Ghar's Self-Care Sundays were unique in that not only was the curriculum arts based, but the methods of implementation and communication were as well. Each week a handout was created that was illustrated to communicate with members who did not read or understand English. Considering that Apna Ghar serves people from over 50 countries and the members speak over 70 different languages, the goal was to avoid excluding anyone who did not speak English or one of the other languages spoken in the group. Figure 7.2 shows an example of one of the directives designed by Jane Kim, an art therapy intern at Apna Ghar. Such instructional sheets were then transformed into handouts, coloring pages, and self-care kits. Self-care was considered an important element of practice for not only the members who attended the group, but also for the staff and advocates who were part of the helping profession.

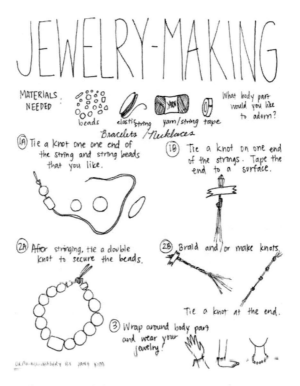

FIGURE 7.2 Visual instructional sheet

Development of the Health and Wellness Center

Self-Care Sundays became so popular within the community that Apna Ghar decided to expand the program as part of the health and wellness center. Health and wellness are often thought to mean visiting the doctor. Apna Ghar engages with the concept of health and wellness from an intersectional framework. For example, when immigrants accessing health and wellness services are from low-income backgrounds, for them time and access to resources are serious considerations.

A generous donation by a board member gave Apna Ghar access to a large open space for the health and wellness program. The space afforded room for the arts-based Self-Care Sundays, yoga, and an employment/economic empowerment program. To overcome language barriers, the programs were required to create image-based materials and translations whenever possible to ensure that information was being communicated to all the community members. The yoga instructor made image-based handouts for the programming and offered trauma-based yoga to the members, including the children. The economic empowerment program was offered in collaboration with various volunteer professionals from the community, from such fields as credit unions, job training programs; credit and money management sessions helped new immigrants and women who needed to establish self-sufficiency.

Apna Ghar additionally sought to include the arts in their programming in other ways. Since the physical space was considered an important part of the wellness program, it was filled with artwork created by members of the community. This included artwork and poetry from people of various age groups and in many languages. All members at the safe home/ shelter, who were fleeing violence, were given a welcome package that included a journal, coloring pages, sewing supplies, and writing/coloring materials to encourage engagement in alternative coping mechanisms during their stay. Finally, to make the arts accessible to all at Apna Ghar, art materials were available in every room. Staff, advocates, visitors, participants and their children used coloring books and art materials alike. Ensuring inclusivity through art making was one of the most effective tools used at Apna Ghar.

Collective Voices, Shared Journeys: *Annual Art Show*

In connection with the programming at Apna Ghar, an annual art show was organized to engage survivors, artists, and activists who were working at the intersections of gender based violence, immigration, mental health, disability, and reproductive justice. The annual show took place at the student center gallery of the University of Illinois at Chicago (Figure 7.3).

The art show lasted a month and was open to all, especially the university community. Along with holding the opening and closing ceremonies at the gallery, the event became a way to collaborate with other Chicago partners engaged in ending gender-based violence. Over the course of the month, the space featured performances and panels dedicated to topics such as police brutality, incarceration,

FIGURE 7.3   *Collective Voices, Shared Journeys* exhibit

and immigration, among other issues. An important part of the programming was to deconstruct the intersectional issues of gender-based violence through work-shops and panel presentations, such as Deferred Action for Childhood Arrivals (DACA) to recruit more Asian American undocumented youth, a dating vio-lence information session by Between Friends, reproductive justice issues by the Wandering Uterus Project, letter writing for Purvi Patel, and a performance on reproductive rights and abortion access by Illinois Caucus for Adolescent Health (ICAH). The art show not only created a platform for visibility surrounding issues of gender based violence addressed through the arts, but also became a safe space to build coalitions with other organizations and community members throughout Chicago. The events became a place to renew everyone's commitment to the movement to end gender based violence. The art show signified solidarity and power. Holding such a gathering at a public university meant creating awareness for people of various ages, races, classes, genders, religions, disability and sexuality groups. The show reached over 1000 people every year, raising awareness of the layered and complex lifetime spiral of gender violence through workshops and education. The show also became a venue celebrating unity and solidarity, factors that are often overlooked in movement building.

Advocacy: Justice for Purvi

Although a lot of the work at Apna Ghar focused on the interpersonal and micro level advocacy for survivors of violence, the case of Purvi Patel connected the advocates at the macro level as well. Since March 2015, I have organized and participated in several "Free Purvi" campaigns that served to educate the general public about the systemic war on women, especially women of color. The Free Purvi campaign was co-sponsored by multiple organizations, including Apna Ghar, i2i: invisible to invincible, FURIE, and others. Participants were asked to explore gender-based violence from a systemic and intersectional perspective, specifically the relationship between identity, reproductive (in)justice, criminalization, and mass incarceration. The workshops were geared towards raising awareness not simply around the injustice done to Purvi by the State of Indiana, but also of the criminalization of reproductive rights.

Using art-based expression to promote solidarity, the workshops were aimed at providing action and support to Purvi. One of the letter writing and art-making campaigns was held at University of Illinois at Chicago, with a predominantly Asian American group of students. Students were introduced to the case and its implications for women's health, bodies, and reproductive justice. A discussion of the prison industrial complex contextualized the disproportionate criminalization of people of color, particularly as it related to Purvi's case and

FIGURE 7.4 Workshop—Wandering Uterus Project: A DIY Movement for Reproductive Justice

other similar cases in Indiana. The workshop resulted in students writing letters and creating art to support Purvi as she served her sentence in prison. A few students began to fold paper to make origami cranes. Following the 2011 Japan earthquake, paper cranes became a popular symbol for healing and hope. In the workshop, one student wanted to create "1000 paper cranes" for Purvi and the entire class joined in the effort. What started as an informational workshop had become a movement. Another workshop was held at the Apna Ghar's annual art show in collaboration with the Wandering Uterus Project: A DIY Movement for Reproductive Justice, dedicated to understanding Purvi's case and how this case complicates the issues of reproductive justice in the U.S. (Figure 7.4).

Conclusion

Sajnani and Nadeau (2006) point out that

> violence against immigrant women of color and aboriginal women, like violence against white women, is treated by the courts, medical and coun-seling systems as a psychological and individual problem, rather than the result of structural violence that can only be remedied by structural and community solutions.
>
> *(p. 46)*

Furthermore, they argue that creating critical consciousness can be the most powerful way to intervene to effect social change and address structural violence enacted through state policies and laws. At Apna Ghar a concerted effort was made to embrace "radical caring" by incorporating the arts for healing and safety at a micro level, as well as to address structural issues to initiate conversations impacting policy changes and advocacy among community members. While the youth program sought to raise awareness among young people, who were often invisible and the most vulnerable in the gender based violence movement, the Self-Care Sundays aimed to reach the entire family in the movement to raise awareness about gender based violence. An important element of intersectional-ity is acknowledging that gender violence is not just a one-time event; rather it is a lifetime cycle. Interventions and raising awareness, therefore, have to happen on an intergenerational level. The Self-Care Sundays became an avenue to reach members in the community who were curious, but were not ready to admit they were survivors. The health and wellness studio became a space to listen to the needs of survivors. The goal was to shift the paradigm of top-down approach to services for survivors of violence, thereby decolonizing the non-profit industrial complex as a whole through a radical caring methodology. By ensuring that the health and wellness studio was a drop-in space with food and child care, Apna Ghar aimed to reduce obstacles often facing immigrant women. Through advocacy for Purvi on the national front and by writing letters to her, the Free

Purvi campaign sought to extend the concept of "service" for gender violence survivors beyond the narrowly defined non-profit world. The annual art show pushed the concept of art based expression beyond just those who sought help in the agency and shelter. The art show became an avenue to acknowledge that gender violence is experienced by more than those labeled as "battered women." It became an avenue to build a movement through cross-coalition organizing and prioritizing intersectional work to address and end the complex spiral of gender violence. Such work cannot be done by throwing certain women into the victim corner while the rest gather as rescuers. The crux of questioning the role of therapists and mental health providers in the non-profit industrial complex means complicating the victim/rescuer binary. A decolonizing framework means understanding the ways in which art therapists have remained complicit in promoting unjust systems of care and continue to participate in the marginalization of the people they serve. In this sense, to envision a paradigm shift means that as mental health providers we cannot address gender violence without taking into consideration the intersection of immigration, reproductive justice, and disability justice as part of the same conversation.

References

Archer, J. (1991). The influence of testosterone on human aggression. *British Journal of Psychology, 82*(1), 1–28.

Bazelon, E. (2015, April 1). Purvi Patel could be just the beginning. *New York Times Magazine.* Retrieved from www.nytimes.com/2015/04/01/magazine/purvi-patel-could-be-just-the-beginning.html?mcubz=0.

Bhattacharjee, A., & Silliman, J. (Eds. 2002). *Policing the national body: Race, gender and criminalization in the United States.* Cambridge, MA: South End Press.

Crenshaw, K. (1991). Mapping the margins: Intersectionality, identity politics, and violence against women of color. *Stanford Law Review, 43*(6), 1241–1299.

Ehrenkranz, J., Bliss, E., & Sheard, M. H. (1974). Plasma testosterone: Correlation with aggressive behavior and social dominance in man. *Psychosomatic Medicine, 36*(6), 469–475.

Fanon, F. (1967). *Black skin, white masks.* New York, NY: Grove press.

Gandhi, L. (1998). *Postcolonial theory: A critical introduction.* New York, NY: Columbia University Press.

George, J., & Stith, S. M. (2014). An updated feminist view of intimate partner violence. *Family Process, 53*(2), 179–193.

Goodman, R. D. (2015). A liberatory approach to trauma counseling: Decolonizing our trauma-informed practices. In R. Goodman & P. Gorski (Eds.), *Decolonizing "multicultural" counseling through social justice* (pp. 55–72). New York, NY: Springer.

Gorski, P. C., & Goodman, R. D. (2015). Introduction: Toward a decolonized multicultural counseling and psychology. In R. Goodman & P. Gorski (Eds.), *Decolonizing "multicultural" counseling through social justice* (pp. 1–10). New York, NY: Springer.

Grzanka, P. (2014). *Intersectionality: A foundations and frontiers reader.* Boulder, CO: Westview Press.

Harasym, S. (Ed. 1990). *The post-colonial critic: Interviews, strategies, dialogues.* London, England: Routledge.

Incite! Women of Color Against. (2006). *Color of violence: The Incite! anthology*. Cambridge, MA: South End Press.

Iyer, D. (2015). *We too sing America: South Asian, Arab, Muslim, and Sikh immigrants shape our multiracial future*. New York, NY: The New Press.

Loewe, B. (2012). An end to self care. *Organizing Upgrade*. Retrieved from www.organizingupgrade.com/index.php/blogs/b-loewe/item/729-end-to-self-care.

Mintzes, B., Hardon, A., & Hanhart, J. (1993). *Norplant: Under her skin*. Amsterdam, Holland: Women's Health Action Foundation and WEMOS.

Mohanty, C. T. (1988). Under Western eyes: Feminist scholarship and colonial discourses. *Feminist Review, 30*, 61–88.

Mohanty, C. T. (2003). *Feminism without borders: Decolonizing theory, practicing solidarity*. Durham, NC: Duke University Press.

Narayan, U. (1998). Essence of culture and a sense of history: A feminist critique of cultural essentialism. *Hypatia, 13*(2), 86.

Narayan, U. (2013). *Dislocating cultures: Identities, traditions, and third world feminism*. New York, NY: Routledge.

Padamsee, Y. M. (2011). YASHNA: Communities of care. *Organizing Upgrade*. Retrieved from www.organizingupgrade.com/index.php/component/k2/item/88-yashna-communities-of-care.

Richie, B. (2012). *Arrested justice*. New York, NY: New York University Press.

Rothenberg, B. (2003). "We don't have time for social change": Cultural compromise and the battered woman syndrome. *Gender & Society, 17*(5), 771–787.

Rudrappa, S. (2004). Radical caring in an ethnic shelter: South Asian American women workers at Apna Ghar, Chicago. *Gender & Society, 18*(5), 588–609.

Sajnani, N., & Nadeau, D. (2006). Creating safer spaces for immigrant women of colour: Performing the politics of possibility. *Canadian Woman Studies, 25*(1), 45–53.

Silliman, J., Fried, M. G., Ross, L., & Gutierrez, E. (2004). *Undivided rights: Women of color organizing for reproductive justice*. Cambridge, MA: South End Press.

Talwar, S. (2002). Decolonisation: Third world women and conflicts in feminist perspectives and art therapy. In S. Hogan (Ed.), *Gender issues in art therapy* (pp. 185–193). London, England: Jessica Kingsley Publication.

Talwar, S. (2010). An intersectional framework for race, class, gender, and sexuality in art therapy. *Art Therapy: Journal of the American Art Therapy Association, 27*(1), 11–17.

Talwar, S. (2015). Culture, diversity, and identity: From margins to center. *Art Therapy: Journal of the American Art Therapy Association, 32*(3), 100–103.

Walker, L. E. (1977). Battered women and learned helplessness. *Victimology, 2*(3–4), 525–534.

Walker, L. E. (1979). *The battered woman*. New York, NY: Harper Perennial.

Young, J. (2015, November 9). *Apna Ghar (Our Home) – The Importance of Cultural Humility*. Retrieved from https://inclusivemigration.wordpress.com/2015/11/09/apna-ghar-our-home-the-importance-of-cultural-humility/.

8

RES(CRIP)TING ART THERAPY

Disability Culture as a Social Justice Intervention

Chun-Shan (Sandie) Yi

It takes people time to connect with a good psychotherapist. It can be especially challenging to find a therapist as a disabled woman of color who, as an art therapist, went through training in art therapy and counseling to master the same talk therapy techniques. After a few conversations about the accessibility of the mental health system for disabled people with my Crip sisters—fellow disabled women who identify disability as their socio-cultural and political identity— who reminded me the importance of self-care, I decided to give talk therapy another try.

I sat before Dr. B., a middle-aged, white woman with 23 years of counseling experience. As I returned to my memories of the traumatic break-up that still haunts me days and nights, I couldn't help but catch Dr. B.'s inquisitive eyes land exclusively on my fingers (I was born with two digits on each limb). This was followed by a frown every few seconds during the therapy session. She would then quickly shift to the professional therapist's body language—making eye contact and giving a few gentle head nods with "uh-huh . . . mmmm" here and there—but then she would return to staring at my fingers as soon as I looked away. As a Crip since birth, I am an expert at recognizing and deciphering strangers' impulses to stare at my body. I tried to stay focused on the issues I was discussing and needed help with, but Dr. B.'s behavior was becoming distracting and annoying.

In the midst of retelling my trauma, I had to shove my vulnerability aside. I pulled myself together and asked, "I noticed that you were looking at my hands. Disability is an important part of me; it is my identity, my politics, and activism. Are you comfortable with disability? Have you worked with disabled people?" Dr. B. smiled and began naming various diagnoses and pathologies she had dealt with in therapy. Then she added, "It's very nice that you can put a positive spin on your disability, not every disabled person can reach that point."

Didn't she hear my questions? It appeared to me that she was unaware of how her compliments on my individual will to "overcome" disability were a patronizing deflection that amounted to a microaggression. I asked her again, "So, YOU WERE looking at my hands?" Dr. B. first denied it, then responded, "Oh, I may have looked two or three times. I wanted to know what they [my fingers] look like and how uncomfortable they might make others feel!"

Her words brought back the years of embarrassment and heavy guilt that I carried in my body for eliciting jaw-dropping bewilderment, sympathetic sighs, screams, and shivers from people who were shocked at seeing my hands. By then, it was getting close to the end of the session and Dr. B. was ready to send me off. I shook off my internal waves of shame; I imagined the presence of my Crip sisters in the room with me as I gathered my strength and asked Dr. B. for her reasons to stare at my hands once again. This time, Dr. B. further justified herself by saying, "I don't want to look straight ONLY at your face while we sit here and talk." She became animated by thrusting her face and upper body towards my face to make a point. She sharpened the timbre of her voice, crossed her arms and then concluded, "It [my recognition of her behavior] may have to do with the sensitivities on your part!"

I walked out of the counseling room in shock and exhaustion. I could feel my brain racing as I recounted the dialogue that I just had with Dr. B., but my body felt cold and numb. I tried not to forget how she had just gaslighted me, negating my experience. If I had not had access to other politicized disabled people during my young adulthood, it would have been too easy for me to fall into the old trap, and allow my defense mechanisms to kick in and make what she said just a blur. As a child, my sense of reality was repeatedly altered whenever strangers intrusively stared and commented on my hands. Adults expected me to be strong and brave; they would tell me, "Oh, that's not true; it's only in your head . . . People mean no harm; they are just concerned!" People's responses have conditioned me to deny, and even shut down, my own feelings at times. It was always about how able-bodied viewers felt about my impairment, never about how I felt as a disabled person.

I wrote about my encounter with Dr. B. on Facebook. Many people responded to my post by sharing their unpleasant, and at times torturous, experiences when their therapists provided counseling based on medical narratives, assumptions, or stereotypes, about disability. My friends offered combative self-care strategies that had worked for them in dealing with the limited options in the existing mental health counseling/therapy service industry. A few of them offered to connect me with their therapists and told me how they had already "groomed" them with "disability 101," so I would not have to deal with ablesplaining. Conversations like these are why my Crip family matters and why a Disability/ Crip Culture community must exist. It comforts me to know that I can seek peer support and community wisdom. While many of us still live in isolation, and the availability of access to each other requires social capital, having access to my Crip peers in person, and/or via social media, has been an essential to my self-care. It angers and saddens me that when disabled people seek help from mental health providers we first need to manage our therapists' failure to recognize disability as something more than a medical issue, and to confront therapists' misuse of disability as a metaphor that only reinforces able-bodied privilege. How much more therapy do disabled people need in order to undo the damage done by professional and licensed therapists, the medical community, and others whose practices are informed by an ableist history?

As an art therapist with a visible congenital disability, I did not always want to affiliate with my Crip family. For me disability had always been a stigma, a source of shame, and a taboo, and I did not even realize that I was trying to ignore it. I was completely oblivious to "disability culture" and "disability identity" before I became politicized at the age of 25. I still have vivid memories of my transformation, of coming out Crip during Bodies of Work: The Chicago Festival of Disability Arts and Culture in 2006 (Ozler, 2006). As a newly minted art therapist, I was enthusiastic about using art as a tool for individual self-expression. My idealistic career vision, however, was shattered soon after attending the festival events, where many self-proclaimed "disabled" or "Crip" artist-activists expressed anger towards art therapy. They were frustrated by the assumption that art made by artists with disabilities is often a subject of psychological assessments or used for rehabilitation purposes, which reinforced the stigmatizing relationship between disabled people and health professionals. I tried to absorb and understand the rage surrounding art therapy from the disabled activists. I was taught to believe that art therapy is a loving, and nurturing profession. But I learned that the notion of "therapy" can be a form of oppression to disabled people. I was flustered, and wondered, have I just become a part of the problem when I naïvely thought I was joining in the solution to help disabled people?

This chapter's proposition—res(crip)ting art therapy with disability culture—grew from my concern about therapeutic practices, including art therapy, that overlook social justice for disabled people. As a self-identified disabled artist, woman of color, disability cultural worker, and art therapist, my roles overlap several boundaries when facilitating consciousness-raising work as a part of the emancipatory actions within the disability culture community. The field of art therapy is accustomed to approaching disability with an interventionist impulse. I question the parameters of art therapy, its assumptions and foundations, and even if art therapy is a culturally appropriate and responsible practice. In this chapter, I critique the deficit model of art therapy, then illustrate a working definition of how disability culture can help broaden the perspective of art therapy. By presenting concepts and theories from disability studies, as well an example from my work at Access Living, an advocacy and disability rights organization in the metropolitan Chicago area, I explore the potential of a community-based art practice informed by the Disability Arts movement and disability culture. I argue that an interventionist analogy of disability in art therapy only works to further the othering of disabled people; by incorporating an intersectional view of disability and Disability Culture in the mental health care industry, art therapists will create long-term systematic change at a grassroots level and a more encompassing, sustainable social justice-based art therapy practice.

Disability Discourse

"Can you do _____ (fill in a daily task)?"

"Did the surgery help with your fine motor skills?"

"You should be grateful that your defect is minor . . . some people can't even walk, right?"

"Are you waiting for a cure for your 'genetic defect?'"

"Have you considered adoption in the future?"

Like many of my Crip brothers and sisters, strangers often question my ability to perform daily tasks and the ramifications of exercising my right to bear children. The questions above reflect the power of the medical model, which sees disability as a defect, a "lack-of," or a dysfunctional and pathological issue situated within the individual (Goodley, 2011). The medical model of disability considers individuals as subjects that require corrective and/or rehabilitative procedures to "fix" the condition. It relies on the concept of normality to differentiate, define, and categorize human differences as abnormalities. It often assigns the individual with a disability to the passive role of a suffering patient. The expectation is for the disabled patient to receive help from trained professionals, who are experts at offering a diagnosis, executing treatment and rehabilitation plans, and ultimately eliminating any abnormality (Mackelprang & Salsgiver, 2009).

Therapy is an institutionalized engagement and agreement between therapists and clients. The current mental health industry is a part of the neoliberal market, which prioritizes productivity and profitability (Gipson, 2017; Kuri, 2017). Most art therapists would agree that art therapy is a practice that focuses on clients' artmaking processes rather than on the final products. But the field of art therapy as a whole is not immune to the product-oriented demand of the capitalist world. Therapists monitor and document patients' diagnoses and progress, not only for treatment, but also as evidence in order to receive insurance reimbursements. As a result, disabled people face not only the inherent stigma leveled against disability, but also the structure of a market of care that expects patients to show progress and get better. As long as the mechanism of neoliberalism operates within the mental health care system, it is inevitable that the threshold for funneling resources to disabled people will be regulated primarily through medical and rehabilitation models, which reduces disability to individual responsibility. Art therapists must be vigilant about how economic factors determine the institutional infrastructure within art therapy, and how they further control the accessibility and quality of therapeutic services allocated to marginalized communities. Essentially, art therapists must begin seeing disability beyond medical terms by moving into a sociological framing of disability (Longmore, 2003).

Disability activists and disability studies scholars (Garland-Thomson, 2011; Kuppers, 2009; Goodley, 2011; Sandahl, 2009) use the social model as a framework, and argue that disability is not a lack of normative functioning. Rather, disability is produced when environmental, architectural, physical, attitudinal, and systemic barriers hinder people with impairments from participating as active members of society. The social model breaks the individualized treatment approach to disability. It acknowledges that a disability is not a singular and isolated human biological attribute. The social models of disability calls attention to how societal, cultural, economic, racial, gender, political, and religious factors both include, and exclude, disabled people. The late disability studies scholar, Paul Longmore (2003) stated, "when devaluation and discrimination happen to one person it is biography, but when in all probability similar experiences happen to millions, it is social history" (p. 39). The term "disabled people" means people who are "disabled" by prejudice, discrimination, and inequality in society. Thus, disability is a systemic and social justice issue.

The social model of disability, however, does not address individuals lived experience of impairments. Removing architectural barriers, rewriting employment policies, and installing lifts on buses will not eliminate the physical and psychological pain, debilitating illness, and chronic fatigue that some people may experience. The political/relational model—a radical social model centered on a feminist framework of disability—acknowledges disability as multifaceted and contextual. It recognizes the need for medical intervention that sustains disabled people's lives (Kafer, 2013). Kafer (2013), in her book *Feminist Queer Crip*, reminds us that ". . . by positioning ourselves only in opposition to the futures imagined through the medical model, and shutting down communication and critique around vital issues, we limit the discourse at our disposal" (p. 8). And, it must be said, advancements in medical technology have improved the physical, psychological, and mental health of disabled people (Mackelprang & Salsgiver, 2009). Nevertheless, art therapists need to be equally cautious when defining disability exclusively by either the medical model or the social model.

Critiquing Art Therapy: A Deficit Model

Art therapy has traditionally drawn its theories and practices from a wide range of disciplines, including psychiatry, psychology, psychotherapy, counseling, education and art, among others (Yi & Talwar, in press). As a cross-disciplinary practice, art therapy has sought to reinvent its approach based on its traditional origins, while making an effort to claim that art therapy can be a stand-alone practice. Art therapists have also taken pains to gain public recognition as professionals whose practice is comparable to that of other prominent mental health services. In doing so, art therapy has inevitably inherited specific paradigms, hierarchies, and power relations from the disciplines it has drawn from (Yi, 2010).

Hall (2000) states that art therapy is a product of its founders' intellectual curiosity. The foundations of art therapy have ignored the marginalization that disabled people have experienced historically. The field of art therapy is founded on the concept of normality versus pathology, thus drawing on a medical interventionist model (Yi, 2010). Disability studies scholars have critiqued art therapy for being an extension of normalization (Kuppers, 2006) and the product of the "epistemologies of able-bodiedness" (Snyder & Mitchell, 2001). This means that the knowledge and working methods behind art therapy inevitably validate and privilege able-bodied people by theorizing "what's wrong" with bodies and their impairments. Disability studies scholars also critique art therapy for employing an individualized approach, which depoliticizes and decontextualizes disabled people's cultural expressions (Kuppers, 2006; Barnes, 2003). Such criticisms ring true when disability is viewed from a medical model of deficiency that needs to be managed, rehabilitated, or simply cured.

It thus behooves art therapists to question the prerequisites mandated for admission to an Art Therapy Master's Program approved by the American Art Therapy Association (AATA). Among other academic credits, a course in "standardized human growth and development," such as developmental psychology and abnormal psychology, is required prior to applying for admission to any art therapy program. During their training, students learn to use the Diagnostic and Statistical Manual (DSM) of Mental Disorders as a main reference. And all too often a majority of the employment sites, such as hospitals, rehabilitation centers, shelters, psychiatric wards, special education schools, and correctional facilities, require art therapists to assess, manage, and treat the client/patient's presenting issues.

Ethical principle 7.1 of the American Art Therapy Association (AATA) states that "Art therapists do not discriminate against or refuse professional service to anyone on the basis of age, gender identity, race, ethnicity, culture, national origin, religion, sexual orientation, disability, socioeconomic status, or any basis proscribed by law" (AATA, 2013). At the same time, AATA largely ignores "disability" as a multicultural community. This is problematic as the organization strives to emphasize multiculturalism in shaping its organizational structure, ethical standards, and accredited training programs. Art therapists have spent over 40 years working with people with disabilities, but there have been few articles within the field's professional journals citing concepts and literature from disability culture and/or Deaf culture perspectives (Spaniol, 1990, 1994; McGraw, 1995). Indeed, only a handful of educators have begun addressing issues of disability beyond the scope of medical and counseling frameworks (Hedley, 2013; Talwar, 2015a, 2015b).

Art therapy has primarily situated itself in a European-American tradition with leaders and educators who have mostly been white, middle-class, and non disabled people (Junge & Asawa, 1994; Kaplan, 2002; Talwar, 2002). The majority of trained art therapists come from privileged socio-economic, cultural, and educational backgrounds. By contrast, a large number of clients/patients with disabilities who are surviving in the current mental health care system are people of color living on the margin. Thus, their quality of care is more likely to be compromised due to race and poverty (McGuire & Miranda, 2008). Rabinow (1984) uses Foucauldian theories to illustrate the mechanism of discipline that art therapists need to be aware of. This includes how their professional roles are part of a system to regulate and reinforce sexism, classism, and racism. Art therapists need to be cautious of reinforcing ableist social norms that rely on stereotypical representations of the disabled as vulnerable people who need to be "helped" or "rescued." It is imperative that the art therapy curriculum and post-graduate training focus on being attuned to gendered and racialized economic power structures. It is especially important to understand how disability is entangled within the web of identity and difference.

Disability Culture, Disability Art, and Identity

What can a cultural identity-based approach of disability offer art therapists working in an ableist society? All individuals, if they live long enough, will experience disability at some point in their lives. However, not all of them will seek out and bond with other disabled people. Disability culture grew out of the International Disabled People's Movement in the 1960s and '70s, when disabled people worked on raising consciousness and fighting for access and civil rights (Barnes, 2003; Kuppers, 2009). As a human manifestation that has been likened to a tool (Levin, 2010), culture can change society. Disability culture is a set of values, shared histories, customs, and ways of being associated with a collective experience. As a minority expression, disability culture reflects disabled people's group consciousness through shared systemic and collective oppression, language, identity, and lifestyle. It is a community response growing out of social injustice, institutional isolation, and segregation. Often, an individual may grow up as the only person with a disability in his/her/their family, so meeting other disabled people, who know what oppression feels like, can be a transformative emotional experience (Garland-Thomson, 2016).

Disability studies scholar and psychologist Carol Gill (1995) describes disability culture as the "emotional unity" of disabled people. Disabled people form a peer support network for each other at community gatherings and political engagement meetings, where they share knowledge and resources, process their experiences, and come up with strategies to confront stigma and discrimination. Connecting with fellow disabled people has thus created a society, and subculture, where participating members forge alliances: brotherhood, sisterhood, and what we might even call "Criphood." As a defense mechanism against oppression, isolation, and discrimination (Barnes, 2003; Kuppers, 2007), disability culture is a phenomenon that reflects disabled people's self-determination, empowerment, and a growing political strength leading to positive changes.

Disability culture is a process of reshaping and redefining the existing social rules and overturning the measures that have excluded and alienated disabled people. It is a relational process of building an interactive, communicative, and responsive system of care-relationships for bodies that do not conform to society's expectation of "normal" and "functional." To disrupt the history of hiding and shaming disability, it is often necessary for people to come out as disabled. This is not only a sign of self-acceptance, but also a desire to reveal the truth through stories and the multiplicity of disability narratives. When the arts are presented in the context of disability politics, they can become a bonding agent and advocacy platform for fellow-disabled people to "undo the history of exclusions" (Kuppers, 2011, p. 4) and use the arts as an agent to cultivate community and solidarity.

Disability Art, as a genre and an art movement, is the work of artists who explore the multiple meanings of disability on a personal, interpersonal, collective, political, and artistic level (Sandahl, 2009). Art that falls under the category of Disability Art examines and critiques traditional representations of disabled bodies. It claims visibility for disability, and may also challenge what access means through artistic expression. Emotional engagement, and accessibility, are central concerns of the disabled artist and disability culture in general (Cooley & Fox, 2014). Disability Art and public events centered on disability culture require accessibility as part of the audiences' participation. Accessibility and disability accommodations intervene in ableist spaces and social structures through physical and sensory changes to spaces from which disabled people are usually excluded. In this way space and accessibility become a way to rescript cultural and social practices by shifting pathology to identity (Garland-Thomson, 1997).

Many of the artists who associate themselves with the Disability Art movement are often inclined to self-identify as "disabled" or even "Crip" as an identity category (Sandahl, 2003). Unless people have access or exposure to other politicized individuals who identify as Disabled or Crip, disability may remain a stigma, perceived pathology, taboo, or label. Disability is a collective experience and a fluid construct when it comes to identity. Feminist disability studies theorists illustrate the parallels between gender and disability as concepts permeating all cultural and social structures (Garland-Thomson, 1997; Hall, 2011). Unlike other biologically inherited or ethnic identities, disability is often reclaimed as a relational identity, not an isolated attribute, or a singular issue/experience. It is interconnected with other identities, (such as race, class, gender, and sexuality, among others) as a sociopolitical reality. It is imperative that we recognize how disability is produced as part of the ideological system that has marginalized disability identity (Garland-Thomson, 1997). Identity politics with regard to disability, therefore, helps to formulate a sense of belonging and solidarity. Examining the social construction of disability from a feminist lens expands the knowledge of disability identity and its multiplicity of interpretation and analysis.

Disability Art and Culture Projects at Access Living

Garland-Thomson (1997) argues that disability culture intervenes in ableist structures and rescripts cultural and social practices by shifting pathology to identity. How would community organizers facilitate such a shift at a grassroots level? At the beginning of my artist-in-residency with the Arts and Culture Project at Access Living, one of the core partners of Bodies of Work (BOW): Network of Disability Art and Culture, I was recovering from my encounter with Dr. B, and was seeking a space to heal and create personal connections outside of institutionalized mental health care services. I launched several exploratory projects that were in line with the independent living and disability culture philosophy at Access Living (www.accessliving.org/). Here, I discuss an advocacy photobooth project and a disabled youth self-advocacy workshop as an example of how the arts can support and cultivate a sense of disability belonging and identity affiliation, and give a voice to disability culture.

Advocacy Photobooth Project

Access Living's International Women's Day celebration in 2013 focused on the intersection of disability and women's issues. With help from the Empowered FeFes, the Access Living advocacy group mainly comprising disabled women of color, we made props for a photobooth and invited people to pose with the props as a way to contribute to disability advocacy by making personal statements (Figures 8.1 and 8.2). Some props were generic—lips, glasses, crowns, mustache, or hearts. Others were more topically focused: a uterus, a megaphone, a microphone inscribed "speak out," a steering wheel with "consumer control," the iconic ADAPT symbol (grass-root disability rights organization's design of wheelchair user ripping off handcuffs), and a solidarity fist. There were also a few blank thought bubbles for people to write in their own messages. Participants in the photobooth sessions, mostly consumers (a word reclaimed by the disability rights movement to denote control over services received as a self-directed participant (DeJong, 1979)), staff, and a few walk-ins, posed for the camera using the props.

Many participants quickly recognized the fun and entertaining aspects of a photobooth. After I introduced the activism themed props to the participants, many of them would pause for a moment as they inspected and drew personal connections to the props. Then they shared with me:

> "Oh, I love the steering wheel, 'consumer control' is what disabled people like me need!"

> "It took me a long time to speak up, but I am learning."

> "How do you spell power? A-D-A-P-T!"[1]

The photographs were then organized into an online album for public viewing. This project lasted only two weeks, but as a part of the larger Arts and Culture Project it sparked the growth of other projects (Figures 8.1 and 8.2).

Disabled Youth Self-Advocacy Workshop

In 2015 the ADA marked its 25th anniversary. One of the programs that the youth advocacy organizers launched at Access Living was working on self-advocacy with students with disabilities from the Chicago Public Schools. This project was co-facilitated by two art therapy graduate student interns from the School of the Art Institute of Chicago, Claudia Angel and Amelia Thomley. A group of high school students in special education made four visits to learn about disability culture and disability accommodations as their rights under the ADA. They visited Access Living's permanent Disability Art collections and learned about my photographic portraits wearing body adornments prior to meeting with me. "Oh, you're THE disabled artist! I saw your art on the wall!" a student identified me excitingly. For our first art workshop together, I decided to use the props from the photobooth to explore self-representation and self-advocacy, which require attending to the self and to social relationships with fellow disabled people.

FIGURE 8.1 Photobooth project

FIGURE 8.2   Photobooth project

Drawing on the approach adapted from the work of drama therapist Josephine Lin, a multidisciplinary artist in Taiwan, I initiated a conversation about a "touch free" zone as the work involves physical interaction with each other's bodies. All of us, the facilitators, students with various physical, developmental, and/or emotional disabilities, and four special education teachers, were active participants. Before the exercise, we created group agreements and encouraged students to express their needs, including leaving or asking for personal space during the group activity. The workshop began by honing in on participants' physical and emotional senses through a partnering exercise in which students took turns creating gestures by positioning another person's body. We reminded students to check in with their partners about appropriate and acceptable physical touch, and to give space and time if their partners used mobility or communication devices.

In the following group performance practice, students began to strike a pose on stage, one by one, without announcing what narratives they intended to create with their bodies. The group exchanged feedback about the "human sculptures." Their collaboration was intuitive and spontaneous. At the end of the exercise, we discussed the experiences and observations, both as audience and as performers. The conversations provided an opportunity to create a dialogue about the interpretation of bodies. Through this process, we re-envisioned the meaning of displaying disability, identifying personal needs and projecting and receiving stares. This exercise allowed the youth to gain knowledge about disability terminology and to name different ways disabled bodies are represented socially.

For the closing activity, participants paired up and shared a secret inspired by the group activity. I asked them to make a "helping space" by being empathic and non-judgmental towards each other. After a moment of silence, Maria (pseudonym) said, tearfully, that she did not like her disability. Jamie (pseudonym) interjected her passionate encouragements. I recognized Jamie's kind intentions, but I asked her to hear Maria's pain before offering something that she considered more positive. Jamie lowered her head, tears ran down her cheeks, and she did not want to engage with me. By then, it was time to wrap up the session. I offered myself as a resource to Jamie. A teacher followed up with her and later confirmed that she was fine. While the interns and other teachers rounded up the students for their bus, a few female students formed a circle around me and said they were afraid that other people would find out about their (non-apparent) learning disabilities. I responded, "It can be scary to experience it alone, let's explore ways to talk about disability in art next week!" Students revealed a sense of relief as they dropped their tight shoulders, smiled, and said goodbye.

The final performance workshop entailed everyone taking turns with a chosen prop and striking poses to express their disability needs. The group then created narratives for what they saw and offered interpretations. During discussion, students got to see how their peers' and teachers' choices of self-expression varied. Many students got excited and kept raising their hands for a chance to speak. The special education teachers later commented on how surprised they were to see students taking the initiative and discussing their ideas about disability. In the end, this project served to help disabled students give a voice to their everyday experiences of disability and build a relationship with their disability activist community (Figure 8.3).

Towards a Social Justice-based Art Therapy

Earlier in the chapter, I discussed the stigmatization of interventionist, medical model approaches in art therapy, and the negative connotation that disabled people's art and cultural products must serve rehabilitation purposes. Sandahl (2006) discusses the lack of quality arts education for students with disabilities, and art therapy is often the only opportunity for them to make art, generally while staying in rehabilitation centers and hospitals. While it is certainly my interest to address the lack of access to creative arts within the disability community, it is also to confront the construction of disability as a taboo.

As illustrated in my artist-in-residency at Access Living, art making was made accessible to the consumers at a physical, emotional, and conceptual level. By creating images and representations of disabled people moving their bodies

FIGURE 8.3 Workshop with special education students

and declaring their needs in public spaces, the two projects sought ways to explore the meaning of self and communal care as activism for social change. At the same time, it was also an opportunity to mine the everyday experiences of disabled people, especially the rhetoric of staring.

Garland-Thomson, in *Staring: How We Look* (2009), discusses staring and its dynamics in creating identities. All people experience staring, both as the one looking and the object of the sustained gaze. It constructs meaning about disability when non-disabled people encounter disabled people. Staring can be a convergence with the unexpected and extraordinary, and it can be a form of communication, perhaps a demonstration of dominance, but it may also stigmatize the object of the stare (Garland-Thomson, 2009). It is a cross-cultural phenomenon. Most parents will tell young kids seeing disabled people to "stop staring." But this imperative never stops the human impulse to do so, since it arises from a desire to know when engaging with the unknown. It may shame the individual's behavior, but, significantly, it carries the implication that disabled bodies are not to be looked at. Disabled people spend a lot of time dealing with ableist staring, but rarely, do disabled people get to spend time looking at each other as a community. Thus, the two projects were about bringing visibility to the often silenced and hidden performative desire of disabled people.

Practicing Self-Reflexivity

Feminist philosopher Judith Butler (1988), who coined the term "performativity," suggests that "language, gesture, and all manner of symbolic social sign" (p. 519) create a social reality in which each individual performs his/her/their identity. Social justice practice requires art therapists to be transparent with regard to their own performativity through multiple identities, including race, gender, class, sexuality, and ability/disability, among other markers of difference. How does the hybrid nature of art therapy speak to therapists' ability to determine what social scripts to follow when working with clients with disabilities? Can art therapists discern the nuances of their social reality in an ableist world and understand how their own performativity intersects or conflicts with a client's/patient's disability?

As a self-identified Crip artist of the disability community, I see working with a young generation of disabled students as an opportunity to model the process of naming and claiming disability. My training and sensitivity as an art therapist have enabled me to stay reflexive as I work with fellow disabled people with whom I share the memories and living history of oppression. Reflexivity is an intra-dynamic processing skill for community organizers and therapists who center their work in a social justice framework. It is not about exercising counseling techniques to provide descriptive solutions as help. Rather, reflexivity requires us to understand how issues of disability impact our personal lives and what sort of social norms surrounding disability we have absorbed. Reflexivity is like a scanner that captures and analyzes the decisions that therapists make when interacting with disabled people, including how and when they ask consumers questions, how they listen and take in information from their consumers. Reflexivity is akin to opening a door, to observing and recognizing how each of us is part of a matrix of power relationships (Collins & Bilge, 2016).

Conclusion: Res(crip)ting Disability Narratives

Rather than writing this chapter as conventional "case studies" for an art therapy audience, my intention was to create snapshots of how we build disability culture and activism as a continuation of the larger disability justice movement at Access Living. Disability narratives in history and contemporary culture have shaped the way art therapists understand disability, but art therapists have also played a role in scripting disability narratives. When art therapists present case studies to illustrate the effectiveness of interventions and results produced for specific "populations," they do so by focusing on symptoms and diagnoses along with other demographic markers.

Art therapists need to recognize how their portrayals of disability paint only "what's wrong" and "what intervention works" when illustrating the individual's story. In the context of institutionalized therapy, disability narratives have become forbidden tales, erasing disabled people's self-representation. Art therapists must commit to seeking alternative ways to represent disability narratives.

If art therapists want to embrace a social justice framework informed by a radical social model of care, they will need to become equal partners with the disability culture community and fellow-activists, shedding the clinical role of the expert. As art therapists, we must keep a versatile practice and begin thinking about ways to make contributions to the Disability Art and Culture movement. Disability culture events are about cultivating a site for disabled people to feel comfortable enough to come out as disabled people. As allies, art therapists can help disabled clients use art to talk through their feelings about the disablement, stigma, and shame they often feel in an ableist society. Art therapists can help connect disabled clients to disability culture communities and support them to develop their own cultural identity by organizing outings and attending disability art and culture events with their clients. Finally, as therapists use self-reflexivity in human engagement, and include an intersectional approach when examining their own uncomfortable feelings about disability, they will have begun the work of deconstructing the ableist myths often held about disabled people. This, in turn, will allow art therapists to use their skills as cultural workers and social practitioners to res(crip)t their dialogues with people with disabilities and their cultural representation.

Note

1 It is a popular chant that disabled people use when protesting with ADAPT, a National disability rights organization.

References

Access Living. (2008, March 11). Retrieved, from www.accessliving.org/

American Art Therapy Association (AATA) (2013). Ethical principles for art therapists. Retrieved from www.sec.state.vt.us/media/522906/AT-Attachment4_Code-of-Ethics.pdf

Barnes, C. (2003). *Effecting change: Disability culture and art.* Retrieved from http://disability-studies.leeds.ac.uk/files/library/Barnes-Effecting-Change.pdf

Butler, J. (1988). Performative acts and gender constitution: An essay in phenomenology and feminist theory. *Theatre Journal, 40*(4), 519–531.

Collins, P. H., & Bilge, S. (2016). *Intersectionality.* Cambridge, MA: Polity Press.

Cooley, J., & Fox, A. M. (2014). Disability art, aesthetics, and access: Creating exhibitions in a liberal arts setting. *Disability Studies Quarterly, 34*(1). Retrieved from http://dsq-sds.org/article/view/3288/3530

DeJong, G. (1979). Independent living: From social movement to analytic paradigm. *Archives of Physical Medicine and Rehabilitation, 60*(10), 435–446.

Garland-Thomson, R. (1997). Disability, identity, and representation: An introduction. In R. Garland-Thomson, *Extraordinary bodies: Figuring physical disability in American culture and literature* (pp. 5–18). New York, NY: Columbia University Press.

Garland-Thomson, R. (2009). *A cultural history. Staring, how we look.* New York, NY: Oxford University Press.

Garland-Thomson, R. (2011). Integrating disability, transforming feminist theory. In K. Hall (Ed.), *Feminist disability studies* (pp. 13–47). Bloomington, IN: Indiana University Press.

Garland-Thomson, R. (2016, August 19). Becoming disabled. *The New York Times.* Retrieved from www.nytimes.com/2016/08/21/opinion/sunday/becoming-disabled.html

Gill, C. (1995). A psychological view of disability culture. *Disability Studies Quarterly, 15*(4), 16–19.

Gipson, L. (2017). Challenging neoliberalism and multicultural love in art therapy. *Art Therapy: Journal of the American Art Therapy Association, 34*(3), 112–117. doi.10.1080/07421656.2017.1353326.

Goodley, D. (2011). *Disability studies: An interdisciplinary introduction.* London, England: Sage Publications Ltd.

Hall, K. (Ed. 2011). *Feminist disability studies.* Bloomington, IN: Indiana University Press.

Hall, N. (2000). Art therapy: Passing through the intersection. *Art Therapy: Journal of the American Art Therapy Association, 17*(4), 247–251.

Hedley, S. (2013). Dominant narratives: Complicity and the need for vigilance in the creative arts therapies. *The Arts in Psychotherapy, 40*(4), 373–381.

Junge, M. B., & Asawa, P. P. (1994). *A history of art therapy in the United States.* Mundelein, IL: American Association of Art Therapy.

Kafer, A. (2013). *Feminist, queer, crip.* Bloomington, IN: Indiana University Press.

Kaplan, F. (2002). Editorial. Cross-cultural art therapy: A now and future therapy. *Art Therapy: Journal of the American Art Therapy Association, 19*(4), 138.

Kuppers, P. (2006). Art therapy. In G. Albrecht (Ed.), *Encyclopedia of disability* (pp. 125–126). Thousand Oaks, CA: Sage Publications.

Kuppers, P. (2007). Performing determinism: Disability culture poetry. *Text and Performance Quarterly, 27*(2), 89–106.

Kuppers, P. (2009). Disability culture. In S. Burch (Ed.), *Encyclopedia of American disability history* (pp. 269–274). New York, NY: Facts on File.

Kuppers, P. (2011). *In disability culture and community performance: Find a strange and twisted shape.* New York, NY: Palgrave Macmillan.

Kuri, E. (2017). Toward an ethical application of intersectionality in art therapy. *Art Therapy: Journal of the American Art Therapy Association, 34*(3), 118–122.

Levin, M. (2010). The art of disability: An interview with Tobin Siebers. *Disability Studies Quarterly, 30*(2). Retrieved from http://dsq-sds.org/article/view/1263/1272

Longmore, P. (2003). *Why I burned my book and other essays on disability.* Philadelphia, PA: Temple University Press.

Mackelprang, R. W., & Salsgiver, R. O. (2009). *Disability: A diversity model approach in human service practice* (2nd Ed.). Chicago, IL: Lyceum.

McGraw, M. (1995). The art studio: A studio-based art therapy program. *Art Therapy: Journal of the American Art Therapy Association, 12*(3), 167–174.

McGuire, T. G., & Miranda, J. (2008). New evidence regarding racial and ethnic disparities in mental health: Policy implications. *Health Affairs, 27*(1), 393–403. doi:10.1377/hlthaff.27.2.393.

Ozler, N. (2006, April 15). *Bodies of work: The Chicago festival of disability arts and culture.* Retrieved from www.dexigner.com/news/7821.

Rabinow, P, (Ed.) (1984). *The Foucault reader.* New York, NY: Pantheon Books.

Sandahl, C. (2003). Queering the crip or cripping the queer? Intersections of queer and crip identities in solo autobiographical performance. *GLQ: A Journal of Lesbian and Gay Studies, 9*(1), 25–56.

Sandahl, C. (2006). Disability arts. In G. Albrecht (Ed.), *Encyclopedia of disability*. (pp. 406–408). Thousand Oaks, CA: SAGE Publications.

Sandahl, C. (2009). Disability art and artistic expression. In S. Burch (Ed.), *Encyclopedia of American disability history* (pp. 264–268). New York, NY: Facts on File.

Snyder, S., & Mitchell, D. (2001). Re-engaging the body: Disability studies and the resistance to embodiment. *Public Culture, 13*(3), 367–390.

Spaniol, S. (1990). Exhibiting art by people with mental illness: Issues, process and principles. *Art Therapy: Journal of the American Art Therapy Association, 7*(2), 70–78.

Spaniol, S. (1994). The power of language in the art therapeutic relationship. *Art Therapy: Journal of the American Art Therapy Association, 11*(4), 266–270.

Talwar, S. (2002). Decolonization: Third world women, conflicts in feminist perspectives and art therapy. In S. Hogan (Ed.), *Gender issues in art therapy* (pp. 185–193). London, England: Jessica Kingsley.

Talwar, S. (2015a). Culture, diversity, and identity: From margins to center. *Art Therapy: Journal of the American Art Therapy Association, 32*(3), 100–103.

Talwar, S. (2015b). Creating alternative public spaces: Community-based art practice, critical consciousness, and social justice. In D. Gussak & M. Rosal (Eds.), *The Wiley Blackwell handbook of art therapy* (pp. 840–847). Hoboken, NJ: John Wiley & Sons.

Yi, C. (2010). From imperfect to I am perfect: Reclaiming the disabled body through making body adornments in art therapy. In C. H. Moon (Ed.), *Materials and media in art therapy: Critical understandings of diverse artistic vocabularies* (pp. 103–118). New York: NY: Routledge.

Yi, S., & Talwar, S. (in press). Disability, art, and art therapy. In C. Sandahl, T. Heller, S.P. Harris, C. Gill, & R. Gould (Eds.), *Disability in American life: An encyclopedia of concepts, policies, and controversies.*

9

"THE SWEETNESS OF MONEY"

The Creatively Empowered Women (CEW) Design Studio, Feminist Pedagogy and Art Therapy

Savneet K. Talwar

> Nobody is just ever a refugee. Nobody is just a single thing. Yet in the public discourse today, we speak of people as a single thing – refugee, immigrant. We dehumanize people when we reduce them to a single thing.
>
> *(Chimamanda Ngozi Adichie)*

A few years ago, the CEW (Creatively Empowered Women) Design Studio was asked to be part of a local collaboration that highlighted the work of the CEW members, along with that of other refugee and immigrant communities in Chicago. The person heading the collaboration had her own vision, which was not explicit in the original invitation for collaboration. As the collaboration continued, I became uncomfortable in the way the members of CEW were represented, as immigrants or refugees. Adichie's words resonated with me, since I, too, am an immigrant. But I am also a woman of color, an educator, cultural worker, step-mother, and U.S. citizen. Being an immigrant is only one dimension of who I am. In this chapter, I want to take a feminist and intersectional perspective to trouble the boundaries of representations that only highlight the displacement and trauma of the members of CEW. In the years I have come to know the women, they have become for me more than just immigrants or refugees. They are as Bosnian or Pakistani, Muslim women, and they are strong and compassionate mothers, grandmothers, wives, sisters, friends, leaders, and the crafters who are an active part of the fabric of CEW (Figure 9.1).

In considering how to write this chapter, I struggled with ways to represent the members of CEW and the community studio collaboration. Questioning the ethics of telling someone else's story, I have tried not to fall into "romanticizing" (Shuman, 2005) a community based art therapy practice. I tell the story of the

FIGURE 9.1   (Left to right) CEW members: Anka, Harija, Fatima, Vera, Halida, Enisa, Fikereta, Barha, Savneet, Emina, and Dzemila

studio from the places of struggle and comradery that have transformed the community members and their interpersonal relationships. For me, as an art therapist, community-based practice has been the most challenging kind of collaborative work I have ever done. I have also tried to avoid representing the CEW members in the "context of the redemptive promise of narrative" (Shuman, 2005, p. 149). The question to ask, therefore, is not how the members of CEW have been served, but rather how the story of the CEW Design Studio has, in different ways, increased each participant's social capital utilizing a collaborative methodology of labor (Sangtin Writers Collective & Nagra, 2006). My contributions of intellectual labor as a university educator, art therapist, researcher, and English speaker, have shaped the direction CEW has taken and helped define its mission. In writing this chapter, I recognize the limitations of objectivity in a community studio practice that predominantly serves non-English speaking women, whose artistic labor is the essential element of the collaboration. At the same time, I also recognize that in describing the stories of the CEW members, I have an obligation to reflect on the essentializing concepts of empathy and trauma in order to tell a story without sensationalism (Shuman, 2005).

I was motivated to start this collaboration by my own interest in crafting practices and as a way to deepen my teaching and scholarship. I have always been interested in exploring how a community-based practice with immigrant and refugee women could support their wellbeing through art making by utilizing a feminist pedagogy, theories of empowerment, hospitality, and restorative self-care practices. I wanted to explore the connection between the making and doing of crafting as a means of building relationships and trust, as well as sharing memories to give experiences of trauma a place in the present. As such, I was interested in how a community studio could offer a social model of art therapy that collapsed the distinction between healing as a private encounter or individual responsibility and one that is collective and political (Cvetkovich, 2003; Talwar, 2015).

To this end, I acknowledge that the stories I tell are filtered through my experience of privilege as a member of CEW, and a researcher, scholar, and educator. I have received attention and respect from the art therapy community for my intellectual labor in initiating CEW. I have presented papers on the group at several universities and conferences across the country. Each presentation has challenged me to think of how to represent the program on behalf of my collaborators.

In this chapter, I share what I learned from the CEW members, and how my collaboration with them, including crafting, has altered and enriched my conceptualization of art therapy. Our collaboration does not have a neat linear narrative, since community collaborations like that of CEW can be messy encounters. Leaning on feminist pedagogy, I concentrate on the role crafting has played to support trauma narratives and wellbeing, in essence, how the joyful act of crafting and community collaboration can play a critical role in envisioning "new paradigms of care" that cultivate a sense of community, wellbeing, and social capital. These concepts are explored through moments that impacted me, including stories of when things went wrong, the moments of conflict that motivated deeper engagement and thinking, moments of miscommunication and lack of adequate translation, as well as the small acts and words of kindness that validate why we are committed to meeting weekly. I begin by outlining feminist pedagogy and its link to labor and crafting. This is followed by a rethinking of models for trauma informed practice in art therapy. I end by contextualizing the feminist pedagogical approach that informs the core values of CEW: hospitality and restorative spaces for wellbeing; empowerment through crafting; and community and social transformation.

Feminist Pedagogy and Materiality of Craft

Feminism, Ahmed argues (2017), is about asking ethical questions and creating relationships that support those who are less supported in society. For her, "feminism is a collective movement" (p. 5). In particular, Ahmed points to the contributions of feminists of color like Audre Lorde, Gloria Anzaldúa, Kimberlé Crenshaw, Patricia Hill Collins, and bell hooks, who advocated for an intersectional analysis to fully grasp the impact of colonial histories on the lives of those who live on the margins. The writings of Anzaldúa, Lorde, hooks, and others brought lessons of the everyday "closer to the skin" (Ahmed, 2017, p. 10). Feminism, therefore, rests on the knowledge of the world and the forces that structure everyday life. Questioning the impact of globalization, capitalism, and neoliberalism means understanding the colonial histories that have exploited labor and marginalized knowledge and practices outside mainstream conceptions of work or therapy.

In the art world, feminist artists and craftivists have offered an extensive critique of the art v. craft binary (Bratich & Brush, 2011; Buszek, 2011; Han Sifuentes, n.d.), which they argue is a false one. Reacting to second wave feminism, many artists have embraced the domestic crafts, such as knitting, crocheting, and embroidery, moving the conversation about domesticity and labor from "old-fashioned and traditional" in order to "challenge contemporary issues" (Black & Burisk, 2011, p. 205). Chansky (2010) argues that third wave feminists moved to reclaim the domestic arts that had been devalued by second wave feminists and patriarchal structures. There is a renewed trend to value domestic arts among a younger generation of women who are learning to knit, sew, and take up abandoned labor practices. The Riot Grrrl movement has been representative of taking back knitting and sewing, which, they know, hearken back to traditional notions of femininity. The younger generation of artists are reclaiming craft practices to inflect the contemporary by using traditional forms of making (in contrast to the outsourcing of fabrication by artists such as Judy Chicago). At the same time, reclaiming traditional craft practices is a move to express and recognize "the irony of using the domestic arts as a way to express contemporary thought" (p. 682), and exploit its political potential.

Pentney (2008) calls attention to DIY culture and craftivism as capitalist's ventures that support consumerism. She argues that only upwardly mobile individuals with a considerable amount of disposable income can afford the cost of yarn, while reminding younger crafters of the subordinate practices that women abandoned in the spirit of gender equality. Fiber artist Han Sifuentes (n.d.) cautions against the self-congratulatory and celebratory nature of the domestic crafts, asking crafters to question the appropriation and fetishization of craft in contemporary culture. She argues that the labor of the artisans who use craft to make a living needs to be separated from the Western history of crafting for leisure. She suggests complicating the notions of traditional and contemporary, so as to not fetishize traditional crafts and their practitioners. Despite the art v. craft debate, Clover (2005) discusses the power of leadership and art-based social learning practices as means of constructing counter-narratives. She claims that imagination and creativity are tools for learning to exercise and challenge power against the backdrop of a neoliberalism in which it is easy to lose hope. There is, however, a strong push to re-contextualize imagination and innovative art-based pedagogies as a means "to educate, empower and demand visibility and justice" (p. 631). As Appadurai (1996) argues, the world today is characterized by disjointed structures of power that have generated acute problems of social wellbeing. The only positive force that encourages emancipation is the imagination.

Feminist theories of empowerment suggest that "power is the increased capacity to engage in meaningful interactions, critical thinking and leadership activities" (Narushima, 2004 as cited in Clover, 2005). In the context of CEW, a feminist pedagogy aims to deepen an understanding of everyday life as a means to reclaim the imaginative and creative power of making and to promote a new paradigm of care. Feminist pedagogies advocate for challenging, recreating, and transforming the world (Greene, 1995; Clover, 2000) to create new learning opportunities, imagining new possibilities, and opportunities for collaboration. In this kind of venture, crafting becomes not only an object, but also a tool for critical learning (Clover, 2005). It is the tactical knowledge that stimulates both verbal and non-verbal interaction to actively engage in a critical arts-based inquiry.

Re-thinking Trauma and Art Making: Joy of Crafting

Several art therapists have written about trauma and the role art therapy can play in addressing the non-verbal aspect of memory (Hass-Cohen & Carr, 2008; King, 2016; Tripp, 2008; Talwar, 2007, among others). Trauma and neurobiology have become a staple of conversation among art therapists, yet trauma has been viewed from the perspective of diagnosis and recovery; the responsibility for wellness falls on the individual rather than on communities. There remains an urgent need to have a better understanding of trauma and how crafting can support health and wellbeing. The early definitions of art therapy reject crafting as an authentic form of therapeutic practice (Kramer, 1966; Ulman, 1975). From a psychoanalytic perspective, trauma created a distinct division between the art v. craft binary. It was argued that the skill involved in crafting inhibited the patient from relaxing enough to induce the regression necessary to uncover pathological material. Ulman (1975) vehemently rejected the use of craft kits, paint by numbers, and coloring books. It is only in the past few years that crafting has made a comeback in art therapy (Cohen, 2013; Collier, Wayment, & Birkett, 2016; Garlock, 2016) by linking it to a form of restorative practice that supports affect regulation.

Researchers like Daniel Siegel and Peter Levine argue that trauma has mostly been reduced to diagnostic traits and categories of the Diagnostic Statistical Manual (DSM) of Mental Health. Both scholars have written extensively, cautioning therapists against reducing trauma to a rubric of Post-Traumatic Stress Disorder (PTSD), arguing that trauma is not a disease "but rather a human experience that is rooted in survival instincts" (p. xiii). According to Levine (2010), trauma, although a fact of life, does not have to be a life sentence. The "psychophysiological systems that govern trauma" (p. xiii) he writes, are also responsible for mediating affect regulation and feelings to facilitate states like empathy, connection, belonging, and feelings of goodness. There are few examples that show the value of community participation, making that involves loving attention, collective sharing, and support as a means of trauma recovery.

My goal is not to dismiss individualized forms of art therapy, but to demonstrate that clinical models are not the only ones responsive to trauma, suffering, and oppression (Talwar, 2015). Rather, social and community models of art therapy support concepts of belonging and wellbeing as a collective endeavor. The CEW Design Studio takes a trauma-informed art therapy approach to deal with systemic barriers affecting the refugee and immigrant women. By using crafting (knitting and crocheting) and economic empowerment, the program has a dual purpose: first, assist the members to overcome language barriers and build communication skills to develop social capital and, second, enjoy the benefits of crafting for health and wellbeing. Drawing on the therapeutic aspects of crafting, making, learning, and sharing skills, CEW members have an opportunity to share stories, as well as insights into how crafting has been a means of coping during difficult times: the stress of relocating, the experience of war, violence, and genocide. At CEW the process of crafting has become one of creative imagining that happens through engagement in repetitive acts of knitting or crocheting. The act of creating with a purpose, which calls for attentive looking and remembering, repetition, and revision, relates to assimilating the unassimilated sensorimotor reaction to trauma. The CEW program can be said to draw on the scientific and social significance of art therapy and crafting to promote wellbeing.

The benefits of crafting that CEW is predicated on are supported by a few different studies. A recent study by a group of neuroscientists reported that crafting could help those who suffer from anxiety, depression, or chronic pain. It may also ease stress, increase happiness, and protect the brain from damage caused by aging. Crafting is being heralded as a natural anti-depressant (Riley, Corkhill, & Morris, 2012). The benefits of craft, especially knitting, have received renewed interest. Most recently, the occupational therapy journal published an article on the therapeutic benefits of knitting. The article concludes that specific skills like knitting have significant psychological, cognitive, and social benefits, and can contribute to wellbeing and quality of life (Riley, Corkhill, & Morris, 2013). La Cour, Josephsson, Tishelman, and Nygard (2007) argue that creativity in everyday life can support, as well as be a means of forging, meaningful connections. According to Dickie (2011) creative activities play a significant role in helping people cope with loss and provide avenues for growth.

Another phenomenological study by Tzandidaki and Reynolds (2011) revealed a sense of competence and achievement that comes from crafting; they also reported a continuity of self in later life. A group of neuroscientists at the National Institutes of Health published an article emphasizing the importance of craft over passive activities, like watching TV, for older adults dealing with mild cognitive impairment (Geda et al., 2011). Examining the current trends in crafting, Kamial, Gonzaga, and Schwachter (2016) ask art therapists to reconsider the divide between fine arts and craft. They state that integrating crafting in an art therapy practice encourages self-expression and can support self-care.

Making and doing are deeply felt human experiences that leave a sensory impression on the maker. The sense of mastery that emerges from this kind of engagement is akin to the kind of self-regulation needed for everyday life (Levine, 2010).

Feminist Pedagogy: Lesson Learned in CEW

The CEW Design Studio started in 2012 and is in its fifth year of programming as I write this chapter. Over the course of the five years, programming at CEW has gone from the simple idea of meeting as a group, crafting for wellness, to embracing crafting as a genuine form of material labor using a feminist pedagogy. In particular, CEW has explored the critical role craft and labor can play in increasing the social capital of its members to promote wellbeing.

The members of CEW are mostly Bosnian or South Asian, Muslim, refugee and immigrant women who live in Chicago. The women range in ages from 64 to 82, and all are currently retired. Before coming to the U.S. some of the Bosnian women held professional jobs as teachers, nurses, or technicians. Upon relocation, many of them had to take up working class jobs (housekeeping, caretaking of older adults, or nurses' assistants) owing to a lack of English or because their degrees from Bosnia were not recognized in the U.S.

The Bosnian and South Asian women have all witnessed genocide. The Bosnian women are survivors of the armed conflict and ethnic cleansing that took place in Bosnia and Herzegovia from 1992 to 1995. As survivors, several of the women have been diagnosed with PTSD, depression, anxiety, and other related issues; in addition, they live on meager incomes as a result of being on disability or social security. Assimilating into a new culture and learning a new language has been the biggest hurdles for the CEW participants and gaining a sense of agency. As in many communities across many cultures, the stigma of mental health remains one of the most powerful for immigrants and refugees (Kramer, Kwong, Lee, & Chung, 2002; Sue & Sue, 2016). Keyes and Kanes (2004) indicate that the impact of the loss of one's home, relocation, and acculturation to a new society, along with taking on new social roles, can have a severe impact on the mental health of the displaced. Cultural factors such as language, age, gender, and other markers of difference can influence acculturation outcomes and access to mental health services. Adopting a perspective that is respectful and unique to each person's adaption process is thus important.

Most of the members of CEW were drawn to the program by their advanced knitting and crocheting skills and their sheer joy in crafting (Figure 9.2). In addition, the chance to earn a supplemental income from their work was appealing. The program was piloted as a ten-week group to explore the potential for crafting as a means to economic justice and wellbeing. The first sale in December 2012 raised $260, which set the stage for developing the program over the next several years (by 2016 sales had risen to $9,300). The success of the pilot project encouraged the collaborators to develop a unique framework for an art therapy

FIGURE 9.2 Vera and Harija

community practice, one that emphasized the significance of labor and crafting in promoting wellbeing. Following the emerging studies that have been cited, the project emphasized providing practical, economic, and emotional support to the CEW members coping with depression, anxiety and related issues.

Founded as it is on a feminist pedagogy, the CEW Design Studio follows three main precepts: hospitality and creating restorative spaces for wellbeing; empowerment through crafting; and community and social transformation.

Hospitality and Creating Restorative Spaces for Wellbeing

It is the day of Eid following the long month of Ramadan. Bàhra brought some baklava to share with the group members for Eid. After greeting and wishing everyone a "Happy Eid," the women settle in to show what they have made. Džemila displays the shawl she has made from the fine silk yarn she took the week before, Emina has made a new design of her famous socks, and Harija has knitted three hats. Bàhra opens her bag and shares the five knitted fingerless gloves, a crotched lace shawl, and some necklaces she has made. Each time a person shares her creations, a loud sound of laughter or applause breaks out. Often the women clap to show their appreciation and support for the finished piece. As the items make their way through the hands of all the members, Harija asks Bàhra to show her how to do the lace stitch for the shawl she made. Bàhra begins to teach Harija the stitch; Sophie is busy checking off the items that were made from the yarn the women took home the week before. I bring the box of tags so the women can label their work for pricing, while one of the interns checks in to ask who would like tea or coffee. As I place the box of tags on the table, Vera asks me to wind some yarn for her. I step by the yarn winder, as Ashley walks over to ask me a question about the upcoming sale.

The hospitality model is drawn from womanist scholarship. Although womanism emerged from the lived experiences of black women (Walker, 1983), Phillips (2006) argues that a womanist methodology "of social transformation cohere[s] around the activities of harmonizing and coordinating, balancing, and healing" (p. xxvi). It focuses on cultivating relationships that incorporate everyday activities, and upholds the idea "that physical and psychological well-being provide a necessary foundation for social justice and commonweal" (p. xxvi). A fundamental focus in such an approach is creating restorative spaces that promote wellbeing through hospitality.

At the CEW Design Studio, hospitality plays an important role in creating space that is welcoming and respectful. The aim is to facilitate positive encounters, and to value the worth and integrity of the members' craft and labor skills. As Phillips (2006) states,

> hospitality is a practice that facilitates a positive encounter between people who are strangers or "others" to one another, setting the stage for possible friendship or collaboration. Hospitality is the fundamental to managing differences . . . providing a means of connection . . . to mediate and reduce conflict through the heartening effect of care, pleasure, and festivity.
>
> *(p. xxviii)*

Hospitality as a method of social transformation has been an age-old form of interaction across cultures and traditions that are invested in caretaking sensibilities and everyday activities of wellbeing.

Empowerment through Crafting

I have been mostly an intuitive knitter, making up patterns on my own. During the Christmas break of 2014 my husband was taken ill and needed surgery. To keep my focus, I decided to challenge myself to learn to knit a triangular shawl from a pattern. I remember making the shawl and waiting to take it to the studio to show my accomplishment to the women after the holidays. On the first day back at the studio, I shared my knitted shawl with the women. Applauding my efforts, the women eagerly started to ask me questions about how I had made the shawl. Proudly, I agreed to share with them my new pattern reading skills in the next session. The following session, I had special yarn and needles for each of the members and began to teach them to make the shawl. After an hour of frustration, I realized that the Bosnian women and I did not have a common language for knitting. The simple process of knit and purl became a confusing and frustrating process of getting lost in translation. This was the first time in two years I realized that I had been taught the British style of knitting, while the Bosnian women used the Continental style of knitting. The following week, two of the CEW members had figured out the pattern on their own and presented finished shawls, starting a whole new shawl knitting movement in the studio.

The word "empowerment" has been frequently used by art therapists to argue for outcomes-approach-based community studios. Most studio approaches to art therapy have focused on empowerment by relying on mental health stigma reduction, raising self-esteem, and building community relationships using the arts to create socially inclusive spaces (Moon & Shuman, 2013; Ottermiller & Awais, 2016; Timm-Bottos, 2006). The concept of empowerment has its roots in the work of Paulo Friere, in that it implies a recognition of "power[s] that embody relations of domination" (as cited in Shrewsbury, 1993, p. 168). Although a few art therapists have written about empowerment, a crucial and not unrelated focus has been on reducing power differentials. At CEW, negotiating and understanding power remains a challenging aspect of community work. While the goal is to decenter the power of the staff and interns through a participatory action approach, policing power relationships remains a complex task. Collaborations are messy encounters and regularly reveal lessons in power. Whenever therapeutic practice moves beyond the four walls of the office with the therapist and a client, to a place where one has to deal with the uncertainty and fluidity of a group, there are no neat outcomes. The process turns to embracing "art therapy practice as a living inquiry."

In an attempt to decentralize power, CEW aims to create a space where multiple voices can emerge by embracing the concept of "membership" over a "client/therapist" model. As a means of decentering power, all participants are considered to be members, including the organizers, who participate in the major decisions in running the studio. The weekly meetings are based on the members' common interest in knitting and crocheting, learning and sharing skills. Each fall, to set the stage, the studio programming begins with a review of the member contract that is signed by all participants, including the staff and interns. The contract outlines the importance of meeting weekly, being open to developing new skills, sharing skills and knowledge, maintaining communication with the staff, being open to conflict resolution, and maintaining a cooperative and supportive space in the studio. Members are also required to help at sales and craft shows. Most importantly, the CEW members participate in pricing their products, to determine what is a fair price for selling them. All materials are provided for the members. They get 70 percent of the proceeds upon sale of their products and 30 percent goes towards purchasing new materials.

Despite good intentions, conflict emerges regularly. For example, the women do not knit from patterns because they have advanced skills and can reproduce an item that they see in a picture. On many occasions, the question has emerged about who gets to claim the design or pattern. Under such circumstances, conversations about ownership and sharing are encouraged. These are the moments in which referring to the membership contract has been helpful. Often, when conflict has arisen between two women due to competition, the group meetings focus on resolving disagreements and welcoming members despite their conflict.

The women served at CEW speak little to no English. To ensure that the members know what they can expect from their participation in the studio, the contract is translated into Bosnian, Urdu, or Hindi. The membership contract allows for the members to know their rights in the studio and maintain the power of creative energy. Another important factor is the role of the translators. For the first few years, CEW operated with minimal translation, the members communicating through crafting and sharing as illustrated in the example above. A translator was engaged only when an issue emerged and communication had come to a standstill. Over the course of time it became essential that a translator be available at all times so the members could communicate openly and feel that their voices were represented at all time.

It is a challenge to understand and negotiate power in a setting like CEW, particularly when new staff members or interns are introduced. Given the long association of the CEW members, the women have a tremendous sense of ownership, claiming the studio as their space. When a new coordinator was hired recently, an initial task was her earning the trust of the women and developing respect for their labor. When new interns enter CEW they are assigned to a mentor to learn how to knit and understand the value of the labor involved in craft practices. In most cases, the relationship with the mentors takes on a special meaning for the students. Yet, on many occasions the art therapy students have expressed disappointment when a typical weekly meeting is not about treating trauma, but seemingly about the practical aspect of making and doing. Some student interns have questioned how making and selling products at CEW can be art therapy.

Such questions go to the heart of how we conceptualize art therapy education and practice. Employing a trauma-informed approach, means focusing on wellness and the creative process that supports everyday life, rather than rekindling the trauma and vulnerability of past experiences of the CEW members for student learning. As Levine (2010) indicates, the capacity to self-regulate is what allows individuals to deal with arousal and difficult emotions. The act of crafting—knitting and crocheting—has been acknowledged by many CEW members as a means of coping and self-regulating (Shefsky, 2016). The arts and craft movement of the eighteenth and nineteenth centuries, inspired by the ideas of John Ruskin and William Morris, was predicated on idea that creative workers must be free to express themselves through their production and have control over their own labor and life. Crafting is a process of transforming materials into meaningful objects. The repetitive action involved in the making, the untangling of wool or thread, or following patterns is part of creative making, attentive looking, and the reworking process (Checinska, 2013); these are coping skills fundamental to everyday life.

Over the course of the program, many interns have witnessed the joy and empowerment the CEW member's experience when their products sell. As one member stated, "I spend money to buy food every day. The money I make from my knitted products is different. I am very careful in how I spend it, as it has the sweetness of my labor." To be paid for one's labor is directly linked to power, self-worth, and self-esteem. At CEW empowerment as a feminist pedagogical principle "embodies a concept of power as energy, capacity, and potential" (Shrewsbury, 1993, p. 168) that the members bring to the studio.

Community and Transformative Learning

It is Monday morning and I am just finishing up my meeting with Cassandra, the program coordinator/artist and Shwetha the fashion designer. I hear the elevator doors open and chattering. The studio door opens and the women walk in, greeting all the staff with laughter and hugs. As they take their seats, chatting with each other, they open their bags to show what they have made. After the show and tell ritual, the CEW members are introduced to the new project for the upcoming holiday season, the "handmade by design" collection. Shwetha has prepared a slide show and talks to the women about product design and color through three story boards she has prepared – new neutrals, decadent darks, and pop art. This morning there is an intensity in the conversation. While the women are excited about the project, they clearly convey their need for the specific yarn colors shown, give advice about the type of yarn that would be best to use, questioning their independence for translating the designs, time involved in the making products, and most importantly pricing the products.

During the first few years of the project, the CEW members made individualized "one of a kind" products. During the early years, any yarn donation was welcomed. There was little uniformity to the products; each was one of a kind. Over the years, as funding improved and sales increased, the CEW members asked that better quality materials be provided. There were conversations about products design and colors, but it was difficult to keep up with "one of a kind" products for online sales. There were just too many things to document. More recently, collaborating with fashion designer Shwetha Shantkumar and artist/photographer Cassandra Davis, the CEW women have engaged in the "handmade by design" line (Figure 9.3). The collaboration and experiments with color and design concepts resulted in a unique fashion line of uniform products.

FIGURE 9.3 Handmade by Design Collection by Shwetha Shantkumar

Photo by Cassandar Davis

The main goal of the CEW Design Studio is to create spaces for transformative learning. Art-based social learning practices are instrumental in constructing counter-narratives for the CEW members. When imagination and creativity become tools of learning, the results can be transformative. By re-contextualizing imagination and innovative art-based pedagogies CEW creates a space "to educate, empower and demand visibility and justice" (Clover, 2005, p. 631). Crafting becomes a source for imagination and creativity as a form of re-creating one's life and work, opening opportunities for people to imagine alternative ways of being and finding meaning. Creating new learning opportunities and imagining new possibilities for action, can enlarge the scope of art therapy practice and develop alternative platforms for wellbeing.

Conclusion

In conclusion, theories of power are intimately linked to theories of community and transformative learning. At the core of feminist pedagogy is a re-imagination of the learning community that allows for "autonomy of self and mutuality with others" (Shrewsbury, 1993, p. 170). Valuing the life experiences, skills, and knowledge of each community member is fundamental to CEW. While the staff initiate new projects, the artisans are equal collaborators in the project and offer their candid advice.

Parker (1984), in *Subversive Stitch*, claims that crafting became a marker of domesticity as a part of the industrialization movement and the marginalization of women's work, which remains true even today. Although in the past decade crafting has gained a renewed interest, reclaiming the traditional arts of femininity

FIGURE 9.4 CEW logo by Sophie Canadé

Photo by Cassandar Davis

and claiming pride in traditional crafting, for middle class women still remains a leisure activity. The CEW Design Studio tries to remain cautious around fetishizing traditional crafts and the labor of the artisans. While on the one hand, the studio space is an intersectional community space where issues of gender, age, culture, family, emotions, and memories can be revisited, on the other, the central focus of the studio remains on material, products, and labor practices. To this end, the raised clenched fist holding knitting needles and crochet hooks (Figure 9.4) has become a symbol for CEW and the labor involved in troubling the boundaries between the domestic and contemporary arts and its relationship to art therapy pratice.

References

Adichie, C. N. (2014). *The danger of a single story*. Retrieved from www.ted.com/talks/chimamanda_adichie_the_danger_of_a_single_story.

Ahmed, S. (2017). *Living a feminist life*. Durham, NC: Duke University Press.

Appadurai, A. (1996). *Modernity at large*. Minneapolis, MI: University of Minnesota Press.

Black, A., & Burisk, N. (2011). Craft hard die free: Radical curatorial strategies for craftivism. In M. E. Buszek (Ed.), *Extra/ordinary: Craft and contemporary art* (pp. 204–221). Durham, NC: Duke University Press.

Bratich, J., & Brush, H. (2011). Fabricating activism: Craft-work, popular culture, gender. *Utopian Studies, 22*(2), 233–260.

Buszek, M. E. (Ed.) (2011). *Extra/ordinary: Craft and contemporary*. Durham, NC: Duke University Press.

Chansky, R. (2010). A stitch in time: Third-wave feminist reclamation of needled imagery. *The Journal of Popular Culture, 43*(4), 681–700.

Checinska, C. (2013). Crafting difference. *Engage: The International Journal of Visual Art and Gallery Education, 33*(Winter), 87–100.

Clover, D. (2005). Sewing stories and acting activism: Women's leadership and learning through drama and craft. *Ephemera, 5*(4), 629–642.

Cohen, R. A. (2013). Common threads: A recovery programme for survivors of gender based violence. *Intervention: Journal of Mental Health and Psychosocial Support in Conflict Affected Areas, 11*(2), 157–168.

Collier, A. D., Wayment, H., & Birkett, M. (2016). Impact of making textile handcrafts on mood enhancement and inflammatory immune changes. *Art Therapy: Journal of the American Art Therapy Association, 33*(4), 178–185. DOI: 10.1080/07421656.2016.1226647.

Cvetkovich, A. (2003). *An archive of feelings: Trauma, sexuality and lesbian cultures*. Durham, NC: Duke University Press.

Dickie, V. A. (2011). Experiencing therapy through doing: Making quilts. *OTJR: Occupational, Participation and Health, 31*(4), 209–215. DOI: 10.3928/15394492-20101222-02.

Garlock, L. R. (2016). Stories in the cloth: Art therapy and narrative textiles. *Art Therapy: Journal of the American Art Therapy Association, 33*(2), 58–66. DOI: 10.1080/07421656. 2016.1164004.

Geda, Y., Topazian, H., Roberts, L., Roberts, R., Knopman, D., Pankratz, V. S., Christianson, T., Boeve, B., Tangalos, E., Ivnik, R., & Petersen, R. (2011). Engaging in cognitive activities, aging and mild cognitive impairment: A population based study. *Journal of Neuropsychiatry and Clinical Neurosciences, 23*(2), 149–154. DOI:10.1176/appi.neuropsych.23.2.149.

Greene, M. (1995). *Releasing the imagination. Essays on education, the arts and social change*. San Francisco, CA: Jossey-Bass Publishers.

Han Sifuentes, A. (n.d.). Steps towards decolonizing craft. *Textile Society of America*. Retrieved from https://textilesocietyofamerica.org/6728/steps-towards-decolonizing-craft/.

Hass-Cohen, N., & Carr, R. (2008). *Art therapy and clinical neuroscience*. Philadelphia, PA: Jessica Kingsley.

Kamial, G., Gonzaga, A., & Schwachter, V. (2016). Craft, health, and wellbeing: Findings from the survey of public participation in the arts and consideration for art therapists. *Art and Health: International Journal for Research, Policy, and Practice, 9*(1), 81–90. DOI: 10.1080/17533015.2016.1185447.

Keyes, E. F., & Kanes, C. F. (2004). Belonging and adapting: Mental health of Bosnian refugees living in the United States. *Issues of Mental Health Nursing, 25*(8), 809–831.

King, J. (2016). *Art therapy, trauma and neuroscience: Theoretical and practical perspectives*. New York, NY: Routledge.

Kramer, E. (1966). Art and craft. *Bulletin of Art Therapy, 5*(4), 149–152.

Kramer, E., Kwong, K., Lee, E., & Chung, H. (2002). Cultural factors influencing the mental health of Asian Americans. *Western Journal of Medicine, 176*(4), 227–231. Retrieved from www.ncbi.nlm.nih.gov/pmc/articles/PMC1071736/.

la Cour, K., Josephsson, S., Tishelman, C., & Nygard, L. (2007). Experiences of engagement in creative activity at a palliative care facility. *Palliative and Supportive Care, 5*(03), 241–250. DOI:10.1017/S1478951507000405.

Levine, P. (2010). *In an unspoken voice: How the body releases trauma and restores goodness.* Berkeley, CA: North Atlantic Books.

Moon, C. H., & Shuman, V. (2013). The community art studio: Creating a space of solidarity and inclusion. In P. Howie, S. Prasad, & J. Kristel (Eds.), *Using art therapy with diverse populations: Crossing cultures and abilities* (pp. 297–307). Philadelphia, PA: Jessica Kingsley Publishers.

Ottermiller, D., & Awais, Y. (2016). A model for art therapists in community based practice. *Art Therapy: Journal of the American Art Therapy Association, 33*(3), 144–150.

Parker, R. (1984). *The subversive stitch: Embroidery and the making of the feminine.* New York, NY: I.B. Tauris & Co Ltd.

Pentney, B. A. (2008). Feminism, activism, and knitting: Are the fiber arts a viable mode for feminist political action? *Thirdspace: A Journal of Feminist Theory and Culture, 8*(1). Retrieved from http://journals.sfu.ca/thirdspace/index.php/journal/article/view/pentney/210.

Phillips, L. (2006). *The womanist reader: The first quarter of a century of womanist thought.* New York, NY: Routledge.

Riley, J., Corkhill, B., & Morris, C. (2012). The benefits of knitting for personal and social wellbeing in adulthood: Findings from an international survey. *The British Journal of Occupation Therapy, 76*(2), 50–58.

Sangtin Writers Collective & Nagar, R. (2006). *Playing with fire: Feminist thought and activism through seven lives in India.* Minneapolis, MI: University of Minnesota Press.

Shefsky, J. (May 5, 2016). Local crafting group knits refugees, immigrants together. Retrieved from http://chicagotonight.wttw.com/2016/05/05/local-crafting-group-knits-refugees-immigrants-together.

Shrewsbury, C. M. (1993). What is feminist pedagogy? *Women's Studies Quarterly, 21*(3–4), 8–15.

Shuman, A. (2005). *Other people's stories.* Chicago, IL: University of Illinois Press.

Sue, D. W., & Sue, D. (2016). *Counseling the culturally diverse: Theory and practice* (7th Ed.). Hoboken, NJ: Wiley and Sons Inc.

Talwar, S. (2007). Accessing traumatic memory through art making: An art therapy trauma protocol (ATTP). *The Arts in Psychotherapy, 34*(1), 22–35.

Talwar, S. (2015). Creating alternative public spaces: Community-based art practice, critical consciousness and social justice. In D. Gussak & M. Rosal (Eds.), *The Wiley-Blackwell handbook of art therapy* (pp. 840–847). Oxford, UK: Wiley Blackwell.

Timm-Bottos, J. (2006). Constructing creative community: Reviving health and justice through community arts. *The Canadian Art Therapy Association Journal, 19*(2), 12–26. DOI: 10.1080/08322473.2006.11432285.

Tripp, T. (2008). A short-term treatment approach to processing trauma: Art therapy and bilateral stimulation. *Art Therapy: Journal of the American Art Therapy Association, 24*(4), 176–183.

Tzandidaki, D., & Reynolds, F. (2011). Exploring the meanings of making traditional arts and crafts among older women in Crete, using interpretative phenomenological analysis. *British Journal of Occupational Therapy, 74*(8), 375–382.

Ulman, E. (1975). Art therapy: Problems of definition. In E. Ulman & P. Dachinger (Eds.), *Art therapy in theory and practice* (pp. 3–13). New York, NY: Schocken Books.

Walker, A. (1983). *In search of my mother's garden: Womanist prose.* New York, NY: A Harvest Book Harcourt, Inc.

INDEX

Made in United States
North Haven, CT
25 February 2025

66259272R00120